COMPILERS
Their Design and Construction
Using Pascal

WILEY SERIES IN COMPUTING

Consulting Editor
Professor D. W. Barron
*Department of Computer Studies, University
of Southampton, UK*

BEZIER · Numerical Control—Mathematics and Applications
DAVIES and BARBER · Communication Networks for Computers
BROWN · Macro Processors and Techniques for Portable Software
PAGAN · A Practical Guide to Algol 68
BIRD · Programs and Machines.
OLLE · The Codasyl Approach to Data Base Management
DAVIES, BARBER, PRICE and SOLOMONIDES · Computer Networks
    and their Protocols
KRONSJO · Algorithms: Their Complexity and Efficiency
RUS · Data Structures and Operating Systems
BROWN · Writing Interactive Compilers and Interpreters
HUTT · The Design of a Relational Data Base Management System
O'DONOVAN · GPSS Simulation Made Simple
LONGBOTTOM · Computer System Reliability
AUMIAUX · The Use of Microprocessors
ATKINSON · Pascal Programming
KUPKA and WILSING · Conversational Languages
SCHMIDT · GPSS—Fortran
PUZMAN and PORIZEK · Communication Control in Computer
    Networks
SPANIOL · Computer Arithmetic
BARRON · Pascal—The Language and its Implementation
HUNTER · The Design and Construction of Compilers
MAYOH · Problem Solving with ADA
AUMIAUX · Microprocessor Systems
CHEONG and HIRSCHHEIM · Local Area Networks—Issues, Products,
    and Developments
BARRON and BISHOP · Advanced Programming—A Practical Course
DAVIES and PRICE · Security for Computer Networks—An Introduction to
    Data Security in Teleprocessing and Electronic Funds Transfer
HUNTER · Compilers—Their Design and Construction using Pascal

COMPILERS
Their Design and Construction Using Pascal

Robin Hunter
Department of Computer Science,
University of Strathclyde

JOHN WILEY & SONS

Chichester · New York · Brisbane · Toronto · Singapore

Library of Congress Cataloging in Publication Data:

Hunter, Robin.
    Compilers: their design and construction using Pascal.

    (Wiley series in computing)
    Bibliography: p.
    Includes index.
    1. Compiling (Electronic computers)   2. PASCAL
(Computer program language)   I. Title. II. Series.
QA76.6.H858   1985   001.64′2   85–609

ISBN 0 471 90720 0

British Library Cataloguing in Publication Data:

Hunter, Robin
    Compilers: their design and construction using
    Pascal. — (Wiley series in computing)
    1. Compiling (Electronic computers)
    I. Title
    001.64′25   QA76.6

ISBN 0 471 90720 0

Photosetting by Thomson Press (India) Limited, New Delhi,
and printed by Page Bros (Norwich) Ltd. Norwich

To

Kate, Andrew, and Ian again

Contents

Preface

As the title suggests, this book is about compilers with emphasis on how they are designed and constructed. The various algorithms described are written in Pascal—hence the final phrase in the title 'using Pascal'. In addition, Pascal is one of the main languages considered from an implementation point of view.

The book is a successor to and is partly based on *The Design and Construction of Compilers* first published in 1981. In view of the compiler work which had taken place in the Computer Science Department of the University of Strathclyde this text was oriented towards the language ALGOL 68 which was used not only in describing algorithms but also to illustrate implementation issues. The present text retains the same basic approach as the previous one but looks at aspects of compiling a wider range of languages, the principal ones considered being FORTRAN, ALGOL 60, ALGOL 68, Pascal, and Ada.

The book can be used as the basis of an undergraduate compiler course for specialist computer science students or others interested more generally in compilers. The exercises at the ends of the chapters are designed to help students to think about the issues more clearly. Outline solutions to the exercises in Chapters 1 to 12 are given at the end of the book.

Chapter 1 introduces the compilation process by describing features of typical high-level languages and machines, and by discussing possible design aims for a compiler project. Chapter 2 is concerned with the formal definition of the syntax of programming languages and includes a section on attribute grammars. Lexical analysis is covered in Chapter 3 and top-down and bottom-up methods of syntax analysis in Chapters 4 and 5.

Chapter 6 introduces the idea of embedding compiler actions in a context-free grammar while Chapter 7 discusses the overall design of compilers. Symbol tables and type tables are discussed in Chapter 8 and Chapter 9 deals with storage allocation and garbage collection.

Chapter 10 is on code generation and Pascal P-code is introduced as an intermediate language. The translation of P-code into assembly code is discussed in Chapter 11. Chapter 12 is concerned with error recovery techniques and Chapter 13 with the production of reliable compilers.

Acknowledgements

I would like to thank Professor A. D. McGettrick and Mr R. R. Patel for many useful discussions on compiler issues; also Miss C. Conlan for typing part of the text and my wife Kate for assistance in preparing the manuscript.

Chapter 1

The Compilation Process

Programs written in high-level (or problem-oriented) programming languages have to be translated into equivalent machine code programs before they can be executed on a computer. High-level languages have existed since the mid-1950's: early examples of such languages were FORTRAN and COBOL, while ALGOL 68, Pascal, and Ada are examples of more recently designed high-level languages. A program which will translate any program written in a particular high-level language into an equivalent program in some other language (usually the code for some particular machine) is called a *compiler*. Compiling a program consists of *analysis*, determining the intended effect of the program, followed by *synthesis*, generating the equivalent machine-code program. In the course of analysis a compiler should be able to detect if the input program is invalid in any sense (i.e. does not belong to the language for which the compiler was written) and if so return an appropriate message to the programmer. This aspect of compilation is referred to as *error detection*.

Compiler technology has made considerable advances over the last twenty-five years. Early compilers used rather *ad hoc* methods, tended to be slow, and were written in a rather unstructured way. (A brief history of compiler writing can be found in Bauer [1974].) More modern compilers tend to use more systematic methods, are relatively fast, and tend to be structured so as to separate out the distinct aspects of compilation as far as possible.

Instead of translating each program into machine code and *then* executing it, an alternative approach is first to translate the program into an intermediate language and then to translate *and* execute each intermediate language statement as it is encountered. A program which will translate and execute a program written in a high-level language in this way is called an *interpreter*. The advantages of an interpreter over a compiler are:

1. It is often easier to communicate error messages to the user in terms of the original program.
2. The intermediate language version of the program is often more compact than the machine code produced by a compiler.
3. An alteration to part of a program need not involve recompiling the whole program.

Interactive languages such as BASIC are often implemented by means of

1

an interpreter, a common intermediate language being some form of Reverse Polish Notation (see Section 10.1). A good text book on implementing interactive languages is Brown [1979]. The chief disadvantage of an interpreter is that programs tend to run relatively slowly since intermediate code statements have to be translated *each* time they are executed, though the time penalty may not be too significant depending on the design of the intermediate language. A compromise is the *mixed-code approach* of Dakin and Poole [1973] in which the part of the program most frequently executed is compiled and the rest interpreted. This tends to save space since that part of the program which is to be interpreted is likely to be much more compact than the compiled code. An extension of this idea, referred to as 'Throw-Away Compiling' is due to Brown [1976].

In this book we will be mainly concerned with compilers rather than interpreters, though many of the ideas could be applied to either. In discussing compilers we will refer to the program to be compiled as the *source program* (or source text), and the machine code produced as the *object code* (Figure 1.1). Similarly, the high-level language may be referred to as the *source language* and the machine language as the *object language*.

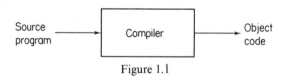

Figure 1.1

In this chapter we discuss the characteristics of high-level languages and typical computers and the various aspects of the compilation process. This leads us on to consider the overall design of compilers.

1.1 Relationship between languages and machines

While the differences between the various high-level languages can be very significant from the users' (and the implementors') point of view, it is the similarities between these languages which we wish to emphasize in this section in order to try to indicate the sort of tasks the compiler has to perform. Typical of the high-level languages we will have in mind are BASIC, FORTRAN, PL/1, Pascal, ALGOL 68, Ada, and (possibly to a slightly lesser extent) COBOL. The program fragments which we use to illustrate points will be in Pascal but could just as well be in any of the other languages and readers unfamiliar with Pascal should not have any great problems in following them.

Languages

Features that most high-level languages have in common are:

1 *Expressions and Assignments*

It is usually possible to evaluate an expression and (amongst other possibilities) assign its value to a variable, e.g.

$$a := (b + c) * (e + f)$$

assuming b, c, e, and f possess suitable values.

2 *Conditionals*

The effect of a statement may depend on a boolean (truth) value:

if $a = b$ **then** $x := x + y$ **else** $x := x - y$

the effect of which is to assign the value of $x + y$ to x if a equals b and the value of $x - y$ to x otherwise.

3 *Loops*

A statement (possibly compound) may be executed a number of times

```
for k : = 1 to 10 do
begin read (i);
      write (i)
end
```

The sequence of statements within the compound statement, i.e.

```
read   (i);
write  (i)
```

is executed 10 times.

4 *Input/Output*

There are usually simple routines for reading in or writing out simple values to standard input/output channels, e.g.

$$read\ (x, y, z)$$

to read in values for x, y, z and

$$write\ (a, b, c)$$

to write the values of a, b, and c.

5 Procedures/Subroutines/Functions

It is usually possible to give a program written in a high-level language some sort of structure by dividing it into subprograms and writing each subprogram as a separate procedure or function. For example if a program involved from time to time the calculation of the average of ten real numbers the following function might be written:

```
function average (row : array 10) : real ;
var sum : real ;
        i : integer ;
begin sum : = 0 ;
      for i : = 1 to 10 do
      sum : = sum + row [i] ;
      average : = sum/10
end
```

Assuming *array 10* had been declared as

type *array 10 =* **array** [1 .. 10] **of** *real*

average could be called as follows

write (average (a))

where *a* had been declared

var *a : array 10*

and had been assigned ten real values.

Variables such as *sum* and *i* can be declared local to functions or procedures in Pascal so that variables with non-overlapping scopes can share storage space. Type identifiers and procedures and functions can also be declared locally. In some languages such as ALGOL 60, ALGOL 68, and Ada identifiers may be declared even more locally at a level equivalent to the compound statement in Pascal. An ALGOL compound statement with declarations is referred to as a block. The implications of block structure on storage allocation will be discussed in Chapter 9.

We will not at this stage say a great deal about the differences between the various high-level languages in, for example, the ways in which loops or conditionals are provided or the types of operators available. For a good summary of language differences from a compiler writer's point of view see Chapter 2 of Aho and Ullman [1977].

One language feature which substantially affects the structure of a compiler is the idea of *type*. In most languages each possible value belongs to one of a finite or infinite number of types, while each type corresponds to a finite or infinite number of values. For example, the set of all integers, real numbers, or characters in some character set might be regarded as a type. In Pascal we can for example define a subtype of type integer

type *upto 100 = 1 . . 100*

being the set of all integer values between 1 and 100 inclusive. Pascal, like most similar languages, also has aggregate types for arrays and records. Modes in ALGOL 68 correspond roughly to types but are more general. For example, there is a mode corresponding to a procedure with one **real** parameter and a **real** result.

Some languages, such as Pascal and ALGOL 68, are said to be *strongly typed* or to have *static types*, i.e. the types of all values in the program are known at compile time. This introduces redundancy into the language and increases the checking which can be done at compile time. For example if x was a character variable

$x := 3$

would be detected as illegal by the compiler. In PL/1, which is also strongly typed, the above 'error' would not be detected since there are so many implicit type conversions (e.g. integer to character).

Languages such as POP-2, APL, and LISP are said to be *weakly typed*, or to have *dynamic types*, since types are not known until run time. For example, in POP-2 the declaration

VARS X, Y;

means that X and Y can take values of any type. An assignment such as

$X \rightarrow Y$

(assignments go from left to right in POP-2) would always be legal. However, in

$X + Y$

the application of the dyadic operator $+$ to X and Y may or may not be legal depending on the *current* types of X and Y. This can only be checked at run time and such run-time checking must be included in the object code with the inevitable cost of slowing down the object program.

A compromise between static and dynamic types is to make the types static in the main part, but to have an extra type (called, for example, *any type* or *general*) the values of which can be any of the other types in the language. This approach is adopted by CPL and ESPOL (Burroughs ALGOL 60 superset).

A third approach to types is that taken by BCPL, which only has one type, which can be thought of as a bit pattern. Distinct types may exist in the mind of the programmer but are unknown to the program or the implementation. It is the programmer's responsibility not to attempt to add a boolean and an integer. No type-checking is possible at compile time or run time.

Machines

As in BCPL, the concept of type is not present in machine code. The computer deals with bit patterns without attaching any meaning to them. Computers, like languages, vary greatly in detail, but it is possible to list a number of typical characteristics in order to illuminate the task which the compiler has to perform. The features of individual machines relate less to their usefulness to the programmer and more to cost–benefit trade-offs in the overall design of the computer. Features common to most machines include:

1 *Linear Main Store*

The main store (or memory) has the capacity to store a large number of bits (binary digits). These are usually grouped into 8-bit bytes arranged sequentially so that each byte can be addressed by an integer in the range 0 to $M - 1$ where M is the number of bytes in the main memory and is usually a power of 2. A byte can be used to represent a character. A group of several bytes (say 2 or 4) may be referred to as a word and in some machines the word is the smallest addressable unit.

2 *Registers*

Like a word in the main store, a *register* can be used for storing data. Registers are usually involved in all arithmetic operations performed by the computer and the time taken to store a value in or retrieve a value from a register is much less than for a word in main store. There are usually only a small (possibly 8 or 16) number of registers in any computer.

3 *Instruction set*

Each machine has a set of *instructions*, referred to as its *machine code*. Each instruction consists of a sequence of binary digits and can usually take several parameters, also sequences of binary digits. These parameters might typically involve the name of a register or an address in the main store. Each instruction (including parameters) usually occupies an exact number of words (or possibly half-words) and can be stored in the main store during execution of the program. Some machine codes have fixed length instructions, others variable length instructions. Using mnemonics in place of binary numbers for instruction codes and decimal numbers in place of sequences of binary digits elsewhere, typical machine code instructions might be

LDX 1 4444

meaning load the contents of address *4444* into register *1*. (Since it may not be known in advance in which part of the main store the program will reside during execution, the address fields are usually not absolute but relative to some base value.),

STO 2 2000

meaning store the contents of register *2* in address *2000*,

ADX 2 102

meaning add the contents of address *102* to what is in register *2*,

BRN 4000

meaning jump (or branch) to address *4000* and continue executing instructions from that address.

Other features of machines, which do not particularly concern us from the compilation point of view, are:

4 *Control unit*

For interpreting the machine code instructions and arranging for them to be executed.

5 *Arithmetic unit*

This is where the various arithmetic operations, tests, etc. are performed.

The job of the compiler, therefore, is to produce executable code from the source code. In some cases the compiler will only go as far as producing assembly code for the particular machine and the final stage of producing machine code will be performed by a separate program called *an assembler*. Assembly code is similar to machine code but mnemonics are used for instructions and address-es, and labels can be used as the destinations of jumps. An assembler has a relatively simple task to perform and most of the compiler's work is concerned with translating the relatively sophisticated constructs of the high-level language into the relatively simple machine code or assembly code of the computer concerned.

A compiler, therefore, involves two languages and in addition there is the language in which the compiler is written. In the simplest cases this is the machine code of the computer on which it is to run. However, we shall see this is not always the case.

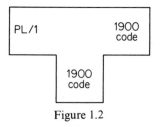

Figure 1.2

A large letter T can be used to represent a compiler. For example, a compiler for PL/1 written in ICL 1900 code to produce 1900 code could be represented as in Figure 1.2, the top left-hand corner giving the source language, the top right-hand corner giving the object language, and the bottom of the T giving the language the compiler is written in. A *cross-compiler* produces code for some machine other than the host machine, for example Figure 1.3 represents a compiler written in 1900 code to compile FORTRAN programs in to PDP-11 code. Using this compiler FORTRAN programs could be compiled on a 1900 and run on a PDP-11.

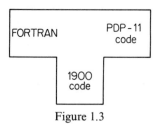

Figure 1.3

It is good practice to try to localize the machine-dependent parts of a compiler as far as possible. This is particularly important if it is intended to move the compiler from one machine to another. For example, if we had a Pascal compiler written in FORTRAN to produce code for machine A (Figure 1.4) then to run the compiler on machine A we would need first of all to translate it into

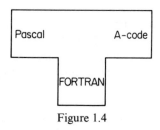

Figure 1.4

A-code by means of a FORTRAN compiler written in A-code and producing A-code (Figure 1.5). From the two compilers illustrated we are able to produce a third compiler by using the second compiler to compile the first one (Figure 1.6). This can be demonstrated by joining the T diagrams together according to simple rules (Figure 1.7) where the rules for combining the T diagrams state that arms of the middle T must refer to the same languages as the adjacent legs of the left and right T, and also the two top T's must have the same languages in the left-hand and right-hand corners. More complex T diagrams can also be produced (e.g. Figure 1.8). The idea of the T diagram is due to Bratman [1961].

By altering the code produced by the original compiler in the previous example to, say, B-code, the code for some machine B, and assuming there is a FORTRAN compiler which runs on machine B to produce B-code, we can also produce a Pascal compiler for machine B.

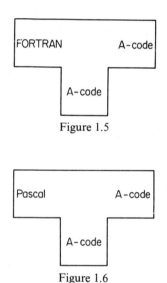

Figure 1.5

Figure 1.6

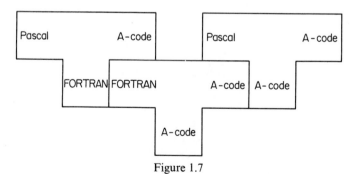

Figure 1.7

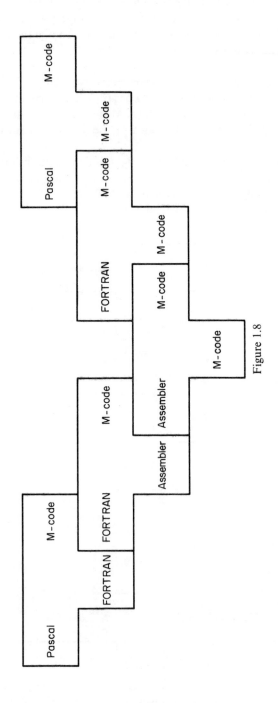

Figure 1.8

1.2 Aspects of the compilation process

From our discussion of typical features of machines and languages we should now have some idea of the sort of tasks the compiler has to perform. There are two main stages. First it has to recognize the structure and meaning of the program to be compiled and then it has to produce a machine (or assembly) code program with the same meaning. The two stages are often referred to as

(a) *analysis*,
(b) *synthesis*.

Conceptually, analysis must take place before synthesis, but in practice they may take place almost in parallel. The source language definition will attribute a meaning to every legal construction in the language (but not to any illegal ones) and having recognized each construction involved in the program the analyser is able to determine what the effect of the program should be. The synthesizer can then produce appropriate object code.

A convenient method of representing the structure of a program is by means of a tree diagram. Consider the piece of program

begin $x := 3$;
        write (x)
    end

The corresponding tree would be as shown in Figure 1.9, which shows more clearly the structure of the piece of program. We can think of the analyser building the tree (usually called the parse tree) and the synthesizer traversing the tree (visiting all the nodes in some predetermined order) to produce machine code.

It might be considered rather arbitrary that the terminal nodes (nodes with no subtrees below them) of the parse tree should be identifiers such as *write*, or language words such as **begin,** and not individual characters. The terminal node labelled *write* could be replaced by the subtree shown in Figure 1.10, but to the human reader at least this would tend to obscure the structure of the program rather than clarify it. As far as the compiler is concerned an initial phase normally performs the task of grouping characters together into what are usually referred to as symbols, e.g.

    write $:=$ **begin end**

This phase of the compilation process is normally known as *lexical analysis* and is discussed further in Chapter 3. The remaining part of the analysis, i.e. building the tree, is referred to as *syntax analysis* or *parsing*.

In order to check certain language requirements, tables have to be built by the compiler. For example, in most languages

    $x := y$

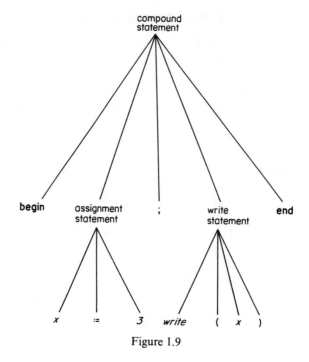

Figure 1.9

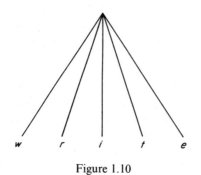

Figure 1.10

is legal only if *x* and *y* are declared to have suitable types. From a declaration such as

var *x* : *integer*

an entry is inserted in a table, normally referred to as the *symbol table*, indicating the type of *x*. The above occurrence of *x* is known as a *defining occurrence*. In the assignment

x := *y*

the occurrence of x is known as an *applied occurrence* and the type of x can be derived from the symbol table. Symbol tables are usually built in parallel with syntax analysis and are required during code generation. Symbol tables are also required to check the validity of programs.

Certain other tables may also be required. During lexical analysis variable length identifiers are usually replaced by fixed length symbols and an *identifier table* is used to provide the correspondence between these symbols and the original identifiers. In Pascal and other languages with complex user-defined types a *type table* will also be required.

The synthesis stage of compilation will involve allocation of storage on the object machine for the values required by the program. Space will be allocated for the values of variables in the program and for working storage required, for example, in the evaluation of expressions such as

$$(a + b) * (c + d).$$

In FORTRAN and Pascal storage requirements are fully known at compile-time. In ALGOL 68 and Ada, however, where arrays may have bounds which are not known until run time (dynamic arrays), storage requirements may not be fully known until run time. Space which can be allocated at compile time is normally referred to as *static space*, and space which has to be allocated at run time is referred to as *dynamic space*.

Storage management is usually organized using a last-in-first-out store called a *stack* and is discussed further in Chapter 9.

Code generation is described in Chapters 10 and 11. In Chapter 10 we discuss the production of a machine-independent intermediate code and in Chapter 11 we discuss how this intermediate code is mapped on to an actual machine. The effect of introducing an intermediate language is to try to separate the machine-dependent and the machine-independent parts of code generation. The intermediate code might consist of statements of the form

ADD address1, address2, address3

meaning add the values in address *1* and address *2* and put the result in address *3*. The intermediate language would probably not be independent of the source language (though attempts have been made to produce universal intermediate languages, see e.g. Poole [1974]) but would reflect the basic actions of the source language and be at a high enough level to be implemented efficiently on a typical computer. Many Pascal implementations make use of P-code as an intermediate language, P-code being code for a hypothetical stack-based machine.

In many compilers there is no explicit separation of the two aspects of code generation. However, if portability is to be a feature of the compiler, it is desirable to keep the machine-dependent and the machine-independent parts of the compiler as separate as possible.

The final code produced should, of course, have the same meaning as the original program. However, expressions will have been broken down into their basic components, types will have disappeared, and all values will be represented as bit patterns. Program structure (such as conditionals and loops) will be represented by tests, jumps, and labels. The program will be much less intelligible but will now be executable on the particular machine.

In this section we have tried to explain some of the various aspects of the compilation process. The details of how the various phases of the compiler are organized and how they fit together are described in later chapters.

1.3 Design of a compiler

We mentioned earlier that a compiler is in some sense defined by the high-level language it accepts and the machine code (more generally some other language) which it produces. However, it does not follow that, for example, all FORTRAN compilers for the PDP-11 series will be identical. Of course, two compilers written by different compiler writers (or teams of compiler writers) could hardly be expected to be identical, though they ought to produce identical, or equivalent, object code from the same source code. One reason why two compilers implementing the same language on the same machine may differ is that the writers may have had different design aims in mind when they were writing them. Possible design aims are

1. to produce efficient object code,
2. to produce small object programs,
3. to minimize the time taken to compile programs,
4. to keep the compiler as small as possible,
5. to produce a compiler with good diagnostic and error recovery capabilities,
6. to produce a reliable compiler.

Unfortunately, these aims are to some extent conflicting. A compiler will almost certainly take a little (or even a lot) longer if it is to produce efficient code. Some of the standard optimizing techniques (Gries [1971]) such as eliminating redundant code, removing code sequences from loops, etc., can be extremely time-consuming. Also a compiler which goes though elaborate optimization routines is bound to be larger than one which does not. The size of the compiler may also be related to the time it takes to compile a program. In computing it is often not possible to optimize both space and time. One is usually done at the expense of the other. The compiler writer has to decide at an early stage which factors he is most anxious to optimize and then be prepared to take deliberate steps to optimize these factors, knowing that it may well be at the expense of other related factors. In addition he may wish to minimize the time spent in writing the compiler, and this factor alone may prevent certain elaborate optimization techniques being included.

Programmers will expect a helpful message indicating where the fault lies when they submit an illegal program and will not be satisfied with a formal reply that their program 'is not in the language which the compiler has been designed to translate'. Also, having detected an error in their program, they will not expect the compiler to give in and stop compiling, but to continue analysing the program in an attempt to spot any further errors. Compilers vary greatly in their diagnostic and error recovery capabilities, though this is not a property which should conflict greatly with the other design aims mentioned above. Admittedly a compiler which gives helpful messages and recovers gracefully after an error has been detected may, as a result, be a little larger but this should be more than compensated for by the increase in programmer efficiency. A compiler with good diagnostic and error recovery capabilities should not as a result take any longer to compile error-free programs. The problem of recovery from errors (especially syntax ones), however, is not simple and no completely satisfactory solution seems to be available. For more details see Chapter 12.

Of course, reliability should be a design aim of every compiler. Compilers are often very large programs and to be confident of the correctness of any compiler in a formal sense is beyond the present state of the art. Good overall design is of paramount importance. If the different phases of the process can be kept relatively distinct and if each phase is structured in as natural a way as possible then reliability is more probable. In addition, if the compiler can be based as far as possible on a clear and unambiguous formal definition of the language, and automatic aids such as *parser generators* are used, then the chances of producing a reliable compiler should be enhanced. The compiler, of course, must be thoroughly tested. This applies not only to the complete compiler but also to the individual parts before they are assembled. Reliability is discussed further in Chapter 13.

It is not uncommon for a manufacturer to offer more than one compiler for a language on a range of machines. An early example of this was the Whetstone and Kidsgrove. ALGOL 60 compilers offered by English Electric for the KDF9 computer. The Whetstone compiler was a fast-compile–slow-run compiler while the Kidsgrove one was slow to compile but produced very efficient machine code. The idea was that users would develop their programs using the Whetstone compiler, and then recompile them using the Kidsgrove compiler for production runs. In the same way IBM produced more than one PL/1 compiler for their 370 range.

The design aims of a compiler will often depend on the environment in which the compiler is to be used. If the compiler is to be used mainly by undergraduate students who will rarely run their programs after the development phase is completed satisfactorily, then the efficiency of the machine code is less important than the speed of compilation and the diagnostic capabilities. In a commercial environment the priorities may be reversed. In a student environment, a batch compiler which remains in main memory while a number of programs are compiled and run leads to an efficient use of the available hardware.

An important design decision in constructing a compiler is the number of *passes* it will have. Each time the source text, or a version of it, is read by the compiler is regarded as a single pass. From a simplicity point of view *single-pass compilers* are attractive. However, not all languages allow single-pass compilation and, from a structural point of view, it may be cleaner and simpler to perform distinct phases of compilation in separate passes. In order to achieve single-pass compilation some compiler writers implement only a subset of the language, for example, by insisting that identifiers are declared before they are used in source programs.

Producing a *multi-pass compiler* would normally involve the design of intermediate languages for inter-pass versions of the source text. There would also be tables built by one pass which would be required for inspection by a subsequent pass or passes. The organization of a multi-pass compiler, therefore, tends to be more complicated than for a single-pass one, though the individual passes may be relatively straightforward and may provide a convenient method of splitting the job between a number of individuals or groups of individuals without introducing unduly complicated interfaces. Finally, it should be added that not all compilers have a fixed number of passes. In some compilers the number of passes required to compile a program depends on whether all identifiers are declared before use, etc., or on the degree of optimization required by the programmer. This topic is discussed further in Chapter 7.

The compiler writer will have to choose a language in which to write his compiler. Increasingly, high-level languages are being used, either general purpose languages such as ALGOL 68, Pascal, or PL/1, or so called software writing languages such as BCPL. There is something to be said for writing a compiler for a language in the language itself. Not only does this mean that the implementor only has to think in terms of one language, but it means that the compiler can be used to compile itself, a good test for any compiler and an aid to portability.

Exercises

1.1 Write down some more typical features of high-level languages and indicate what sort of machine code instructions would be generated when they were translated.

1.2 A compiler translates Pascal into ICL 1900 machine code and is written in ALGOL 68. What further piece of software would be required in order to run Pascal programs on an ICL 1900 machine? Illustrate your answer by means of a T diagram.

1.3 Some compilers generate code to check array subscripts at run time to see they are within the declared bounds of the array. Discuss the arguments for and against implementing such checks
    (a) during program development,
    (b) during production runs.

1.4 A FORTRAN compiler has to be implemented within a relatively short timescale. Which of the six design aims in Section 1.3 do you think would be hardest to achieve?

1.5 Which of the following high-level language facilities do you think would be useful to the compiler writer:

(a) arrays,

(b) real arithmetic,

(c) procedures?

1.6 Give arguments in favour of using an interpreter rather than a compiler in a student environment.

1.7 What possible problem do you see in offering separate compilers for development and production work?

1.8 In some languages the programmer is able to choose the relative priorities of operators. How might this affect the parse tree of a particular program?

1.9 What would you expect to be the chief design aims for a compiler for a software writing language?

1.10 What particular feature would you expect in a compiler for an interactive language such as BASIC?

Chapter 2

Language Definition

Before writing a compiler it is necessary (or at least highly desirable) to have a clear and unambiguous definition of the source language. Unfortunately, however, while methods for defining some aspects of programming languages are well-developed, full and clear definitions of languages to be implemented are not always available. Furthermore, the formal definition of a programming language cannot necessarily be used directly by the compiler writer. In this chapter we introduce a few of the methods used to define programming languages. For a fuller discussion on the topic see Marcotty, Ledgard, and Bochmann [1976]. We also discuss the parsing problem—how to decide whether a sequence of symbols belongs to a particular language or not.

2.1 Syntax and semantics

A language can be thought of as consisting of a number of strings (sequences of symbols); and the definition of a language defines which strings belong to the language (the syntax of the language) and the meaning of these strings (the semantics of the language). For a finite language (i.e. one consisting of only a finite number of strings) the syntax of the language could be defined by giving a list of the strings. For example, a language might consist of the strings

abc
xyz

Those strings which belong to a language are usually referred to as sentences of the language. Most languages of interest consist of an infinite number of sentences so that their syntax cannot be defined by listing the sentences. For example, the sentences of a language might be 'all strings consisting only of 0's and 1's', for example

101 1100 11001

would be in the language, in which case the phrase in quotes would seem a reasonable definition of the syntax. However, English is not very suitable

18

for defining the syntax of more complex languages, and it is usual to adopt a more formal approach in defining the syntax of programming languages, as we will see later.

The semantics of a language attribute a meaning to all sentences of the language. For example

```
program sample (input, output);
var k : integer;
begin read  (k);
      write  (k + 1)
end.
```

is a sentence of Pascal and from the semantics of Pascal the meaning of the above program in terms of declaring an identifier, reading a value for it, evaluating, and printing an expression could be deduced. As with syntax, the semantics of a language are usually described in a fairly formal way. However, methods of defining semantics are not so well-developed as those for syntax, and further developments in this area are required before completely satisfactory formal definitions of programming languages will be a reality. Further progress in this field may eventually lead to the possibility of producing compilers automatically from the formal definition. In the next section we discuss the problem of specifying the syntax of a language.

2.2 Grammars

We begin by introducing some terminology. Curly brackets are used to denote sets, e.g.

$$\{1,2,3\}$$

denotes the set containing the integers 1, 2, and 3. Union ($\cup$) and intersection ($\cap$) of sets are defined as usual:

$$\{1,2,3\} \cup \{3,4,5\} = \{1,2,3,4,5\}$$
$$\{1,2,3\} \cap \{3,4,5\} = \{3\}.$$

We say set A includes ($\supseteq$) set B if every element of B is an element of A, e.g.

$$\{3,4,5\} \supseteq \{3\}.$$

Similarly set B is included in ($\subseteq$) set A if every element in B is also in A, e.g.

$$\{3\} \subseteq \{3,4,5\}.$$

We use $\in$ to indicate that an element is contained in a set, e.g.

$$3 \in \{3,4,5\}$$

The empty set is denoted by $\varnothing$. Therefore,

$$\{1,2\} \cap \{3,4,5\} = \varnothing.$$

If A is the set

$$\{2,4,9,8\}$$

and we define B as

$$B = \{x \mid x \in A \text{ and } x \text{ is even}\}$$

then B is the set

$$\{2,4,8\}.$$

B is defined by a predicate, in this case '$x \in A$ and x is even'.

We define an *alphabet* (or *vocabulary*) to be a set of symbols. For example, it might be the Roman or the Greek alphabet or the decimal digits 0–9. An alphabet D could be

$$D = \{0,1,2,3,4,5,6,7,8,9\}$$

If A is an alphabet, A^* (the closure of A) is used to denote the set of all strings (including the empty string consisting of zero symbols) composed of symbols from A. A^+ is used to denote the set of all strings (excluding the empty string) composed of symbols from A. The empty string is usually denoted by ε.

The syntax of a language can be defined using set notation, e.g.

$$L = \{0^n 1^n \mid n \geq 0\}$$

In English, the language consists of all strings consisting of zero or more 0's followed by the same number of 1's. The empty string is included in the language.

Other syntaxes which could be defined in this way include

1. $\{a^n b^n c^n \mid n \geq 0\}$
2. $\{a^m b^n \mid m, n \geq 0\}$

i.e. a number of a's followed by a number (not necessarily the same) of b's, e.g.

aaabb

would be in the language.

3. $\{x^m \mid m \text{ is prime}\}$
4. $\{a^m b^n c^p \mid m = n \text{ or } n = p\}$.

All these syntaxes are a good deal less complex than those of most programming languages and a more useful way of defining the syntax of a programming language is by means of a *grammar*. A grammar consists (in part) of a set of rules for generating sentences of a language. Take, for example, the syntax defined earlier in this section:

$$\{0^n \, 1^n \mid n \geq 0\}.$$

The following rules can be used to generate the sentences:

1. $S \to 0S1$
2. $S \to \varepsilon$

To derive a sentence of the language proceed as follows. Start with the symbol S and replace it by $0S1$ or ε. If S still appears in the resultant string it may again be replaced using one of the rules, and so on. Any string produced in this way which does not contain S is a sentence of the language. For example

$$S \Rightarrow 0S1 \Rightarrow 00S11 \Rightarrow 000S111 \Rightarrow 000111$$

The sequence of steps above is referred to as a *derivation* of the string 000111, and the symbol $\Rightarrow$ is used to separate the steps in the derivation. All sentences in the language can be derived using the two rules and any string which cannot be derived using the two rules is not a sentence of the language. A grammar is often (and aptly) referred to as a rewriting system. We now define a grammar more formally.

A grammar is defined to be a quadruple

$$(V_T, V_N, P, S)$$

where V_T is an alphabet whose symbols are known as *terminal symbols* (or simply *terminals*), V_N is an alphabet whose symbols are known as *nonterminal symbols* (or *nonterminals*), and V_T and V_N have no symbols in common, i.e.

$$V_T \cap V_N = \varnothing$$

V is defined to be $V_T \cup V_N$.

P is a set of *productions* (or *rules*), each element of which consists of a pair (α, β) where α is in V^+ and β is in V^*. α is normally known as the left part of the production and β is known as the right part, and a production is written

$$\alpha \to \beta$$

$S \in V_N$ and is normally referred to as the sentence symbol (or axiom) and is the starting point in producing any sentence in the language.

A grammar generating the language

$$\{0^n 1^n \mid n \geq 0\}$$

is G_0 where

$$G_0 = (\{0,1\}, \{S\}, P, S)$$

and

$$P = \{S \rightarrow 0S1,\ S \rightarrow \varepsilon\}$$

A grammar generating strings in the set

$$\{a^m b^n \mid m, n \geq 0\}$$

is $\quad G_1 = (\{a,b\}, \{S, A, B\}, P, S)$

where the elements of P are

$$S \rightarrow AB$$
$$A \rightarrow aA$$
$$A \rightarrow \varepsilon$$
$$B \rightarrow bB$$
$$B \rightarrow \varepsilon$$

Starting with the sentence symbol S and successively using one of the productions to replace a nonterminal in the derived string, we can generate the string *aaabb*:

$$S \Rightarrow AB \Rightarrow aAB \Rightarrow aaAB \Rightarrow aaa\,AB \Rightarrow aaaB \Rightarrow aaabB$$
$$\Rightarrow aaabb\,B \Rightarrow aaabb$$

Each string which can be derived from the sentence symbol (e.g. *aAB. aaaB* above) is called a *sentential form*. A sentence is a sentential form containing only terminal symbols.

$$\gamma \overset{+}{\underset{G}{\Rightarrow}} \delta$$

means that the string (of symbols) δ can be derived from the string γ by one or more applications of productions of the grammar G. (G can be omitted if it is clear which grammar is intended.) It can be seen from the above that

$$aAB \overset{+}{\underset{G_1}{\Rightarrow}} aaabB$$

Similarly,

$$\gamma \underset{G}{\overset{*}{\Rightarrow}} \delta$$

means that the string δ can be derived from the string γ by zero or more applications of productions of the grammar G (again G can be omitted in appropriate circumstances). For example

$$aAB \underset{G_1}{\overset{*}{\Rightarrow}} aaabB$$

$$aAB \underset{G_1}{\overset{*}{\Rightarrow}} aAB$$

Where *exactly* one application of a production is involved the symbol $\Rightarrow$ is used, e.g.

$$AB \underset{G_1}{\Rightarrow} aAB$$

or, omitting the G_1,

$$AB \Rightarrow aAB$$

In this book we will normally use small letters (or strings of small letters) to denote terminals of a grammar and capital letters (or strings of capital letters) to denote nonterminals of a grammar. Where ambiguity might arise with sequences of letters denoting terminals or nonterminals, spaces will be used to separate the symbols in a production. Strings of terminals and/or nonterminals will usually be represented by Greek letters.

The sentences of a language can usually be generated by more than one grammar; two grammars generating the same language are said to be equivalent. For example, G_1 is equivalent to G_2 defined as follows:

$$G_2 = (\{a,b\}, \{S, Y\}, P, S)$$

where the elements of P are

$$S \to aS$$
$$S \to a$$
$$S \to b$$
$$S \to bY$$
$$Y \to b$$
$$Y \to bY$$
$$S \to \varepsilon$$

From the compiler writer's point of view one grammar may be much more suitable than another as a basis for the syntax analysis phase of compilation.

In the examples so far, the left parts of productions have always consisted of a single nonterminal. However, it is clear from the definition of a grammar that this need not be so. Consider the grammar

$$G_3 = (\{a\}, \{S, N, Q, R\}, P, S)$$

where the elements of P are

$$S \rightarrow QNQ$$
$$QN \rightarrow QR$$
$$RN \rightarrow NNR$$
$$RQ \rightarrow NNQ$$
$$N \rightarrow a$$
$$Q \rightarrow \varepsilon$$

The language generated is

$$\{a^{(2^n)} | n \geq 0\}$$

A typical derivation is

$$S \Rightarrow QNQ \Rightarrow QRQ \Rightarrow QNNQ$$
$$\Rightarrow QRNQ \Rightarrow QNNRQ \Rightarrow QNNNNQ$$
$$\overset{+}{\Rightarrow} aaaa$$

The reader should be able, by considering the roles of N, Q, and R in the above derivation, to convince himself that the language generated is the one stated. It should be noticed, for example, that R serves to duplicate N.

By restricting the types of productions which can appear in a grammar we can define a number of special classes of grammars. One standard classification is known as the *Chomsky hierarchy*, which may be described as follows.

Any grammar of the form defined previously is referred to as a type-0 grammar.

If, however, a grammar has the property that for all productions of the form

$$\alpha \rightarrow \beta \quad \text{we have} \quad |\alpha| \leq |\beta|$$

where $|\alpha|$ denotes the length of α, i.e. the number of symbols in α, and similarly for $|\beta|$, then the grammar is said to be of *type 1* or *context sensitive*.

If the grammar has the further property that all left parts consist of a single nonterminal symbol then the grammar is said to be of *type 2* or *context free*.

If each production of the grammar is of one of the forms

$$A \rightarrow a$$
$$A \rightarrow aB$$

where a is a terminal symbol and A and B are nonterminal symbols then the grammar is said to be of *type 3* or *right linear* or *regular*.

A *left linear grammar* defined analogously to a right linear grammar, i.e. with all rules of either of the forms

$$A \rightarrow a$$
$$A \rightarrow Ba$$

is also said to be of type 3 or regular.

Clearly the hierarchy is inclusive, that is all type-3 grammars are type-2 grammars and all type-1 grammars are type-0 grammars, etc. Corresponding to the hierarchy of grammars is a hierarchy of languages. For example, if a language can be generated by a type-2 grammar it is referred to as a type-2 language and if a language can be generated by a type-3 grammar it is referred to as a type-3 language. Again the hierarchy is inclusive. Also the inclusions are proper in that there exist languages which are type i but not type $(i + 1)$ $(0 \leq i \leq 2)$.

For example, it can be shown that the language generated by G_3 above is context sensitive and not context free i.e. no context-free grammar exists which generates the language. Similarly the language generated by G_0 is context free and not regular. However, the fact that a language can be generated by a nonregular context-free grammar does not necessarily mean that it is nonregular. For example, grammar G_1 is context free but not regular, but the language generated by it is regular since it can also be generated by grammar G_2. (Strictly speaking, it is $L(G_2) - \varepsilon$ which is regular but it is usual to extend the definitions of type-3 grammars to include productions of the form $S \rightarrow \varepsilon$ where S is the sentence symbol.) The Chomsky hierarchy is significant as far as programming languages are concerned. The fewer the restrictions put on the grammar the finer the constraints that can be put on the language generated.

Type-3 grammars can be used to describe certain features of programming languages. For example, the following productions can be used to generate identifiers as defined in many programming languages:

$$IDENT \rightarrow letter$$
$$IDENT \rightarrow letter\ REST$$
$$REST \rightarrow letter$$
$$REST \rightarrow digit$$
$$REST \rightarrow letter\ REST$$
$$REST \rightarrow digit\ REST$$

where *letter* and *digit* are terminals. It is sometimes convenient to group right-hand sides of productions with the same left-hand side together. The above grammar could also be written as

$$IDENT \rightarrow letter|letter\ REST$$
$$REST \rightarrow letter|digit|letter\ REST|digit\ REST$$

where the vertical bar can be read as 'or'.

Many 'local' features of programming languages can be represented by type-3 grammars, e.g. constants, language words, and strings. However, it can be shown that type-3 grammars are strictly limited in the types of languages they can generate. We now define *regular expressions* and state without proof that type-3 grammars generate exactly all regular expressions (see Aho and Ullman [1972], page 118).

Given an alphabet A, then the following are regular expressions:

1. an element of A (or the empty string).

If P and Q are regular expressions then so also are:

2. PQ (P followed by Q).
3. $P|Q$ (P or Q).
4. $P*$ (zero or more occurrences of P).

Over the alphabet $\{a,b,c\}$

$$a*b|ca*$$

is a regular expression describing a language including the following strings (amongst others):

aab
c
caa
ab
ca

If we think of regular expressions being built using the three operators

concatenate (represented by juxtaposition)
|
*

then in writing regular expressions * has the highest priority followed by concatenation followed by |.

The operator | (alternatively represented by +) is commutative and associative, i.e. for regular expressions P, Q, R

$$P|Q = Q|P \qquad \text{(commutative)}$$
$$(P|Q)R = P|(Q|R) \quad \text{(associative)}.$$

Concatenation is associative but not commutative.

Brackets may be used to override the priorities normally associated with these operators. Thus over the alphabet $\{a, b\}$

$$(aab|ab)*$$

is a regular expression describing a language including the following strings:

ε
aababaab
ababab
aabaabaabab

A regular expression describing an identifier would be

$$L(L|D)*$$

where L stands for a letter and D for a digit.

A regular expression is said to generate a *regular set*. For example, the regular expression

$$(a|b)c$$

generates the regular set $\{ac, bc\}$. Clearly a regular set can be generated by more than one regular expression (if only because '|' is commutative). Normally we will not distinguish between a regular expression and the set it generates.

Other properties of regular sets are:

1. There exists an algorithm to determine whether a string belongs to a given regular set (defined by a regular expression).
2. There exists an algorithm to determine whether two regular expressions generate the same regular set.

The above properties turn out to be extremely useful from the compiler writer's point of view.

Regular expressions, however, do have their limitations. For example, patterns of matching brackets of arbitrary length cannot be defined by a regular expression and consequently cannot be generated by a type-3 grammar. Consider the language consisting of strings of opening and closing brackets-plus the empty string with the following properties:

1. on reading from left to right the number of closing brackets encountered never exceeds the number of opening brackets encountered,
2. each string contains the same number of opening and closing brackets.

For example, the following strings would be in the language:

    ((( )))
    ( )( )(( ))
    (( )( )(( )( )))

but the following would not:

    ( ))(( )   —rule 1
    ((( )( )) —rule 2

There is no way the above language can be expressed as a regular expression (see Minsky [1967], p. 72) or generated by a type-3 grammar.

However, the context-free grammar with the following productions generates the language:

$$S \rightarrow (S)$$
$$S \rightarrow S S$$
$$S \rightarrow \varepsilon$$

In most programming languages there are a number of pairs of brackets which have to be matched, e.g.

( ), [ ], **begin end**

and, of course, each opening bracket must be matched by the appropriate closing bracket, e.g.

begin ( ) **end**

is a suitable bracket structure whereas

begin (**end**)

is not. A context-free grammar is able to specify these sorts of constraints. Context-free grammars go a long way towards describing the syntactic properties of programming languages and are normally used as the basis of the syntax analysis phase of compilation. However, there are some properties of typical programming languages which cannot be expressed by means of a context-free grammar. For example, the assignment

$$x := y$$

may only be legal if x and y have been declared to have appropriate types. If x and y have been declared as

var $x : integer$;
  $y : char$

the assignment (at least in Pascal) would be illegal. This sort of condition cannot be specified by a context-free grammar and compilers normally perform type checking, etc., separate from but in parallel with the formal syntax analysis phase. We shall see in the next section, however, that it is possible to extend the idea of a context-free grammar to include some non-context-free properties of languages.

It appears, therefore, that the more general the class of grammar used, the more features of typical programming languages we are able to describe. However, the more general the grammar, the more complex is the machine (or program) required to recognize the strings of the corresponding language. We will see in Chapter 3 that the class of recognizer associated with a type-3 grammar is a finite automaton or a finite state machine—a machine with a finite number of states between which control passes as the symbols of a string are read, the string being accepted or not depending on which state the machine reaches finally. For a language generated by a context-free grammar a pushdown automaton is (in general) required, i.e. a finite automaton plus a stack; while for context-sensitive languages a linear bounded automaton is required, i.e. a Turing machine with a finite amount of tape. Finally, a type-0 language requires a Turing machine as a recognizer.

For a full description of these machines and proofs of the equivalence of the various classes of languages and their related automata see Hopcroft and Ullman [1979].

2.3 Formal definition of programming languages

By the formal definition of a programming language we mean the complete description of the syntax and semantics of the language.

Formal definitions of programming languages are useful in the areas of program proving and language design, and it could be argued that certain languages contain features which reflect the method of formal definition used at the design stage. However, as far as we are concerned here there are two main reasons why formal definitions of programming languages are desirable.

1. Programmers wish to be able to find authoritative answers to questions they may have about the syntax and semantics of the language. Language manuals and text books may provide some information about the language but are often ambiguous or uninformative on the finer points of the language.
2. Compiler writers wish a precise definition of the language they are implementing, preferably in a form which can be readily implemented.

These two needs tend to be conflicting. (1) suggests that the definition should be readable, and that a programmer familiar with the method of definition should not have too much difficulty in obtaining an answer to a question about the language. (2) suggests that the definition should be in a form from which an analyser (at least) can be readily built with as little human intervention as possible. In Chapter 4 we will see that the most natural (and readable) grammars are not always in a form from which a parser can be built automatically. In particular certain parsing methods nearly always require the grammar to be transformed before it can be used to build a syntax analyser.

One of the first attempts to define a language formally was the ALGOL 60 report. Much of the syntax was described by means of a context-free grammar, the remainder of the syntax and the semantics being described in English. The original report contained many ambiguities and even the revised report (Naur [1963]) was not free from them (Knuth [1967]).

A further development in the techniques of formal definition was the ALGOL W report (Bauer, Becker, Graham, and Satterthwaite [1968]) in which an attempt was made to include some type information in the formal part of the syntax. The revised report on ALGOL 68 (van Wijngaarden *et al.* [1975]) used a two-level grammar (W-grammar—named after its inventor A. van Wijngaarden) to define the complete syntax of the language. The idea of using a two-level grammar is that, just as the production rules of a conventional grammar provide a finite way of describing a language consisting of an infinite number of strings, so in the ALGOL 68 Report a second grammar is used to generate an infinite number of productions which in turn generate the sentences of the language ALGOL 68. In other words, although ALGOL 68 cannot be generated by means of a context-free grammar, which by definition may only have a finite set of productions, the (simple?) extension of allowing the grammar to have an infinite set of productions is a sufficient generalization for a grammar generating ALGOL 68 to be specified. In fact any type-0 language can be generated by such a grammar. This means we are dealing with rather a powerful concept and, in view of the type of recognizer required for type-0 languages, possibly too powerful a concept for defining programming languages whose non-context-free features tend to be of a fairly simple nature.

Attribute Grammars

Attribute grammars have been used to define the syntax of a number of languages and the partial definition of Pascal which follows is based on the work of Watt [1977] and McGettrick [1980]. Attribute grammars are based on context-free grammars and we will first use a context-free grammar to define part of Pascal and then extend this grammar to define certain non-context-free aspects of the language by means of attributes. The productions of the grammar will be given in Extended Backus–Naur notation which will allow us to avoid using upper case letters which can be reserved for use in connection with attributes. Nonterminals in the grammar will be enclosed in angle brackets, e.g.

⟨ *with statement* ⟩

and

$$::=$$

will be used in place of the arrow to separate the left and right sides of a production.

A program will therefore be defined as

$\langle program \rangle ::=$ **program** $\langle name \rangle$
$(\langle program\ parameters \rangle);$
$\langle block \rangle$

where

$\langle block \rangle ::= \langle label\ declaration\ part \rangle$
$\langle constant\ definition\ part \rangle$
$\langle type\ definition\ part \rangle$
$\langle variable\ declaration\ part \rangle$
$\langle procedure\ and\ function\ declaration\ part \rangle$
$\langle statement\ part \rangle$

$\langle statement\ part \rangle ::= \langle compound\ statement \rangle$

$\langle compound\ statement \rangle ::=$ **begin** $\langle statement \rangle$
$\{; statement\}$
end

where the curly brackets are used to denote zero or more occurrences of whatever they enclose.

$\langle statement \rangle ::= \langle unlabelled\ statement \rangle |$
$\langle label \rangle : \langle unlabelled\ statement \rangle$

$\langle label \rangle ::= \langle unsigned\ integer \rangle$

$\langle unlabelled\ statement \rangle ::= \langle simple\ statement \rangle |$
$\langle structured\ statement \rangle$

$\langle simple\ statement \rangle ::= \langle assignment\ statement \rangle |$
$\langle procedure\ statement \rangle |$
$\langle goto\ statement \rangle |$
$\langle empty\ statement \rangle$

$\langle structured\ statement \rangle ::= \langle compound\ statement \rangle |$
$\langle conditional\ statement \rangle |$

$$\langle \textit{repetitive statement} \rangle |$$
$$\langle \textit{with statement} \rangle$$

$$\langle \textit{assignment statement} \rangle ::= \langle \textit{variable} \rangle$$
$$:=$$
$$\langle \textit{expression} \rangle$$

and so on.

The context-free syntax is unable to specify certain features of Pascal programs, for example that variables have to be declared appropriately, and we will show how the context-free grammar may be extended to include some of these features. At the same time it should be stated (without proof or demonstration) that the mechanism of attribute grammars is powerful enough to define the complete syntax of Pascal.

An attribute grammar will restrict the programs that can be generated by the underlying context-free grammar to those in which the non-context-free aspects of the language are observed. This is done by associating attribute variables with certain terminals and nonterminals in the context-free grammar. The value of an attribute variable might typically be a set of identifiers and their types or a set of labels. Where a variable appears two (or more) times in a production each occurrence will have the same value. In this way information may be passed from the sentence symbol towards the sentence (or program) being generated. An attribute used in this way is said to be *inherited*. Alternatively an attribute variable may be used to pass values from the sentence towards the sentence symbol, in which case the attribute is said to be *synthesized*. Such attributes are usually initialized by the lexical analyser. A production of an attribute grammar may have a rule or rules associated with it specifying relationships which *must* hold between the values of attribute variables appearing in the production. For a program to be generated by an attribute grammar it must be able to be generated by the underlying context-free grammar *and* at each stage of the derivation any such rules associated with the production being used must be observed. Thus the programs generated by an attribute grammar are a subset of those generated by the underlying context-free grammar.

We now proceed by adding attributes to the context-free productions discussed earlier

$$\langle \textit{program} \rangle ::= \textbf{program} \ \langle \textit{name} \rangle \uparrow NAME$$
$$(\langle \textit{program parameters} \rangle);$$
$$\langle \textit{block} \rangle \downarrow STANDARDENV \downarrow \{ \ \} \downarrow \{ \ \}$$

where attribute variables are in upper case following a terminal or nonterminal. A variable name is preceded by an upward arrow for a synthesized attribute and a downward arrow for an inherited attribute. The value of $NAME$ is thus a synthesized attribute obtained from the lexical analyser and passed 'up' to the program. $STANDARDENV$ is an inherited attribute and its value is the set of standard identifiers and their meanings. A block will have two other attributes associated with it: any formal parameters local to the block and any global labels. The values of these two attributes in the above case is the empty set $\{\ \}$.

$\langle block \rangle \downarrow GLOB \downarrow FORM \downarrow GLOBLAB$
$::= \langle label\ declaration\ part \rangle \uparrow LOCLAB$
$\quad\langle constant\ definition\ part \rangle \downarrow GLOB \downarrow FORM \uparrow NEWLOC1$
$\quad\langle type\ definition\ part \rangle \downarrow GLOB \downarrow NEWLOC1 \uparrow NEWLOC2$
$\quad\langle variable\ declaration\ part \rangle \downarrow GLOB \downarrow NEWLOC2 \uparrow NEWLOC3$
$\quad\langle procedure\ and\ function\ declaration\ part \rangle$
$\quad\quad\downarrow GLOB \downarrow NEWLOC3 \downarrow LABELS \uparrow NEWLOC$
$\quad\langle statement\ part \rangle \downarrow ENV \downarrow LABELS \uparrow STMLAB$

in which the following rules are observed:

(1) To form ENV all identifiers in $GLOB$ which are not in $NEWLOC$ should be added to $NEWLOC$.
(2) To form $LABELS$ all labels in $GLOBLAB$ which are not in $LOCLAB$ should be added to $LOCLAB$.
(3) $STMLAB$ is a subset of $LABELS$.

The attributes in the production ensure for example that applied occurrences of local identifiers always occur after their defining occurrences, local constants but not local variables may appear in type definitions, and so on.

$\langle statement\ part \rangle \downarrow ENV \downarrow LABELS \uparrow STMLAB$
$::= \langle compound\ statement \rangle \downarrow ENV \downarrow LABELS \uparrow STMLAB$

$\langle compound\ statement \rangle \downarrow ENV \downarrow LABELS \uparrow STMLAB$
$::= \mathbf{begin}\ \langle statement \rangle \downarrow ENV \downarrow LABELS \uparrow STMLAB |$
$\quad\quad\{ ; \langle statement \rangle \downarrow ENV \downarrow LABELS \uparrow STMLABi\}$
$\quad\mathbf{end}$

where the $STMLABi$ are all disjoint and $STMLAB$ is their union.

$\langle statement \rangle \downarrow ENV \downarrow LABELS \uparrow STMLAB$
$::= \langle unlabelled\ statement \rangle \downarrow ENV \downarrow LABELS \uparrow STMLAB |$
$\quad\langle label \rangle \uparrow LABEL : \langle unlabelled$
$\quad\quad\quad statement \rangle \downarrow ENV \downarrow LABELS \uparrow STMLAB |$

where $STMLAB = LABEL \cup STMLAB |$

$\langle unlabelled\ statement \rangle \downarrow ENV \downarrow LABELS \uparrow STMLAB$
$::= \langle simple\ statement \rangle \downarrow ENV \downarrow LABELS \uparrow STMLAB |$
$\quad\langle structured\ statement \rangle \downarrow ENV \downarrow LABELS \uparrow STMLAB$

$\langle\,simple\,statement\,\rangle\downarrow ENV\downarrow LABELS\uparrow\{\ \}$
$\quad::=\langle\,assignment\ statement\,\rangle\downarrow ENV|$
$\qquad\langle\,procedure\ statement\,\rangle\downarrow ENV|$
$\qquad\langle\,goto\ statement\,\rangle\downarrow LABELS|$
$\qquad\langle\,empty\ statement\,\rangle$

Notice that a simple statement cannot contain any labels other than as part of a goto statement.

$\langle\,structured\ statement\,\rangle\downarrow ENV\downarrow LABELS\uparrow STMLAB$
$\quad::=\langle\,compound\ statement\,\rangle\downarrow ENV\downarrow LABELS\uparrow STMLAB|$
$\qquad\langle\,conditional\ statement\,\rangle\downarrow ENV\downarrow LABELS\uparrow STMLAB|$
$\qquad\langle\,repetitive\ statement\,\rangle\downarrow ENV\downarrow LABELS\uparrow STMLAB|$
$\qquad\langle\,with\ statement\,\rangle\downarrow ENV\downarrow LABELS\uparrow STMLAB$

$\langle\,assignment\ statement\,\rangle\downarrow ENV::=\langle\,variable\,\rangle\downarrow ENV\uparrow TYPE1$
$\qquad\qquad\qquad\qquad\qquad :=$
$\qquad\qquad\qquad\qquad\qquad\langle\,expression\,\rangle\downarrow ENV\uparrow TYPE2$

where *TYPE1* is the type of the variable in *ENV* and *TYPE1* and *TYPE2* are assignment compatible.

Attribute grammars have the advantage of looking like context-free grammars but of being able to specify non-context-free features of languages. In fact any type-0 language can be described by means of an attribute grammar. The fact that programming languages are naturally thought of as context-free languages with non-context-free constraints added means that attribute grammars are well suited to describing them. Techniques are also available for producing efficient analysers automatically from suitable attribute grammars, and this together with their readability means that attribute grammars come close to meeting the two main aims of language definition mentioned at the beginning of this section.

Other well-known methods of describing the syntax of programming languages include the *Vienna Definition Language* for PL/1 (Lucas and Walk [1969]) and Ledgard's Production Systems (Ledgard [1974]).

2.4 The parsing problem

We have shown how a grammar can be used to generate programs in a given programming language. However, the problem which the compiler has to deal with is not how to generate programs but how to check strings of symbols to see if they belong to the language and, if they do, to recognize the structure of the strings in terms of the productions of the grammar. This problem is known as the *parsing problem* and, before investigating it more deeply, we introduce one or two new ideas.

Consider the grammar with productions

1. $E \rightarrow E + T$
2. $E \rightarrow T$
3. $T \rightarrow T \times F$
4. $T \rightarrow F$
5. $F \rightarrow (E)$
6. $F \rightarrow x$
7. $F \rightarrow y$

(E is the sentence symbol).

Clearly the string

$$(x + y) \times x$$

is in the language. In particular it could have been derived as follows:

$E \Rightarrow T$
$\Rightarrow T \times F$
$\Rightarrow F \times F$
$\Rightarrow (E) \times F$
$\Rightarrow (E + T) \times F$
$\Rightarrow (T + T) \times F$
$\Rightarrow (F + T) \times F$
$\Rightarrow (x + T) \times F$
$\Rightarrow (x + F) \times F$
$\Rightarrow (x + y) \times F$
$\Rightarrow (x + y) \times x$

Alternatively it could have been derived as follows:

$E \Rightarrow T$
$\Rightarrow T \times F$
$\Rightarrow T \times x$
$\Rightarrow F \times x$
$\Rightarrow (E) \times x$
$\Rightarrow (E + T) \times x$
$\Rightarrow (E + F) \times x$
$\Rightarrow (E + y) \times x$
$\Rightarrow (T + y) \times x$
$\Rightarrow (F + y) \times x$
$\Rightarrow (x + y) \times x$

Notice that at each stage in the first derivation the leftmost nonterminal in the sentential form was replaced using one of the productions of the grammar. This derivation is, therefore, known as a *leftmost derivation*. In the second

36

derivation the rightmost nonterminal in the sentential form was replaced at each stage using one of the productions. This is, therefore, known as a *rightmost derivation*. There are also other derivations of the sentence which are neither leftmost nor rightmost.

We define the *leftmost parse* of a sentence to be the sequence of productions used to generate the sentence by a leftmost derivation. In the above case the leftmost parse might be written

2,3,4,5,1,2,4,6,4,7,6

The rightmost parse of a sentence is the reverse of the sequence of productions used to generate the sentence by a rightmost derivation, e.g. in the above case the rightmost parse would be

6,4,2,7,4,1,5,4,6,3,2

The reason why the sequence of productions is given in reverse order is related

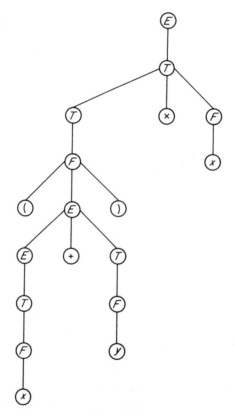

Figure 2.1

to the fact that rightmost parsing is normally associated with reducing a sentence to the sentence symbol rather than generating a sentence from the sentence symbol (see bottom-up parsing later). Note that each production is used the same number of times in the two derivations (or parses).

We can also describe a derivation in terms of building a tree known as the syntax tree (or parse tree). In the case of the string

$$(x + y) \times x$$

the syntax tree is as shown in Figure 2.1. The parsing problem can be expressed as

1. finding a leftmost parse,
2. finding a rightmost parse,
3. building the syntax tree.

In most cases the left and right parses and the syntax tree are unique. However, consider the grammar with productions

$$S \rightarrow S + S$$
$$S \rightarrow x$$

The sentence $x + x + x$ has two syntax trees (Figure 2.2) and two left (and right) parses

$$
\begin{array}{ll}
S \underset{L}{\Rightarrow} S + S & \qquad S \underset{L}{\Rightarrow} S + S \\[4pt]
\underset{L}{\Rightarrow} S + S + S & \qquad \underset{L}{\Rightarrow} x + S \\[4pt]
\underset{L}{\Rightarrow} x + S + S & \qquad \underset{L}{\Rightarrow} x + S + S \\[4pt]
\underset{L}{\Rightarrow} x + x + S & \qquad \underset{L}{\Rightarrow} x + x + S \\[4pt]
\underset{L}{\Rightarrow} x + x + x & \qquad \underset{L}{\Rightarrow} x + x + x
\end{array}
$$

where $\underset{L}{\Rightarrow}$ means 'derives in a leftmost manner'.

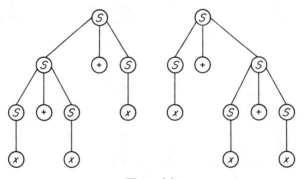

Figure 2.2

If any sentence generated by a grammar has more than one parse tree the grammar is said to be ambiguous. An equivalent condition is that a sentence should have more than one left or right parse. The problem of whether an arbitrary grammar is ambiguous or not is undecidable. That is, no algorithm exists which will accept *any* grammar as input and determine whether or not it is ambiguous (though special cases like productions which contain both left and right recursion can be detected). Some languages are inherently ambiguous, i.e. they cannot be generated by an unambiguous grammar. On the other hand, some ambiguous grammars can be transformed into unambiguous grammars generating the same language. For example, the grammar with productions

$$S \rightarrow x$$
$$S \rightarrow S + x$$

is unambiguous and generates the same language as the ambiguous grammar discussed earlier. For most parsing methods an unambiguous grammar is required. If there exists an algorithm to determine whether a given grammar is suitable for a particular parsing method, *and* the parsing method can only be applied to a subset of the unambiguous grammars, then we have an algorithm which may be used to show that a grammar is unambiguous (but not to show that it is ambiguous).

DeRemer [1974] has compared the parsing problem to kind of dominoes game. In the game there is a piece for each production in the grammar, the top and the bottom of each piece corresponding to the left- and right-hand sides of the production respectively. For the grammar discussed at the beginning of this section the pieces would be as in Figure 2.3. To play the game we start

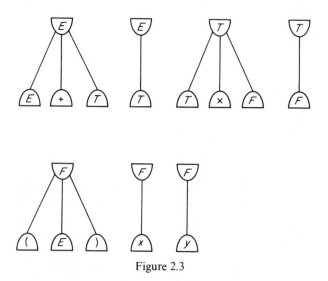

Figure 2.3

Figure 2.4

with a large board with the sentence symbol enclosed in a flat-bottomed semi-circle at the top and the symbols in the sentence enclosed in flat-topped semi-circles along the bottom of the board. For example, to parse the sentence

$$(x + y) \times x$$

the initial position would be as in Figure 2.4. The object of the game is to use the pieces illustrated to link up the sentence and the sentence symbol. The following points should be noted:

1. There are as many copies of each piece as are required.
2. The pieces are elastic and may be stretched as desired.
3. No piece may be played upside down.
4. Pieces meet by joining flat-bottomed edges to flat-topped edges denoting the same symbol.

The solution in the case of the above example is given in Figure 2.5.

The dominoes problem could be solved in a number of ways. One could start at the top of the board with the sentence symbol and try and work downwards to the sentence. Alternatively one could start with the sentence and try to work upwards towards the sentence symbol. One could work from the left-hand side of the board towards the right-hand side or from the right-hand side to the left-hand side or, say, from the top left corner to the bottom right corner of the board. One might wish to solve the problem without ever lifting a piece once laid, or one might be prepared to undo a partial solution and start again.

Most of these methods of tackling the problem correspond to particular parsing methods. Parsing methods are usually either top-down, i.e. work from the sentence symbol towards the sentence, or bottom-up, i.e. work from the sentence towards the sentence symbol, although it is possible to mix the two appro-

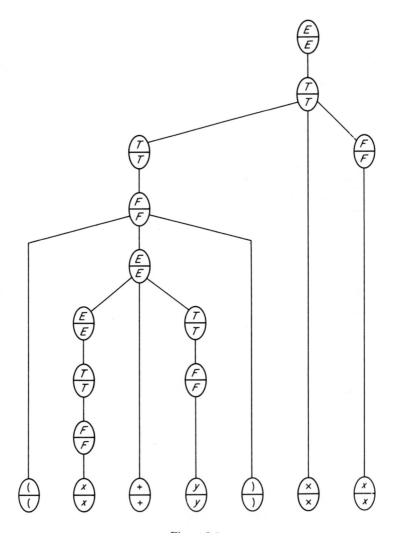

Figure 2.5

aches. It is normal to read the sentence being parsed from left to right, though
from a parsing point of view it may be as simple (or simpler) to read it from right
to left. The idea of never lifting a piece once laid in the dominoes game corresponds to that of never going back on a decision to apply a particular production
in the parsing process. Going back on a parsing decision is sometimes known
as backtracking. Parsing methods are said to be nondeterministic or deterministic depending on whether backtracking can take place or not. Nondeterministic parsing methods can be very expensive in space and time, and
make it very difficult to insert compile-time actions in the parser which might
later have to be undone, such as building the symbol table, etc. In this book

we deal almost entirely with deterministic parsing methods. In Chapter 4 we describe the LL method, which is top-down and uses leftmost derivations, and in Chapter 5 we describe the LR method, which is bottom-up and uses rightmost derivations. We deal mainly with context-free parsing but the techniques can generally be extended to deal with certain classes of more general grammars such as attribute grammars (Watt [1974]) and affix grammars (Koster [1974]).

Exercises

2.1 Give grammars for the following languages:

$$L_1 = \{a^m b^n c^p \mid m,n,p \geq 0\}$$
$$L_2 = \{a^m b^m c^p \mid m,p \geq 0\}$$
$$L_3 = \{x^n a y^n \mid n \geq 0\} \cup \{x^n b y^n \mid n \geq 0\}$$

2.2 State with reasons which, if any, of the above languages are regular.

2.3 Find a regular grammar generating the same language as the grammar with the following productions (S is the sentence symbol):

$$S \to AB$$
$$A \to X \mid Y$$
$$X \to x \mid xX$$
$$Y \to y \mid yY$$
$$B \to b \mid bB$$

2.4 Write down the regular expression generated by the grammar in Exercise 2.3.

2.5 Show that the grammar with the following productions is ambiguous:

$$S \to \textbf{if } b \textbf{ then } S \textbf{ else } S$$
$$\to \textbf{if } b \textbf{ then } S$$
$$\to a$$

2.6 In a certain grammar S is the sentence symbol and the productions are

$$S \to \textbf{real } IDLIST$$
$$IDLIST \to IDLIST, ID$$
$$IDLIST \to ID$$
$$ID \to a$$
$$ID \to b$$
$$ID \to c$$

Give the parse tree for the sentence

real a, b, c

2.7 Derive a grammar generating all strings (including the empty string) over the alphabet $\{0,1\}$.

2.8 Consider the following grammar with sentence symbol *PROGRAM*:

$$PROGRAM \rightarrow \textbf{begin } DECS\,; STATS \textbf{ end}$$
$$DECS \rightarrow d\,; DECS$$
$$d$$
$$STATS \rightarrow s\,; STATS$$
$$s$$

Give the leftmost and the rightmost derivations of

begin $s\,; s\,; d\,; d$ **end**

2.9 An identifier in FORTRAN consists of a sequence of up to six letters and digits, of which the first character must be a letter. Derive
(a) a regular expression for an identifier,
(b) a type-3 grammar generating exactly all the FORTRAN identifiers.

2.10 Most languages have a conditional clause or statement similar to that described in Exercise 2.5. Explain how the potential ambiguity is avoided or resolved in some languages with which you are familiar.

Chapter 3

Lexical Analysis

Conceptually the first phase of the compilation process is Lexical Analysis, i.e. the grouping together of strings of characters denoting identifiers, constants, or language words, etc., into single symbols. In single-pass compilers, of course, the process will take place in parallel with other compilation phases. However, whether or not lexical analysis constitutes a distinct pass of the compiler, it is convenient in describing the construction of a compiler, as well as in constructing one, to think of lexical analysis as a distinct phase of compilation. In this chapter we discuss how the various symbols are recognized, and we describe the tables which the lexical analyser has to build for its own use, and for use by later phases of the compiler. We also discuss particular problems encountered in writing lexical analysers for FORTRAN and other languages.

3.1 Recognition of symbols

The process of lexical analysis is greatly simplified by the nature of the strings which have to be recognized. Examples are identifiers, e.g.

first   *date1*   *no1234*

real numbers, e.g.

1.23   *6.0*   *34.29e – 20*

language words, e.g.

begin   **for**   **case**

All these strings can be generated by regular expressions. For example, real numbers might be generated by the regular expression

$(+|-|)$ *digit*. digit digit*(e(+|-|) digit digit*|)*

from which it is seen that a real number consists of

1. an optional sign,

43

2. a sequence of zero or more digits,
3. a decimal point,
4. a sequence of one or more digits,
5. an optional exponent part consisting of
    (a) an exponent (e)
    (b) an optional sign
    (c) a sequence of one or more digits
  in that order.

    Regular expressions are, of course, equivalent to type-3 grammars (Section 2.2). For example, a type-3 grammar corresponding to the regular expression for a real number given above has productions

$$
\begin{aligned}
R \rightarrow\ & + S|\\
& - S|\\
& digit\ S|\\
& . P\\
S \rightarrow\ & digit\ S|\\
& . P\\
P \rightarrow\ & digit\ F|\\
& digit\\
F \rightarrow\ & digit\ F|\\
& e\ A|\\
& digit\\
A \rightarrow\ & + N|\\
& - N|\\
& digit\ N|\\
& digit\\
N \rightarrow\ & digit\ N|\\
& digit
\end{aligned}
$$

where R is the sentence symbol.

    There is also a one-to-one correspondence between regular expressions (and therefore type-3 grammars) and *finite automata*, which are defined as follows.

    A finite automaton is a device for recognizing strings of a particular language. It has a finite set of states, some of which are termed final states, and control passes from state to state as each character of the string is read, according to a given set of transitions. If, after reading the final character of a string, the automaton is in one of the final states the string is said to belong to the language accepted by the automaton. Otherwise the string does not belong to the language accepted by the automaton.

    More formally, a finite automaton is defined by five characteristics:

1. A finite set of states, K.
2. A finite input alphabet, Σ.

3. A set of transitions, δ
4. A starting state S ($S \in K$).
5. A set of final states F ($F \subseteq K$).

We can write a finite automaton as a 5-tuple

$$M = (K, \Sigma, \delta, S, F)$$

Consider the following example where

the states are A and B,
the input alphabet is $\{0,1\}$,
the starting state is A,
the set of final states is $\{A\}$,
the transitions are

$\delta(A,0) = A$
$\delta(A,1) = B$
$\delta(B,0) = B$
$\delta(B,1) = A$

meaning 'on reading a 0 in state A, control is passed to state A' and so on.

On reading the string

01001011

control will pass successively through the states

$A, A, B, B, B, A, A, B, A$

in that order. Since A is a final state the string is accepted by the finite automaton, However, on reading the string

00111

the automaton passes through the states

A, A, A, B, A, B

in that order and, since B is not a final state, the string is not accepted, i.e. the string does not belong to the language accepted by the automaton. Since zeros do not affect the state of the automaton but each one changes its state from A to B or B to A, and the initial state is the same as the final state, it follows that the language accepted by the automaton consists of exactly those strings which contain an even number of ones.

Another way of representing the transitions is by means of a table (see Table 3.1) or diagrammatically (see Figure 3.1).

Table 3.1

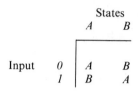

		States	
		A	B
Input	0	A	B
	1	B	A

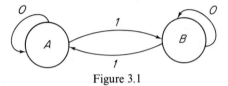

Figure 3.1

The above automaton is said to be deterministic since each entry in the transition table contains a single state. In a nondeterministic finite automaton this is not necessarily the case. Consider the finite automaton defined as follows:

$$M_1 = (K_1, \Sigma_1, \delta_1, S_1, F_1)$$

where

$$K_1 = \{A, B\}$$
$$\Sigma_1 = \{0, 1\}$$
$$S_1 = \{A\}$$
$$F_1 = \{B\}$$

and the transitions are given by Table 3.2

Table 3.2

	A	B
0	$\varnothing$	$\{B\}$
1	$\{A, B\}$	$\{B\}$

or diagrammatically (Figure 3.2).

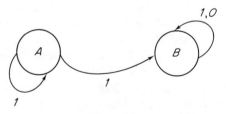

Figure 3.2

M_1 accepts a string if and only if it begins with a one. The string

011

cannot be accepted as there is no transition from A on reading a *0*.
The string

1

will be accepted since there is a transition (more generally a sequence of transitions) leading to a final state on reading the string. There is also a transition leading to a nonfinal state (A to A) but this does not affect the acceptability of the string. For a nondeterministic finite automaton therefore it is necessary to try all possible sequences of transitions before concluding that a string cannot be accepted by the automaton. This can be done either by trying all possibilities in parallel or one after the other. If only one route can be tried at a time (as is usually the case) then backtracking is required, i.e. it is necessary to re-read all or part of the string while another route is investigated. This can clearly be very time consuming.

Corresponding to M_1 there is a deterministic finite automaton M_2 accepting the same language where

$$M_2 = (K_2, \Sigma_2, \delta_2, S_2, F_2)$$

and

$$K_2 = \{A, B, C\}$$
$$\Sigma_2 = \{0, 1\}$$
$$S_2 = \{A\}$$
$$F_2 = \{B\}$$

and the transitions are given by Table 3.3

Table 3.3

	A	B	C
0	C	B	C
1	B	B	C

or diagrammatically (Figure 3.3).

Like M_1, M_2 accepts a string of zeros and ones if and only if the string begins with a *1*. However, in attempting to recognize a string using M_2, backtracking is never required since from any state there is exactly one transition to another state on reading a particular input symbol. This means that using M_2 the time taken to recognize a string is proportional to the length of the string.

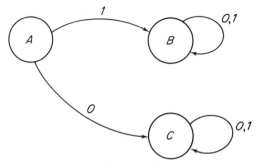

Figure 3.3

It can be shown that corresponding to each nondeterministic finite automaton there corresponds a deterministic finite automaton accepting the same language. The proof involves letting the states in the deterministic automaton correspond to subsets of the states of the nondeterministic one. For example, state B in M_2 corresponds to the set of states $\{A, B\}$ of M_1 and state C in M_2 corresponds to $\emptyset$, the empty set of states of M_1.

The relevance to lexical analysis is that corresponding to each type-3 language there is a deterministic finite automaton which recognizes strings of the language. For example, strings generated by the grammar G_1 with productions

$$A \rightarrow 1A$$
$$A \rightarrow 1B$$
$$A \rightarrow 1$$
$$B \rightarrow 0B$$
$$B \rightarrow 1B$$
$$B \rightarrow 0$$
$$B \rightarrow 1$$

where A is the sentence symbol, are recognized by M_1 or M_2. The grammar is obtained from the nondeterministic finite automaton, M_1, as follows:

1. The starting state of the automaton becomes the sentence symbol of the grammar.
2. Corresponding to the transitions

$$\delta(A, 1) = A$$
$$\delta(A, 1) = B$$
$$\delta(B, 0) = B$$
$$\delta(B, 1) = B$$

we have the productions

$$A \rightarrow 1A$$

$$A \rightarrow 1B$$
$$B \rightarrow 0B$$
$$B \rightarrow 1B$$

and corresponding to the fact that in state A there is a transition on reading a 1 to a final state (B) we have

$$A \rightarrow 1$$

and similarly

$$B \rightarrow 1$$
$$B \rightarrow 0$$

Conversely, the automaton M_1 could have been deduced from the grammar. The automaton M_2 corresponds to the grammar G_2 with productions

$$A \rightarrow 1B$$
$$A \rightarrow 0C$$
$$A \rightarrow 1$$
$$B \rightarrow 0B$$
$$B \rightarrow 1B$$
$$B \rightarrow 0$$
$$B \rightarrow 1$$
$$C \rightarrow 0C$$
$$C \rightarrow 1C$$

which contains the useless nonterminal C but is equivalent to G_1. The grammar G_2 is said to be 'unclean' since it contains a nonterminal which does not generate any terminal symbols.

Writing a lexical analyser consists in part of simulating the various automata to recognize identifiers, numbers, reserved words, etc. A finite automaton to recognize a real number would be given by Figure 3.4. R is the starting state and F and *Finish* the final states. *Error* is the failure state. The automation is deterministic and can be obtained from the type-3 grammar at the beginning of the section.

From the automation a function to recognize a real number can be written. The value of the function is true or false depending on whether a real number is recognized or not. The states in the automation are numbered as shown in Figure 3.4.

```
function realno: bool;
var in:char;
    i:integer;
```

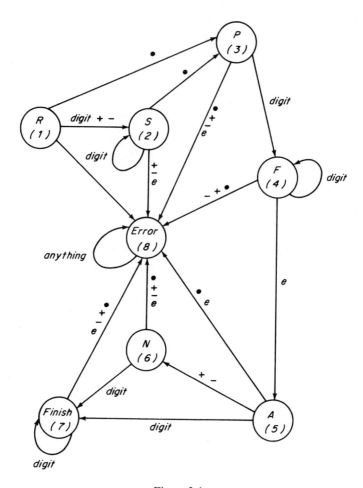

Figure 3.4

```
begin i := 1;
   read(in);
   while digit(in) or sign(in) or
      (in = '.') or (in = 'e') do
   begin case i of
      1 : if sign(in) or digit(in)
         then i := 2
         else if in = '.'
            then i := 3
            else i := 8;
```

```
2 : if digit(in)
     then i := 2
     else if in = '.'
          then i := 3
          else i := 8;
3 : if digit(in)
     then i := 4
     else i := 8;
4 : if digit(in)
     then i := 4
     else if in = 'e'
          then i := 5
          else i := 8;
5 : if digit(in)
     then i := 7
     else if sign(in)
          then i := 6
          else i := 8;
6 : if digit(in)
     then i := 7
     else i := 8;
7 : if digit(in)
     then i := 7
     else i := 8;
8 : i := 8
end;
read(in)
end;
realno := (i = 4) or (i = 7)
end
```

The existence of the functions *digit*, which tests a character to see if it is a digit, and *sign* which tests for a '+' or a '−' are assumed. The function terminates when it comes to a character which cannot be contained in a real number.

Where two symbols can begin with the same character, or string of characters, it may be necessary to 'merge' their recognition procedures.

We have demonstrated that, given a finite automaton accepting strings of a regular language, it is not difficult to write a function to recognize such strings. Of course, for every finite automaton there is a corresponding regular expression, which for a real number was given earlier as

$$(+|-|) \; digit^* . digit \; digit^* \; (e(+|-|) \; digit \; digit^*|)$$

A procedure to recognize a real number can be written from the regular expression

```
procedure realno;
var in:char;
begin read(in);
  if sign(in)
  then read(in);
  while digit(in) do
  read(in);
  if in = '.'
  then read(in)
  else error;
  if digit(in)
  then read(in)
  else error;
  while digit(in) do
  read(in);
  if in = 'e'
  then begin read (in);
            if sign(in)
            then read(in);
            if digit(in)
            then read(in)
            else error;
            while digit(in) do
            read(in)
       end
end
```

error is a procedure which is assumed to take appropriate action when an error situation arises.

Recognizers can be written from regular expressions or finite automata almost as fast as one can write and it is not difficult to automate the process.

3.2 Output from the Lexical Analyser

The lexical analyser will transform the source program in to a sequence of symbols. In doing so, arbitrary length identifiers and constants will be replaced by fixed length symbols. Language words, too, will be replaced by some standard representation. For example, language words might be replaced by integers, identifiers by the letter *I* followed by an integer, constants by the letter *C* followed by an integer, and so on. The integers involved cannot of course be of arbitrary length and therefore it is usual to limit the number of identifiers and constants that may appear in a program to be less than some reasonably large integer. This restriction should not be noticed by the vast majority of users. However, if the limit is ever reached a clear message should be output by the compiler.

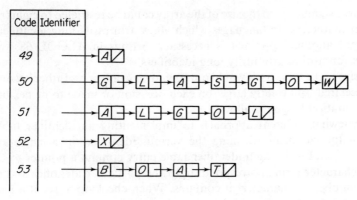

Figure 3.5

The codes produced for language words will be program independent. For example, **begin** might be replaced by *11* and **for** by *22*. In the case of identifiers, however, the standard identifiers such as *read, sin, sqr* will always have the same codes but user-defined identifiers will be allocated codes by the lexical analyser in the order in which they are encountered, the first identifier being e.g. *I1*, the second *I2*, and so on. Each occurrence of a particular identifier (at whatever block level) will be replaced by the same code. This means that an identifier table giving the code for each identifier must be kept by the lexical analyser. After lexical analysis each identifier will have been consistently replaced and, strictly speaking, there will be no further need for the identifier table. However, it may be useful for providing diagnostics to the user in terms of the source language if errors are discovered at a later stage of compilation. For this reason the identifier table is usually retained throughout the compilation process.

Storage of the identifier table usually requires a data structure capable of holding arbitrary length identifiers. An obvious solution is to use lists, where each list element corresponds to a letter of an identifier and ☑ represents the null pointer (Figure 3.5).

In Pascal the identifier table would require the following type declarations:

```
type list = ↑listel;
     listel = record l:char;
                     next:list
            end;
     idtable = array [1..100] of record code:integer;
                                        ident:list
            end;
```

The large number of pointers used in such a table would seem to waste space. Alternatively a character array could be used to store the actual characters of each identifier. In Pascal, only the first eight characters of an identifier are often considered significant so the size of the array could be restricted to eight (possibly packed) characters. In languages which allow arbitrarily long identifiers to be significant another approach is necessary. Strings in ALGOL 68 would be suitable for storing arbitrarily long identifiers.

The size of the table itself would not be known in advance. Either it would need to be declared 'sufficiently large' on each occasion or made to be flexible if the implementation language allowed.

A somewhat different approach to implementing an identifier table is to store all the characters forming the various identifiers in a single array of characters, and to let each identifier table entry contain a pointer to the start of the character string corresponding to the particular identifier and a count of the number of characters it contains. When checking to see if a particular identifier is already in the table it is only necessary to do a character-by-character comparison with those identifiers already in the table which happen to be of the appropriate length (Figure 3.6).

A similar type of table is required for constants. Some compilers check the lengths of constants and evaluate them during lexical analysis. The length of constant which is allowable, however, usually depends on the host machine, and it would seem more satisfactory just to store the arbitrary length constants in a table at the lexical analysis stage rather than to introduce machine dependencies at such an early stage of the compilation process. The constant table will be required at a later stage of compilation, but what the lexical analyser must pass to the syntax analyser is that a constant of a particular type has been stored in the constant table at a specific address. The value at the address may not be required until the final phase of code generation but its type will be required during the analysis stage. The lexical analyser will pass to the syntax analyser a code of the form $TXXX$ (where XXX denotes the

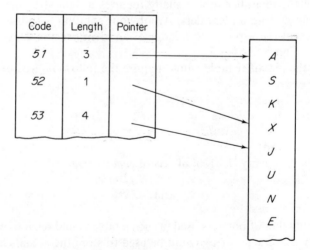

Figure 3.6

constant table entry where the value is to be found and *T* its type). As an alternative, 'small' integer constants may be passed as literals rather than as pointers to the constant table. For example, *C001* to *C009* could represent the integers 1 to 9.

ALGOL 68 programs may contain user-defined bold identifiers (or bold tags) such as

list, max

which are used to define modes or operators. The lexical analyser treats these in a similar way to identifiers by putting them in a table which is passed on to later passes for diagnostic purposes.

3.3 Comments, etc.

As well as passing on a representation of the symbols in the source program the lexical analyser may insert additional information into the source text or remove strings of characters from the text. An example of the former is line numbers. For diagnostic purposes, especially in a multi-pass compiler, it is useful to be able to refer to program errors by means of line numbers in the original source text. It is simple for the lexical analyser to insert line numbers into the program as it is being processed, and these line numbers can be passed on to subsequent passes as long as program errors are liable to be detected (probably as far as machine-code generation if constants are not checked until this stage).

Comments are included in programs solely for the benefit of the human reader. They do not concern the compiler in any way and will normally be removed by the lexical analyser. ALGOL 68 and Ada programs may also include pragmatic remarks which, like commentary, do not affect the meaning of programs. However, pragmatic remarks are of interest to the compiler and may affect the manner in which compilation takes place. They are used to convey messages from the programmer to the compiler concerning, for example, whether a particular section of program should be optimized with respect to execution time or whether a particular method of error recovery should be used. Pragmatic remarks may concern one particular phase of the compiler, such as the lexical analyser or the code generator, or they may concern more than one phase of the compiler. Where a pragmatic remark concerns only the lexical analyser then it will be removed at this stage. Otherwise it will be passed on.

3.4 Problems concerning particular languages

For the main part a lexical analyser will base its decisions on information contained in the symbol it is processing. One would normally expect a lexical analyser to accept (and to be happy with) any sequence of symbols belonging to the language being compiled. In recognizing an integer constant, for example, the lexical analyser would not be concerned whether it followed an operator or a **begin** symbol or whether it occurred within a procedure declaration or a **for** statement. A problem can arise when the way in which characters are combined to form symbols depends on the context. In FORTRAN, for example, in the sequence

$$DO\ 7\ I = 1,\ 5$$

up till the moment when the comma has been read 'DO' could be the language word or alternatively part of the identifier

$$DO\ 7\ I$$

Similarly

$$IF(I) = I$$

is an *assignment* whereas

$$IF(I)\ 1,\ 2,\ 3$$

is an *arithmetic IF* statement.

To resolve these ambiguities the lexical analyser has to do some lookahead. The problem arises because in FORTRAN spaces are not significant.

In PL/1 language words are (in the main) not reserved and certain ambiguities can require an arbitrary amount of lookahead to resolve. For example

$$IF(I) = THEN + THEN;$$

where the 'expression' I can be arbitrarily complex, is an *assignment-statement* whereas

$$IF(I) = THEN + THEN\ THEN\ldots$$

is an *if-statement*. Also

$$DO\ WHILE(P = 0);$$

is a *DO WHILE statement* whereas

$$DO\ WHILE(P) = 0\ldots$$

is a *DO statement* with control variable $WHILE(P)$

In COBOL and Pascal, language words (over 100 of them in COBOL) are reserved and cannot be used as identifiers. In BASIC and ALGOL 68 language words take a different form from identifiers and cannot be confused with them.

In Pascal programs separators are required between consecutive identifiers, numbers, or language words. These may be spaces, new lines, or comments. Separators may not, however, appear within identifiers, numbers, or language words. With these restrictions a Pascal lexical analyser requires very little context information to operate. A minimum amount of context can be used to distinguish between

    and   ..

or

    :   and   :=

which are all single symbols to the syntax analyser.

ALGOL 68, however, illustrates how problems can arise. Assuming operators to be symbols of the language, the sequence of characters

    $<=$

might be interpreted as an operator (usual meaning 'less than or equal to'). However, the same sequence of characters could also occur in an ALGOL 68 program within the declaration of the operator $<$, e.g.

op $<=$ ...

In this case '$<$' is an operator and '$=$' is a symbol separating the operator name from the routine defining it.

In this case the lexical analyser would be expected to pass on '$<$' and '$=$' as two distinct symbols. For the lexical analyser to be able to distinguish between the compound symbol

    $<=$

and the pair of symbols '$<$' and '$=$' appearing in succession it is necessary for the lexical analyser to have some context information. Clearly if **op** precedes '$<=$' it should be treated as two separate symbols. Similarly in the following context where we have a sequence of operator declarations separated by commas

op $>=$ ..., $<=$

'$<$' and '$=$' are distinct symbols. To cope with these sorts of situations it is occasionally necessary (at least to avoid complications at a later stage) for a lexical analyser for ALGOL 68 to know something about the context in which it is operating.

Formats also cause complications in ALGOL 68. Within a format (used for input/output) certain letters such as X, Y, L have well-defined meanings whereas elsewhere they might be taken to be identifiers (or parts of identifiers). Each format is surrounded by a pair of format symbols (usually dollar symbols) so that the lexical analyser always knows whether it is within a format or not and can interpret the letters X, Y, L, etc. accordingly. A complication arises in that formats can contain closed clauses (blocks) inside which, of course, the normal interpretation should again be used for these characters. In

$$\$ \, n \, (x - 1) \, x, \, dd \, \$$$

$x - 1$ spaces (the second x is an alignment symbol denoting a space) are taken before writing (assuming the format is being used in connection with output) a two-digit integer.

It is also possible for a closed clause within a format to contain a format, and so on to any depth. A suitable structure for a lexical analyser to deal with the situation would be for it to consist of two mutually recursive procedures, one corresponding to each of the modes in which it is required to operate.

We have already mentioned that an ALGOL 68 program may contain user-defined bold tags denoting modes or operators. However, as far as the lexical analyser is concerned, the context information necessary to distinguish between user-defined modes and user-defined operators is not available and bold tags are simply passed on as such. Each implementation of ALGOL 68 will have a method of representing bold tags (and languages words) in a program, the two most common representations of the language word **begin** being

$$\text{'}BEGIN\text{'} \text{ and } . BEGIN$$

The lexical analyser could be designed to accept more than one representation of bold symbols, with one particular representation being assumed unless the programmer indicated otherwise by means of a pragmat. A standard representation for ALGOL 68 is described in Hansen and Boom [1977].

Were it not for points like those described in this section, the production of lexical analysers would be a fairly straightforward process and lexical analysers could be produced automatically by means of a lexical analyser generator, which accepted as input the syntax of the various symbols of a particular language and output a lexical analyser for the language.

Lexical analysis may be relatively straightforward, but as far as compilation time is concerned it turns out to be rather expensive. For many compilers around half the time taken to compile a program is taken up by lexical analysis. This is largely unavoidable because of the character nature of the input and if it were not so, for some particular compiler, this would tend to suggest that some of the other phases of the compiler were not as efficient as they might be.

Exercises

3.1 Write down the productions of a type-3 grammar generating the regular expression

$(101)* (010)*$

3.2 Derive a finite automaton corresponding to the regular expression in Exercise 3.1.

3.3 Derive a nondeterministic finite automaton accepting the regular expression

$(101)* (110)*$

3.4 Derive a deterministic automaton accepting the regular expression in Exercise 3.3.

3.5 Give a type-3 grammar corresponding to the finite automaton described by Figure 3.7, where A is the starting state and C the final state. How would you describe the language?

3.6 Write a procedure to recognize strings of the language accepted by the automaton in Exercise 3.5.

3.7 A fixed point number is defined to be an optional sign followed by a string of zero or more digits, followed by a point, followed by a string of zero or more digits; containing at least one digit (before or after the point). Write a procedure to recognize such a number.

3.8 A goods train may have one or two engines at the front, followed by one or more trucks, followed by a guards van. Write a procedure to recognize a goods train.

3.9 Suggest data structures suitable for implementing a constant table.

3.10 Suggest an alternative to mutually recursive procedures for dealing with the two lexical analysis modes required for ALGOL 68 (i.e. within and outside formats).

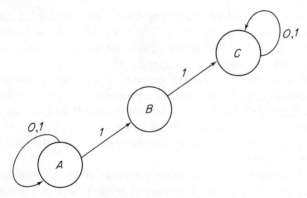

Figure 3.7

Chapter 4

Context-Free Grammars and Top-Down
Syntax Analysis

In the last chapter we discussed the recognition problem for type-3 languages, and showed that a finite automaton could be used to recognize any type-3 language. Furthermore, we found that we could always use a deterministic automaton, so that backtracking was never required. While type-3 grammars are suitable for generating the symbols which are constructed during lexical analysis, they are not so suitable for describing the ways in which these symbols can be combined to form sentences of typical programming languages. For example, as we have already mentioned in Chapter 2, bracket matching cannot be specified by means of a type-3 grammar. Context-free grammars, although not able to specify all properties of typical programming languages, are more general and therefore more suitable as a basis for the syntax analysis (parsing) phase of compilation.

In this chapter we discuss the properties of context-free grammars and their relation to automata theory. We also describe top-down methods of syntax analysis. Bottom-up methods are described in Chapter 5.

4.1 Context-free grammars

Traditionally, context-free grammars have been used as a basis for the syntax analysis phase of compilation. Where a programming language cannot be generated by a context-free grammar it is always possible to find a context-free grammar which generates a superset of the language, i.e. generates a language which contains the given programming language. Using this grammar as a basis for syntax analysis means that certain restrictions in the actual language (e.g. that all identifiers in the program are declared) will not be checked by the parser. However, it is usually not difficult to incorporate other actions in the compiler (e.g. by the use of a symbol table) to perform the necessary checks on the source program.

From the definition of a context-free grammar given in Chapter 2 it is clear that the class of context-free grammars is more powerful (i.e. can generate more languages) than the class of regular grammars but less powerful than the context-sensitive grammars. The language

60

$$\{a^n b^n \mid n \geq 0\}$$

is context free but not regular. It is generated by the grammar with productions

$$S \to aSb$$
$$S \to \varepsilon$$

On the other hand, the language

$$\{a^n b^n c^n \mid n \geq 0\}$$

is context sensitive but not context free.

There are a number of characteristics of context-free grammars, and proofs of most of the following results can be found in Hopcroft and Ullman [1979].

1. Canonical form

(a) Every context-free grammar is equivalent to (i.e. generates the same language as) a grammar in *Chomsky Normal Form*, i.e. with all productions of the form

$$A \to BC$$
$$A \to a$$

with the usual convention regarding terminals and nonterminals.

(b) Every context-free grammar is equivalent to a grammar in *Greibach Normal Form*, i.e. with all productions of the form

$$A \to b\alpha$$

where α is a (possibly empty) string of nonterminals.

2. Self-embedding

Self-embedding is defined as follows. If in a grammar G there is a nonterminal, A say, for which

$$A \underset{G}{\overset{*}{\Rightarrow}} \alpha_1 A \alpha_2$$

where α_1 and α_2 are non-empty strings of terminals and/or nonterminals then the grammar is said to *contain self-embedding*. For example, the following two grammars contain self-embedding:

1. $G_1 = (\{S\}, \{a, b\}, P, S)$
   where the elements of P are

$$S \rightarrow aSb$$
$$S \rightarrow \varepsilon$$

2. $G_2 = (\{S, A\}, \{\textbf{begin}, \textbf{end}, [,]\}, P, S)$
   where the elements of P are

$$S \rightarrow \textbf{begin } A \textbf{ end}$$
$$S \rightarrow \varepsilon$$
$$A \rightarrow [S]$$

In the latter case both A and S are said to exhibit the self-embedding property. A theoretical result states that any context-free grammar which does not contain self-embedding is equivalent to a regular grammar or (alternatively) generates a regular language. It is also the case that a regular grammar cannot contain self-embedding. It is self-embedding that effectively distinguishes between context-free (nonregular) languages and regular languages. As can be seen from the second example above, matching brackets, etc., involves self-embedding and therefore cannot be specified by a regular grammar.

3. *Pumping lemma*

For any context-free language, L, there exists a constant k such that any sentence z of the language whose length is not less than k can be written in the form

$$z = uvwxy \quad \text{where} \quad |vwx| \leq k$$

and v and x are not both the empty string and the string

$$uv^i wx^i y \quad (\text{for } i \geq 0)$$

is in L.

This lemma can be used to show that certain languages are not context free. Consider the language

$$\{\alpha\alpha \,|\, \alpha \in \{0, 1\}^*\}$$

($\{0, 1\}^*$ is the closure of $\{0, 1\}$ as defined in Section 2.2).

Assume the language is context free. From the lemma any string z of length $\geq k$, can be written

$$uvwxy$$

where $|vwx| \leq k$, $|vx| \neq 0$ and $uv^i wx^i y (i \geq 0)$ is in the language
Let α consist of k 0's followed by k 1's so that z is of the form

$$000 \ldots 01111 \ldots 1000 \ldots 01111 \ldots 1$$

This string can be written in the form

$uvwxy$

but since $|vwx| \le k$ either

1. v and x are both in the first half of z or are both in the second half, or
2. vx contains 1's from the first half of the string and 0's from the second half of the string.

In the first case uwy will be formed by removing 0's and 1's from the first half or the second half of z (but not both). Thus uwy will not be in the language.

In the second case uwy will be formed from z by removing 1's from the first half and 0's from the second half of z. Again the resultant string will not be in the language.

We have thus shown that the given string cannot be expressed in the form

$uvwxy$

in such a way that uwy is also in the language. This contradicts the pumping lemma and therefore the language is not context free.

Similarly it can be shown that the languages

$$\{a^n b^n c^n \,|\, n \ge 0\}$$
$$\{a^i \,|\, i \text{ is prime}\}$$

are not context free.

From a parsing point of view it is important to know what type of automaton is capable of recognizing a context-free language. The answer is a *push-down automaton* which is equivalent to a finite automaton with the addition of a push-down store or stack. A move of the push-down automaton consists of either

(a) reading an input symbol, replacing the top symbol on the stack by a (possibly empty) string of symbols, and changing state, or
(b) as (a), but without reading an input symbol.

A push-down automaton may be represented by a tuple

$$(K, \Sigma, \Gamma, \delta, q_0, Z_0)$$

where
K is a finite set of states
Σ is the input alphabet
Γ is the push-down alphabet
δ is a set of transitions
q_0 is the initial state
Z_0 is a push-down symbol which is initially on the stack.

For example, consider the push-down automaton M defined as follows:

$$K = \{A\}$$
$$\Sigma = \{`(`,`)`\}$$
$$\Gamma = \{O, I\}$$
$$q_0 = \{A\}$$
$$Z_0 = I$$

δ is given by

$$\delta(A, I, `(`) = (A, IO)$$

(meaning in state A with I on top of stack on reading '(' goto state A and replace I by IO).

$$\delta(A, O, `(`) = (A, OO)$$
$$\delta(A, O, `)`) = (A, \varepsilon)$$
$$\delta(A, I, \varepsilon) = (A, \varepsilon)$$

M recognizes matched pairs of brackets. Opening brackets (represented by O) are put on the stack and removed when a corresponding closing bracket is encountered. The bracket string is accepted if reading the complete string leaves the stack empty. This is the normal way by which push-down automata accept strings, though it is also possible to define push-down automata that accept by final state, and the two types can be shown to be equivalent.

The push-down automaton described above was deterministic, i.e. for each admissible input symbol there was a unique transition. As for finite automata, we can also define nondeterministic push-down automata which may contain a *set* of transitions for a given input, state, and stack contents.

Consider the language

$$\{\alpha\alpha^r \mid \alpha \text{ in } \{0, 1\}^*\}$$

α^r denotes α reversed.

The language is accepted by the following nondeterministic push-down automaton

$$M = (\{A, B\}, \{0, 1\}, \{I, 0, 1\}, \delta, A, I)$$

where transitions are given by

$$\delta(A, I, 0) = \{(A, I0)\}$$
$$\delta(A, I, 1) = \{(A, I1)\}$$
$$\delta(A, 0, 0) = \{(A, 00), (B, \varepsilon)\}$$
$$\delta(A, 1, 1) = \{(A, 11), (B, \varepsilon)\}$$
$$\delta(A, 0, 1) = \{(A, 01)\}$$

$$\delta(A,1,0) = \{(A,10)\}$$
$$\delta(B,0,0) = \{(B,\varepsilon)\}$$
$$\delta(B,1,1) = \{(B,\varepsilon)\}$$
$$\delta(B,I,\varepsilon) = \{(B,\varepsilon)\}$$
$$\delta(A,I,\varepsilon) = \{(A,\varepsilon)\}$$

State A corresponds to having read less than half the string and state B to having read more than half the string. As the first half is being read symbols are put on the stack (state A), and, as the second half is being read, each symbol is checked against the top symbol of the stack and one symbol is removed from the stack. The problem is knowing when the midpoint of the string has been reached. A necessary condition is that two consecutive ones or two consecutive zeros are read. However, this is not a sufficient condition. Consider, for example, the string

01011011011010

The two ones in position 4 and 5 might be thought to mark the middle of the string and without (in general) an arbitrary amount of lookahead there is no way of telling whether it is the middle or not. Hence the alternative transitions in state A when the incoming symbol and the top of the stack are identical. This makes the push-down automaton nondeterministic and it is difficult to see how it could be otherwise. Indeed, this is borne out by the theory which asserts that there exist nondeterministic push-down automata which accept context-free languages which are not accepted by any deterministic push-down automata. Thus, while for a regular language we could always find a deterministic automaton which would accept it, the corresponding result does not hold for context-free languages. Thus, it is not possible to find deterministic automata corresponding to some context-free languages. When it is recalled that deterministic finite automata were produced from nondeterministic ones by merging states where two or more transitions led to different states, it is not surprising that the same approach does not work with push-down automata when alternative transitions may affect the stack in different ways.

Parsing involves effectively simulating the appropriate push-down automaton and the effect of the above is that some context-free languages cannot be parsed deterministically (i.e. without backtracking). How important this is from the compiler writer's point of view depends on whether typical programming languages can be parsed deterministically or not. We define a *deterministic language* to be one which can be parsed deterministically; it turns out that most programming languages are deterministic, or at least almost so.

There is a one-to-one correspondence between context-free grammars and push-down automata and it may depend on which grammar we use to generate a language as to whether the corresponding push-down automaton is deterministic or not. We say that a parsing method is deterministic (for a particular grammar) if no backtracking is involved in parsing the grammar. Some languages can be parsed deterministically by one parsing method but not by another. In particular, some languages can be parsed deterministically from the bottom up but not from the top down. In this book we will be concerned almost entirely with deterministic parsing methods. Nondeterministic methods may not be too intolerable for line-oriented languages such as BASIC or FORTRAN but for highly recursive languages such as ALGOL 68 or Pascal, where the compiler may have to backtrack over not just the current line but over a large part of a program, the overheads are just not acceptable. Another disadvantage of backtracking is that it may involve undoing compiler actions which take place in parallel with syntax analysis.

4.2 Method of recursive descent

A well-known and easy-to-implement top-down deterministic parsing method is known as the method of recursive descent. Using it, a syntax analyser can be written from a suitable grammar and, furthermore, can be written almost as fast as one can write.

Consider, for example, the language generated by the grammar with the following productions:

> $PROGRAM \rightarrow begin\ DECLIST\ comma\ STATELIST\ end$
> $DECLIST \rightarrow d\ semi\ DECLIST$
> $DECLIST \rightarrow d$
> $STATELIST \rightarrow s\ semi\ STATELIST$
> $STATELIST \rightarrow s$

We first modify the grammar to the following:

> $PROGRAM \rightarrow begin\ DECLIST\ comma\ STATELIST\ end$
> $DECLIST \rightarrow d\ X$
> $X \rightarrow semi\ DECLIST$
> $X \rightarrow \varepsilon$
> $STATELIST \rightarrow s\ Y$
> $Y \rightarrow semi\ STATELIST$
> $Y \rightarrow \varepsilon$

Now we write a procedure to recognize each nonterminal. Starting with the sentence symbol ($PROGRAM$) we have

```
procedure PROGRAM;
begin    if symbol <> beg
         then error;
         symbol:=lexical;
         DECLIST;
         if symbol <> comma
```

```
          then error;
          symbol := lexical;
          STATELIST;
          if symbol < > fin
          then error
    end;

    procedure DECLIST;
    begin if symbol < > d
          then error;
          symbol := lexical;
          X
    end;

    procedure X;
    begin if symbol = semi
          then begin symbol := lexical;
                     DECLIST
               end
          else if symbol = comma
               then
               else error
    end;

    procedure STATELIST;
    begin if symbol < > s
          then error;
          symbol := lexical;
          Y
    end;

    procedure Y;
    begin if symbol = semi
          then begin symbol := lexical;
                     STATELIST
               end
          else if symbol = fin
               then
               else error
    end
```

Notice the use of the dummy statement (i.e. do nothing) after the final '**then**'. In Pascal a forward directive has to be used if a function or procedure is called before it is fully declared. The above sequence of procedure declarations would be legal in Pascal if preceded by

procedure *DECLIST*; *forward*;
procedure *STATELIST*; *forward*;
procedure *X*; *forward*;
procedure *Y*; *forward*;

In the above procedures a number of assumptions have been made:

1. *error* is a procedure to deal with syntax errors; the details do not concern us here,
2. *lexical* is a function which reads characters of source text and whose value is the next symbol. Alternatively, if lexical analysis is performed by a previous pass *lexical* simply reads the next symbol,
3. *semi, comma,* etc. are identifiers whose values are the compile-time representations of the corresponding terminals, similarly *beg* and *fin* correspond to the symbols *begin* and *end* respectively.
4. before *PROGRAM* is called the following assignment has taken place:

   symbol := *lexical*.

Parsing a sentence of the language could involve many recursive calls of the procedures corresponding to the nonterminals in the grammar. If we choose to represent the grammar in a slightly different way this recursion can be replaced by iteration:

   PROGRAM → *begin DECLIST comma STATELIST end*
   DECLIST → *d* (*semi d*)*
   STATELIST → *s* (*semi s*)*

where (*x*)* means zero or more occurrences of *x*. The procedures for *DECLIST* and *STATELIST* then become

```
proc DECLIST;
begin if symbol < > d
      then error;
      symbol: = lexical;
      while symbol = semi do
      begin symbol: = lexical;
            if symbol < > d
            then error;
            symbol: = lexical
      end
end;

proc STATELIST;
begin if symbol < > s
      then error;
      symbol: = lexical;
```

```
      while symbol = semi do
      begin symbol : = lexical;
            if symbol < > s
            then error ;
            symbol : = lexical
      end
end ;
```

Replacing recursion by iteration is likely to make the analyser more efficient and also (arguably) more readable.

The advantages of writing a recursive descent parser are fairly obvious. The main one is the speed at which the parser can be written from the corresponding grammar. Another is that, because of the close correspondence between the grammar and the parser, there is a high probability that the parser will be correct, or at least any errors will be of a simple nature. The disadvantages of the method, though perhaps less obvious, are no less real. The high incidence of procedure calls during syntax analysis are likely to make the parser relatively slow, and, compared with some table-driven parsing methods to be described later, the parser is likely to be rather large. Although the method is well suited to the insertion of code generation actions in the parser, this inevitably leads to different phases of compilation becoming intermixed. This does not lead to reliable or to easily maintainable compilers and tends to introduce machine dependencies into the parser. The recursive descent parsing method is, however, related to another well-known top-down parsing method which avoids most of the problems and is discussed in the next section.

4.3 LL(1) grammars

An LL(1) grammar is one type of grammar from which a top-down deterministic parser can be produced. As a preliminary to defining an LL(1) grammar more precisely we introduce the idea of an *s*-grammar.

Definition An *s*-grammar is one in which:

1. The right-hand side of each production begins with a terminal.
2. Where a nonterminal appears on the left-hand side of more than one production, the corresponding right-hand sides begin with different terminals.

Condition (1) is similar to saying the grammar is in Greibach Normal Form except that the terminal at the start of each right-hand side may be followed by nonterminals *and/or* terminals.

Condition (2) is what helps us to write a deterministic top-down parser, since, in deriving a sentence of the language, it is always possible to distinguish between the alternative productions for a leftmost nonterminal in the sentential form by examining a single lookahead symbol.

The grammar with productions

$$S \rightarrow pX$$
$$S \rightarrow qY$$
$$X \rightarrow aXb$$
$$X \rightarrow x$$
$$Y \rightarrow aYd$$
$$Y \rightarrow y$$

is an *s*-grammar whereas the following grammar which generates the same language is not:

$$S \rightarrow R$$
$$S \rightarrow T$$
$$R \rightarrow pX$$
$$T \rightarrow qY$$
$$X \rightarrow aXb$$
$$X \rightarrow x$$
$$Y \rightarrow aYd$$
$$Y \rightarrow y$$

since two of the right-hand sides do not begin with terminals.

It is extremely easy to detect whether a given grammar is an *s*-grammar or not, and in some cases a grammar which is not an *s*-grammar can be transformed into an *s*-grammar without affecting the language generated.

Consider the problem of parsing the string

   paaaxbbb

using the *s*-grammar above. Starting with the sentence symbol S we try to generate the string. A leftmost derivation is used and the result is shown below.

Source string	Derivation
paaaxbbb	S
$p_\uparrow aaaxbbb$	$=> pX_\uparrow$
$pa_\uparrow aaxbbb$	$=> paXb_\uparrow$
$paa_\uparrow axbbb$	$=> paaXbb_\uparrow$
$paaa_\uparrow xbbb$	$=> paaa_\uparrow Xbbb$
$paaaxbbb_\uparrow$	$=> paaaxbbb_\uparrow$

As the derivation takes place initial terminals in the sentential form are checked off against symbols in the source string. At each stage of the derivation the upward arrow indicates the point up to which the source has been read and the initial terminals of the derivation checked. Where the leftmost nonterminal in the sentential form can be replaced using more than one production the appropriate production can always be chosen by examining the next symbol of the input string for, since we are dealing with an s-grammar, the right-hand sides of the alternative productions will begin with distinct terminals.

We see therefore that it is always possible to write a deterministic top-down parser for a language generated by an s-grammar. An LL(1) grammar is a generalization of an s-grammar and we will see that the way in which it is generalized will still allow us to construct deterministic top-down parsers.

The two L's in LL(1) refer to the fact that strings are parsed from Left to right and Leftmost derivations are used. The 1 denotes the fact that alternative productions are chosen by means of a single symbol of lookahead. The terminology is due to Knuth [1971] and the properties of LL(1) grammars have also been investigated by Foster [1968]. We first note that, even though the right-hand side of a production does not start with a terminal, it may be possible to deduce that a given alternative for some nonterminal symbol may only give rise to strings which begin with one of a particular set of terminals. For example, from the productions

$$S \rightarrow RY$$
$$S \rightarrow TZ$$
$$R \rightarrow paXb$$
$$T \rightarrow qaYd$$

it can be deduced that the production

$$S \rightarrow RY$$

should only be applied in a top-down parse (assuming there are no other productions for R) when the lookahead symbol is p. Similarly the production

$$S \rightarrow TZ$$

should only be applied when the lookahead symbol is q.

This leads us to introduce the idea of sets of *starter symbols* defined as follows:

$$a \in S(A) \Leftrightarrow A \overset{+}{\Rightarrow} a\alpha$$

where A is a nonterminal symbol, α is a string of terminals and/or nonterminals, and $S(A)$ denotes the set of starter symbols of A. In the grammar with productions

$$P \rightarrow Ac$$

$$P \rightarrow Bd$$
$$A \rightarrow a$$
$$A \rightarrow aA$$
$$B \rightarrow b$$
$$B \rightarrow bB$$

a and b are starter symbols for P. We also define the set of starter symbols for string of terminals and/or nonterminals as follows:

$$a \in S(\alpha) \Leftrightarrow \alpha \overset{*}{\Rightarrow} a\beta$$

where α and β are strings of terminals and/or nonterminals (β may be empty).

A necessary condition for a grammar to be LL(1) is that the sets of starter symbols for alternative right-hand sides of productions are disjoint.

Care should be taken when a nonterminal at the start of a right-hand side can generate the empty string. For example, in

$$P \rightarrow AB$$
$$P \rightarrow BG$$
$$A \rightarrow aA$$
$$A \rightarrow \varepsilon$$
$$B \rightarrow c$$
$$B \rightarrow bB$$

we have

$$S(AB) = \{a, b, c\}$$

since A can generate the empty string, and

$$S(BG) = \{b, c\}$$

so the grammar is not LL(1).

Consider also the grammar with productions

$$T \rightarrow AB$$
$$A \rightarrow PQ$$
$$A \rightarrow BC$$
$$P \rightarrow pP$$
$$P \rightarrow \varepsilon$$
$$Q \rightarrow qQ$$
$$Q \rightarrow \varepsilon$$
$$B \rightarrow bB$$
$$B \rightarrow e$$
$$C \rightarrow cC$$
$$C \rightarrow f$$

giving

$$S(PQ) = \{p,q\}$$

and

$$S(BC) = \{b,e\}$$

However, since PQ can generate the empty string, the lookahead symbol on applying the production

$$A \to PQ$$

could be b or e, possible follower symbols of A; and a single lookahead symbol is not sufficient to distinguish between the two alternative right-hand sides for A since b and e are also starter symbols for BC

For this reason, we introduce what Griffiths [1974] calls '*director symbols*', defined as follows. If A is a nonterminal the director symbols of A are

> $S(A) +$ (if A can generate the empty string
> then all the symbols which can follow A).

More generally, for a given alternative α of a nonterminal $P(P \to \alpha)$ we have

$$DS(P, \alpha) = \{a \,|\, a \in S(\alpha) \; or \; (\alpha \overset{*}{\Rightarrow} \varepsilon \text{ and } a \in F(P))\}$$

where $F(P)$ is the set of symbols which can follow P. In the previous example the sets of director symbols are

$$DS(A, PQ) = \{p,q,b,e\}$$
$$DS(A, BC) = \{b,e\}$$

Since the sets are not disjoint, the grammar cannot form the basis of a deterministic top-down parser using one lookahead symbol to distinguish between alternative right-hand sides.

We are now ready to define an LL(1) grammar. A grammar is said to be LL(1) if, for every nonterminal appearing on the left-hand side of more than one production, the sets of director symbols corresponding to the right-hand sides of the alternative productions are disjoint. All LL(1) grammars can be parsed deterministically from the top down.

For a given grammar there exists an algorithm for determining whether it is LL(1) or not and we now describe such an algorithm.

First it is necessary to determine which nonterminals can generate the empty string. To do this we set up a one-dimensional array with one element for each nonterminal. Each element of the array may take one of three values, *YES*, *NO*, or *UNDECIDED*. Initially all the elements are set to *UNDECIDED*. We scan the grammar as many times as are required to set each element to *YES* or *NO*.

On the first scan all productions containing terminals are eliminated. If this leads to the elimination of all productions for some nonterminal the value

NO is assigned to the appropriate element of the array. Secondly, for each production with ε on the right-hand side the value *YES* is assigned to the array element corresponding to the nonterminal on the left-hand side and all productions for that nonterminal are removed from the grammar.

If subsequent scans are required (i.e. some array elements still have the value *UNDECIDED*) the following actions take place:

1. Each production with a symbol on the right-hand side which cannot generate the empty string (as given by the values of the appropriate array element) is eliminated from the grammar. If there are no other productions for the nonterminal on the left-hand side of the eliminated production then the value of the array element corresponding to that nonterminal is set to *NO*.
2. Each nonterminal on the right-hand side of a production which can generate the empty string is deleted from the production. If the right-hand side of a production becomes empty the value *YES* is assigned to the array element corresponding to the nonterminal on the left-hand side and all productions for that nonterminal are removed from the grammar.

This process is continued until a complete scan of the grammar produces no change in the values of the array elements. Assuming the grammar was clean in the first instance (i.e. all nonterminals could generate terminal strings, or the empty string) the array elements will now all be set to *YES* or *NO*. As an example of the process, consider the grammar

1. $A \rightarrow XYZ$
2. $X \rightarrow PQ$
3. $Y \rightarrow RS$
4. $R \rightarrow TU$
5. $P \rightarrow \varepsilon$
6. $P \rightarrow a$
7. $Q \rightarrow aa$
8. $Q \rightarrow \varepsilon$
9. $S \rightarrow cc$
10. $T \rightarrow dd$
11. $U \rightarrow ee$
12. $Z \rightarrow \varepsilon$

After the first pass the array will be as shown in Table 4.1, and the grammar

Table 4.1

A	X	Y	R	P	Q	S	T	U	Z
U	U	U	U	Y	Y	N	N	N	Y

U—UNDECIDED
Y—YES
N—NO

will be reduced to

1. $A \to XYZ$
2. $X \to PQ$
3. $Y \to RS$
4. $R \to TU$

After the second pass the array will be as shown in Table 4.2, and the grammar becomes

Table 4.2

A	X	Y	R	P	Q	S	T	U	Z
U	Y	N	N	Y	Y	N	N	N	Y

1. $A \to XY$

A further pass completes the array (Table 4.3).

Table 4.3

A	X	Y	R	P	Q	S	T	U	Z
N	Y	N	N	Y	Y	N	N	N	Y

The next step is to form a matrix showing all the *immediate starters* of each nonterminal, the term immediate starter being used to denote those symbols which can be seen to be starters by the inspection of a single production. For example, from the productions

$P \to QR$
$Q \to qR$

it is deduced that Q is an immediate starter of P and q is an immediate starter of Q. The starter matrix will have a row for each nonterminal and a column for each terminal and nonterminal. If the nonterminal A, for example, has immediate starters B and C, ones will be placed in the Ath row in the Bth and Cth columns (Table 4.4).

Table 4.4

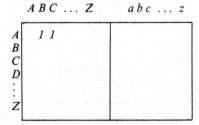

Where the right hand side of a production begins with a nonterminal, the empty string array should be used to check whether the nonterminal can generate the empty string. If so, the symbol following the nonterminal (if any) is an immediate starter of the nonterminal on the left hand side, and so on.

Once the immediate starters have been entered in the matrix further deductions can be made. For example, from the productions

$$P \to QR$$
$$Q \to qV$$

it can be deduced that q is a (non-immediate) starter symbol of P. Alternatively, from the matrix of immediate starters, a one in the Pth row, Qth column together with a one in the Qth row, qth column implies that, if we wish to form the complete starter matrix (not just immediate ones), we should put a one in the Pth row, qth column. More generally we may say that whenever a one occurs in the (i,j)th position *and* the (j,k)th position we should insert a one in the (i,k)th postion. However, suppose there is also a one in the (k,l)th position, then the process should be applied again to produce a one in the (i,l)th position. This process should be continued until there are no instances of a one appearing in the (i,j)th position and the (j,k)th position without a one also appearing in the (i,k)th position.

The algorithm is illustrated by the set of productions

$$A \to BC$$
$$B \to XY$$
$$X \to aa$$

from which three ones can be readily inserted in the immediate starter matrix and, by deduction, three further ones can be inserted in the complete starter matrix corresponding to the fact that X is a non-immediate starter of A, and a is a non-immediate starter of B and also of A (Table 4.5). Non-immediate starters are circled in the table.

The process is known as finding the *transitive closure* of the matrix and has an analogy in graph theory. For example, from Figure 4.1 we can produce

Table 4.5

	A	B	C	...	X	Y	a	...
A	1				①	①		
B					1	①		
C								
⋮								
X						1		
Y								

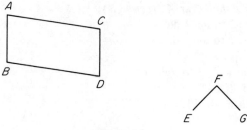

Figure 4.1

a matrix, known as the adjacency matrix, which contains ones to indicate neighbouring vertices, e.g. *A* is a neighbour of *C*, so a one will be inserted in position (*A*, *C*) and so on. (*A* is assumed to be a neighbour of itself.) From the adjacency matrix the transitive closure operation may be performed to produce the reachability matrix which has ones corresponding to vertices which have paths joining them (Tables 4.6 and 4.7).

Table 4.6 Adjacency matrix

	A	*B*	*C*	*D*	*E*	*F*	*G*
A	1	1	1				
B	1	1		1			
C	1		1	1			
D		1	1	1			
E					1	1	
F					1	1	1
G						1	1

Table 4.7 Reachability matrix

	A	*B*	*C*	*D*	*E*	*F*	*G*
A	1	1	1	1			
B	1	1	1	1			
C	1	1	1	1			
D	1	1	1	1			
E					1	1	1
F					1	1	1
G					1	1	1

A well-known algorithm to perform transitive closure is Warshall's algorithm (Warshall [1962]).

A Pascal version of the algorithm follows. Initially the array *A* is the adjacency matrix (or contains immediate starters) and finally it is the reachability matrix (or contains complete starters).

```
procedure Warshall (var A : rectangle);
begin for j := 1 to upb1 do
    for i := 1 to upb1 do
        if A[i, j] = 1
        then for k := 1 to upb2 do
            if A[j, k] = 1
            then A[i, k] := 1
end;
```

where *rectangle* has been defined as

type *rectangle* = **array** [*1..upb1, 1..upb2*] **of** *integer*.

It might be thought that an outer loop would be required in the procedure to repeat the process until there was no change in A. However, due to a theorem by Warshall [1962] this is not necessary. Warshall's algorithm will require time proportional to n^3 for an $n \times n$ matrix. However, it can be shown using the work of Strasen (Strasen [1969]) that an algorithm requiring time proportional to $n^{2.81}$ exists. It is also possible to take advantage of the relatively sparse nature of the immediate starter matrix to produce a more efficient algorithm (Griffiths [1969]).

If it were not for the problem of nonterminals generating the empty string, the LL(1) test would only involve examination of the complete starter matrix. However, we have seen that in computing the director symbols it may be necessary to consider the symbols which can legitimately follow a particular nonterminal. We therefore set up a follower matrix from the productions of the grammar. For example, from the production

$$S \rightarrow ABC$$

it can be deduced that B can follow A and so the element (A, B) is set to 1 in the follower matrix. Similarly C can follow B and the element (B, C) is set to 1. If B can generate the empty string it should also be deduced that C can follow A and the element (A, C) set to 1.
Less obviously, the productions

$$P \rightarrow QR$$
$$Q \rightarrow VU$$

lead to the conclusion that R is a follower of U or, more generally (from the second production), 'any follower of Q is a follower of U'.

It should also be noted that if, for example, B is a follower of A and b is a starter of B then b is also a follower of A. Thus the starter matrix may be used to deduce more follower symbols and the follower matrix augmented accordingly.

From the empty string array, the starter matrix, and the follower matrix the LL(1) condition may be tested. Where a nonterminal appears on the left-hand side of more than one production the director symbols of the various alternative right-hand sides must be evaluated. If, for any such nonterminals, the various sets of director symbols are not disjoint, the grammar is not LL(1). Otherwise it is LL(1).

The grammar transformation which was performed at the beginning of section 4.2 transformed a non-LL(1) grammar (consider the alternatives for *DECLIST* and *STATELIST*) into an LL(1) grammar, viz:

$PROGRAM \rightarrow begin\ DECLIST\ comma\ STATELIST\ end$
$DECLIST \rightarrow d\ X$
$X \rightarrow semi\ DECLIST$
$X \rightarrow \varepsilon$
$STATELIST \rightarrow s\ Y$
$Y \rightarrow semi\ STATELIST$
$Y \rightarrow \varepsilon$

To check the LL(1)-ness of this grammar we form the various matrices (Tables 4.8–4.10). It is only necessary to consider the alternatives for X and Y.

Table 4.8 Empty string array

PROGRAM	DECLIST	STATELIST	X	Y
N	N	N	Y	Y

Table 4.9 Complete starter matrix

PROGRAM DECLIST STATELIST X Y begin d s comma semi end

	PROGRAM	DECLIST	STATELIST	X	Y	begin	d	s	comma	semi	end
PROGRAM						1					
DECLIST							1				
STATELIST								1			
X										1	
Y										1	

Table 4.10 Follower matrix

PROGRAM DECLIST STATELIST X Y begin d s comma semi end

	PROGRAM	DECLIST	STATELIST	X	Y	begin	d	s	comma	semi	end
PROGRAM											
DECLIST									1		
STATELIST											1
X								1			
Y											1

The first alternative for X has director symbol set $\{semi\}$. The second alternative is the empty string so we have to consider what can follow X. The only follower symbol is *comma* so the director symbol set is $\{comma\}$. The director symbol sets are disjoint and so it can be deduced that there is no violation of the LL(1) condition as far as the productions for the nonterminal X are concerned. In a similar manner it can be shown that the director symbol sets for Y are $\{semi\}$ and $\{end\}$ and therefore the grammar is LL(1).

4.4 LL(1) languages

We have seen that there is an algorithm to determine whether a grammar is LL(1) or not. Two questions now arise:

1. Do all languages posses an LL(1) grammar?
2. If not, is there an algorithm to determine whether a language is LL(1) (i.e. can be generated by an LL(1) grammar) or not?

The answer to the first question is no. For example, the language

$$\{ \alpha \alpha^r | \alpha \text{ in } \{0,1\}^* \}$$

generated by the grammar with productions

$$S \rightarrow 0S0$$
$$S \rightarrow 1S1$$
$$S \rightarrow \varepsilon$$

is not LL(1). As we saw in Section 4.1 the language generated is not acceptable by any deterministic push-down automaton (this point was not actually proved) and is therefore not generated by any LL(1) grammar. Thus we see that a grammar which is not LL(1) may or may not generate an LL(1) language or, expressed another way, given a non-LL(1) grammar it may or may not be possible to transform it into an LL(1) grammar generating the same language. This is where the second question arises. Is there an algorithm to determine whether a language is LL(1)? The answer is no and the problem is said to be *undecidable* or *unsolvable*. That is, it is known from theoretical considerations that no such algorithm exists, at least not one which is guaranteed to work in every case. Any attempt at such an algorithm is liable to loop indefinitely in certain cases.

How important is this result in practice? It turns out that the 'obvious' grammar for most programming languages is not LL(1). However, it is usually possible to represent the vast majority of the context-free features of a programming language by means of an LL(1) grammar. The problem then is, given a grammar which is not LL(1), to find an equivalent LL(1) grammar. Since there is no algorithm to tell us whether such an LL(1) grammar exists it follows that there is none to find out if suitable transformations exist *and* to perform them. In certain cases, however, the transformations can be readily spotted. For example, the transformations required to transform the grammar introduced at the beginning of Section 4.2 were fairly simple. Many compiler writers with suitable experience have little difficulty in transforming grammars manually to remove their non-LL(1) features. However, there are considerable dangers associated with manual transformations, the chief one being that, with the best will in the world, the person performing a transformation may inadvertently alter the language generated by the grammar. If our aim is to produce reliable compilers then it is wise to avoid manual transformations as far as possible.

However, if there is no completely general automatic process available to transform grammars into LL(1) form, what alternative is available to us? The lack of general solution to the problem does not mean that it cannot be solved for special cases. Before considering how to do this, let us look at what is involved in transforming a grammar into LL(1) form.

1 Removal of left recursion

A grammar containing left recursion is not LL(1). Consider the rules

$$A \rightarrow A \alpha \quad \text{(left recursion in } A)$$
$$A \rightarrow a$$

In this case a is a starter symbol for both alternatives of the nonterminal A. In a similar way it can be shown that a grammar containing a left recursive cycle cannot be LL(1), e.g.

$$A \rightarrow BC$$
$$B \rightarrow CD$$
$$C \rightarrow AE$$

It can be shown that a grammar containing a left recursive cycle can be transformed into one containing only *direct* left recursion, and further, by the introduction of additional nonterminals, left recursion can be removed completely (in fact it is replaced by right recursion which is not a problem as far as the LL(1) property is concerned). The two results follow in fact from the Greibach Normal Form theorem mentioned in Section 4.1

As an example, consider the grammar with productions

$$S \rightarrow Aa$$
$$A \rightarrow Bb$$
$$B \rightarrow Cc$$
$$C \rightarrow Dd$$
$$C \rightarrow e$$
$$D \rightarrow Az$$

which has a left recursive cycle involving A, B, C, D. To replace this cycle by direct left recursion we can proceed as follows. Impose an ordering on the nonterminals, viz:

S, A, B, C, D

Consider all productions of the form

$$X_i \rightarrow X_j \gamma$$

where X_i and X_j are nonterminals and γ is a string of terminal and nonterminal symbols. No action is taken for those rules for which $j \geq i$. However, this inequality cannot hold for all the rules if a left recursive cycle is present. For the ordering we have chosen, the only rule which we deal with is

$D \rightarrow Az$

since A *precedes* D in the ordering. The procedure now is to substitute for A using all productions with A on the left-hand side. This gives

$D \rightarrow Bbz$

Since B precedes D in the ordering the process is repeated to give

$D \rightarrow Ccbz$

and once more to give two rules

$D \rightarrow ecbz$
$D \rightarrow Ddcbz$

The transformed grammar is now

$S \rightarrow Aa$
$A \rightarrow Bb$
$B \rightarrow Cc$
$C \rightarrow Dd$
$C \rightarrow e$
$D \rightarrow ecbz$
$D \rightarrow Ddcbz$

All productions are now of the required form and the left recursive cycle has been replaced by direct left recursion.

To remove the direct left recursion we proceed as follows.

Introduce a new nonterminal symbol Z and replace the productions

$$D \rightarrow ecbz$$
$$D \rightarrow Ddcbz$$

by

$$D \rightarrow ecbz$$
$$D \rightarrow ecbzZ$$
$$Z \rightarrow dcbz$$
$$Z \rightarrow dcbzZ$$

Notice that before and after the transformation D generates the regular expression

$$(ecbz)\,(dcbz)^*$$

More generally it can be shown that if a nonterminal A appears on the left-hand side of $r + s$ productions, r of which involve direct left recursion and s of which do not, i.e.

$$A \rightarrow A\alpha_1, A \rightarrow A\alpha_2, \ldots, A \rightarrow A\alpha_r$$
$$A \rightarrow \beta_1, A \rightarrow \beta_2, \ldots, A \rightarrow \beta_s$$

then it can be shown (Hopcroft and Ullman [1979]) that these productions can be replaced by

$$\left. \begin{array}{l} A \rightarrow \beta_i \\ A \rightarrow \beta_i Z \end{array} \right\} 1 \leq i \leq s \qquad \left. \begin{array}{l} Z \rightarrow \alpha_i \\ Z \rightarrow \alpha_i Z \end{array} \right\} 1 \leq i \leq r$$

An informal proof consists of noting that before and after the transformation A generates the regular expression

$$(\beta_1|\beta_2|\ldots|\beta_s)(\alpha_1|\alpha_2|\ldots|\alpha_r)^*$$

An alternative method of removing left recursion (due to Foster) is given in Griffiths [1974].

It is always possible to remove left recursion from a grammar and it is not difficult to write a program to deal with the general case.

2 Factorization

In many cases non-LL(1) grammars can be made LL(1) by a process of factorization. An example of this can be seen at the beginning of Section 4.2 Similarly, the productions

$$S \rightarrow aSb$$
$$S \rightarrow aSc$$
$$S \rightarrow \varepsilon$$

can be transformed by factorization into

$$S \rightarrow aSX$$
$$S \rightarrow \varepsilon$$
$$X \rightarrow b$$
$$X \rightarrow c$$

the resultant grammar being LL(1)

However, this process cannot be automated to deal with the general case. If it could then this would contradict the unsolvable nature of the problem of determining whether a language is LL(1) or not. The following example illustrates the sort of thing which can happen.

Consider the productions

1. $P \rightarrow Qx$
2. $P \rightarrow Ry$
3. $Q \rightarrow sQm$
4. $Q \rightarrow q$
5. $R \rightarrow sRn$
6. $R \rightarrow r$

The director symbol sets for the two alternatives for P both contain s and in an attempt to 'factorize out' s we substitute for Q and R on the right-hand sides of 1. and 2., giving

$$P \rightarrow sQmx$$
$$P \rightarrow qx$$
$$P \rightarrow sRny$$
$$P \rightarrow ry$$

which can be replaced by

$$P \rightarrow qx$$
$$P \rightarrow ry$$
$$P \rightarrow sP_1$$
$$P_1 \rightarrow Qmx$$
$$P_1 \rightarrow Rny$$

The productions for P_1 are similar to the original ones for P and have nondisjoint director symbols. We could deal with these productions in a similar way to that in which we dealt with the P ones

$$P_1 \rightarrow sQmmx$$
$$P_1 \rightarrow qmx$$
$$P_1 \rightarrow sRnny$$
$$P_1 \rightarrow rny$$

and factorizing

$$P_1 \rightarrow qmx$$
$$P_1 \rightarrow rny$$
$$P_1 \rightarrow sP_2$$
$$P_2 \rightarrow Qmmx$$
$$P_2 \rightarrow Rnny$$

P_2 is again like P_1 and P but longer, and by now it should be apparent that the process will not terminate. Any algorithm which attempts to transform a grammar into LL(1) form is bound to fail (or loop) for certain inputs. The cleverer (and more complicated) the algorithm, the more cases with which it may be able to deal, but there will always be some inputs which defeat it. How then is a compiler writer to find an LL(1) grammar on which to base his syntax analyser for the language he has to compile? The answer probably is by using an (imperfect) tool to transform the grammar he has for the language. An example of such a tool is SID (Syntax Improving Device), due to Foster [1968]. Though 'imperfect', SID is able to transform many non-LL(1) grammars into LL(1) form and has proved an invaluable tool for compiler writers (including the author) in Britain and elsewhere.

The question may be asked as to what the compiler writer should do when his grammar transformer is unable to produce an LL(1) grammar. He must then try to identify, from the output of the transformer, which part of the grammar is causing the problem, and either transform this part of the grammar manually into LL(1) form or rewrite it in a form with which the transformer can cope. This is always assuming the language is LL(1). If it is not, then an LL(1) parser cannot be produced without altering the language being implemented. If the language is not LL(1) the output from the transformer may indicate why this is so.

From a user's point of view, there are four situations which can arise from using a typical grammar transformer corresponding to whether the language is LL(1) or not and whether the transformer is 'clever' enough to do the 'correct' thing for the given input, i.e. convert the grammar to LL(1) form if possible or give a suitable diagnostic if not. The possibilities are represented diagrammatically in Table 4.11.

The top half of the table corresponds to the more satisfactory outputs from the transformer, and the bottom half to the less satisfactory ones. The more ingenious the transformer program the more often the output will be satisfactory but, due to the unsolvable nature of the problem, any transformer will have inputs which will defeat it.

Table 4.11

Language LL(1)	Language not LL(1)
Grammar transformed successfully	Suitable message given
Transformer loops or halts explaining why grammar cannot be transformed	Transformer loops

For a language such as ALGOL 68, relatively few aspects of the syntax seem to defeat a good transformer. The sort of thing which has caused problems with at least one transformer is illustrated by the following piece of syntax for a structure actual declarer:

$$STRAD \rightarrow \textbf{struct } orb\ LIST\ crb$$
$$LIST \rightarrow EL$$
$$LIST \rightarrow EL\ comma\ LIST$$
$$EL \rightarrow ad\ FIELDS$$
$$FIELDS \rightarrow tag$$
$$FIELDS \rightarrow tag\ comma\ FIELDS$$

where ad can be **real** or **int**, a tag is an identifier and orb and crb denote the characters '(' and ')' respectively. A typical string generated might be

struct (**int** a, b, **real** x, y)

The problem lies in the double use of the comma (to separate EL's and tag's). The syntax can be rewritten in such a way as to generate the same language but with the comma appearing only once in the productions.

$$STRAD \rightarrow \textbf{struct } orb\ LIST\ crb$$
$$LIST \rightarrow ad\ tag\ TAIL$$
$$TAIL \rightarrow comma\ ITEM\ TAIL$$
$$\rightarrow \varepsilon$$
$$ITEM \rightarrow ad\ tag$$
$$\rightarrow tag$$

and the grammar is LL(1) so no further transformations are required. Other areas of ALGOL 68 where similar problems arise involve the many uses of opening round brackets and some aspects of formats. If a context-free grammar for ALGOL 68 (or at least the context-free aspects of it) is taken from the Revised Report then with the aid of a few simple manual transformations, like the one described above, it should be possible for a good grammar transformer to produce an LL(1) grammar for the language on which a parser can be based. It might be noted in passing that almost all the problems in parsing ALGOL 68 (whatever method is used) arise from the overloading of symbols, mainly the opening round bracket and the comma. Pascal offers few problems for a top-down parser and most implementations are based on a recursive descent parser.

4.5 LL(1) parsing table

Having found an LL(1) grammar for the language, the next stage is to use the grammar to drive the parsing phase of the compiler. The method is similar to recursive descent except that we avoid the numerous procedure calls by representing the grammar in a tabular form (the parse table or parsing table) and using a source-language independent module of the compiler to drive through the table as the source text is read. This module, which we will refer to as the driver, will always point to the place in the syntax which corresponds to the current input symbol. The driver will require a stack to remember return addresses each time it enters a new production corresponding to some nonterminal. The representation of the syntax should be such as to make the parser efficient both with respect to space and time.

We first describe a possible form of the parsing table which should be fairly easy to understand and, later, we consider possible optimizations with respect to space, etc.

The parsing table is represented as a one-dimensional array of structures of the form

```
type parsel = record terminals : list;
                      jump      : integer;
                      accept, stack,
                      return, error : boolean
              end;
```

where

```
type list = record term : string;
                    next : ↑ list
            end;
```

string being a suitable user-defined type.
The type corresponding to the parsing table is defined as

```
type ptable = array [1..ptsize] of parsel;
```

where *ptsize* is a suitable constant.
The parser requires a stack and a stack pointer declared as

```
var stack : array [0..upb] of integer ;
    sptr : integer ;
```

sptr is initialized to zero before parsing commences.

There will be one element of the parse table corresponding to each step of the parsing process. There are a number of different types of steps in the process, namely:

1. Checking whether the lookahead symbol is a director symbol for a particular right-hand side of a production. If it is not, and there is an alternative right-hand side, this can be checked next. In the special case where the right-hand side begins with a terminal then the director symbol set will consist only of this terminal.
2. Checking a terminal appearing on the right-hand side of a production.
3. Checking a nonterminal. This will involve checking that the lookahead symbol is contained in one of the director symbol sets for the nonterminal, stacking a return address, and jumping to the first production for the nonterminal. In the case of a nonterminal appearing at the end of the right-hand side it is not necessary to stack a return address.

There will therefore be one element of the parsing table for each production of the grammar and for each occurrence of a terminal or nonterminal on the right-hand side of a production. In addition there is a parsing table element for each occurrence of the empty string on the right hand side of a production.

The driver will consist of a loop, the body of which will process an element of the parsing table and identify the next element to be processed. The jump field will normally give the next element to be processed unless the return field is true, in which case the address of the next element is taken from the stack (this corresponds to the end of a production). Also, if the lookahead symbol is not contained in the list of terminals and the error field is false, the following parsing table element should be processed with the same lookahead symbol (this is how alternative right-hand sides are dealt with).

In the function which follows, *la* is a boolean which determines whether a new lookahead symbol is to be read before processing the next parse table element. It is set to *false* for example, when the lookahead symbol is not a director symbol for a particular right-hand side and the director symbol set corresponding to another right-hand side is to be tried. If the lookahead symbol is not contained in the current set of director symbols *and* the error field of the *parsel* is *true* a syntax error will be indicated. If the stack field of the *parsel* being processed is *true* the next *parsel* address is stacked prior to jumping to the address given by the jump field.

A call

   parse (pt)

of function *parse* will start the driver where

```
function parse (pt :ptable):boolean ;
var i: integer ;
    la :boolean ;
    lookahead :string ;
begin i := 1 ;
    push(0) ;
    lookahead := lexread ;
    while (lookahead < > '⊥') and (i < > 0) do
    begin if oneof(lookahead, pt[i].terminals)
        then begin la := pt[i].accept ;
            if pt[i].return
            then i := pop
            else begin if pt[i].stack
                    then push (i + 1) ;
                    i := pt[i].jump
                end
            end
        else if pt[i].error
            then syntaxerror
            else begin i: = i + 1 ;
                    la := false
                end ;
        if la
        then lookahead := lexread
    end ;
    parse := (i = 0) and (lookahead = '⊥')
end
```

'⊥' is assumed to be a special symbol appearing after the end of the sentence.
The procedure *push* and functions *pop* and *oneof* are defined as follows:

```
procedure push (x :integer) ;
begin if sptr > upb
    then overflow
    else begin stack[sptr] := x ;
            sptr := sptr + 1
        end
end

function pop :integer ;
begin sptr := sptr − 1 ;
    if sptr < 0
    then empty ;
    pop := stack [sptr]
end
```

```
function oneof (la : string ; l : list) : boolean ;
var result : boolean ;
    ll : list ;
begin result : = false ;
    ll : = l ;
  while(ll < > nil) and not result do
  if la = ll↑.term
  then result : = true
  else ll : = ll↑.next
  oneof : = result
end
```

nil denotes the end of a list in Pascal.

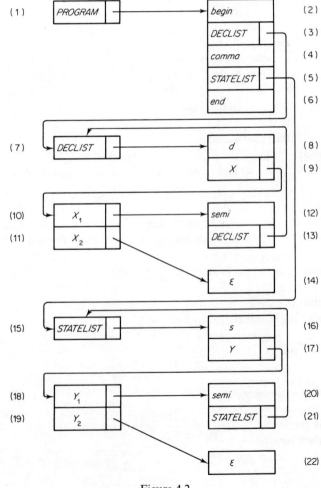

Figure 4.2

In addition, *syntaxerror overflow* and *empty* are suitable procedures for dealing with these situations, and *lexread* delivers a string corresponding to a single symbol of the language.

The driver is completely independent of the language being parsed and can be used in a number of compilers. It is relatively small so that most of the space occupied by the parser relates to the parse table whose size will be proportional to that of the grammar (language). For 'large' languages therefore the size of the parser is roughly proportional to the size of the grammar. As an illustration we derive the parsing table for the following grammar:

(1)   *PROGRAM → begin DECLIST comma STATELIST end*
(2)   *DECLIST → d X*
(3)   *X → semi DECLIST*
(4)   *X → ε*
(5)   *STATELIST → s Y*
(6)   *Y → semi STATELIST*
(7)   *Y → ε*

First we represent the grammar diagrammatically as in Figure 4.2. The numbers in brackets on the left and right of the figure give the indexes of the corresponding elements of the parse table. From the figure the parse table can be formed (Table 4.12). *0* appears in jump field where this field is irrelevant.

Table 4.12

	terminals	jump	accept	stack	return	error
1	{begin}	2	false	false	false	true
2	{begin}	3	true	false	false	true
3	{d}	7	false	true	false	true
4	{comma}	5	true	false	false	true
5	{s}	15	false	true	false	true
6	{end}	0	true	false	true	true
7	{d}	8	false	false	false	true
8	{d}	9	true	false	false	true
9	{semi, comma}	10	false	false	false	true
10	{semi}	12	false	false	false	false
11	{comma}	14	false	false	false	true
12	{semi}	13	true	false	false	true
13	{d}	7	false	false	false	true
14	{comma}	0	false	false	true	true
15	{s}	16	false	false	false	true
16	{s}	17	true	false	false	true
17	{semi, end}	18	false	false	false	true
18	{semi}	20	false	false	false	false
19	{end}	22	false	false	false	true
20	{semi}	21	true	false	false	true
21	{s}	15	false	false	false	true
22	{end}	0	false	false	true	true

Consider the sentence (followed by '⊥')

begin d semi d comma s semi s end ⊥

The sentence is parsed as follows.

i	action	parse-stack
1	*begin is read and checked;* *go to pt[2]*	0
2	*begin is checked and accepted;* *go to pt[3]*	0
3	*d is read and checked;* *4 is stacked;* *go to pt[7]*	4 0
7	*d is checked;* *go to pt[8]*	4 0
8	*d is checked and accepted;* *go to pt[9]*	4 0
9	*semi is read and checked;* *go to pt[10]*	4 0
10	*semi is checked;* *go to pt[12]*	4 0

12	semi is checked and accepted; go to pt[13]	4 0
13	d is read and checked; go to pt[7]	4 0
7	d is checked; go to pt[8]	4 0
8	d is checked and accepted; go to pt[9]	4 0
9	comma is read and checked; go to pt[10]	4 0
10	comma does not check with semi; error is false—go to pt[11]	4 0
11	comma is checked; go to pt[14]	4 0
14	comma is checked; return is true—pop 4; go to pt[4]	0
4	comma is checked and accepted; go to pt[5]	0

(*Contd.*)

5	*s is read and checked;* *6 is stacked;* *go to pt[15]*	6 0
15	*s is checked;* *go to pt[16]*	6 0
16	*s is checked and accepted;* *go to pt[17]*	6 0
17	*semi is read and checked;* *go to pt[18]*	6 0
18	*semi is checked;* *go to pt[20]*	6 0
20	*semi is checked and accepted;* *go to pt[21]*	6 0
21	*s is read and checked;* *go to pt[15]*	6 0
15	*s is checked;* *go to pt[16]*	6 0
16	*s is checked and accepted;* *go to pt[17]*	6 0

17	*end is read and checked;* *go to pt[18]*	6 0
18	*end does not check with semi;* *error is false—go to pt[19]*	6 0
19	*end is checked;* *go to pt[22]*	6 0
22	*end is checked;* *return is true—pop 6;* *go to pt[6]*	0
6	*end is checked and accepted;* *return is true—pop 0;* *i := 0*	
0	*parse terminates*	

Notice that some terminals are checked more than once. This could perhaps be avoided if one was prepared to delay in terms of parsing steps (though not in terms of source text read) the detection of certain syntax errors. It is also possible to cut down on the number of elements in the parse table.

It is desirable to keep the parsing table elements as small as possible and, in return for restricting the number of terminals in the grammar and the range of jumps within the parse table, it may be possible to pack each parse table element into a machine word. This is likely to slow down the parser at compile time because of the unpacking which has to be done but, in return, the parse table can probably be kept as small as a few thousand words even for quite large languages like ALGOL 68. As we will see again later, when we discuss bottom-up parsing methods, parsing table size is more often a problem to the compiler writer than is the speed of the parser.

Given an LL(1) grammar a program can be written to produce the corresponding parsing table. The algorithm involved has much in common with the LL(1) test and the two are often combined, as, for example, in the SID/SAG package produced by RSRE at Malvern. The driver module, of course, can be used over and over again for different compilers so that, given suitable software tools, it should be possible to produce an LL(1) parser from a grammar with a minimum of effort.

The LL(1) parsing method possesses a number of desirable features:

1. It is deterministic, i.e. backtracking is never required.
2. Parsing time is (roughly) proportional to the length of the program. We will see later that this may not be true for the compilation process as a whole since some compile-time actions, such as table searching, may take time dependent on the size of the tables which in turn depends roughly on the size of the program.
3. The method is associated with good diagnostic and error recovery capabilities since syntax errors are recognized at the first inadmissible symbol and the parsing table will then have available a list of possible continuation symbols. Error recovery techniques are discussed in Chapter 12.
4. The parsing tables tend to be small compared with those associated with other parsing methods.
5. LL(1) parsing can be applied to a wide class of languages—all those with LL(1) grammars. However, it should be added that in most cases the 'obvious' grammar for a programming language is not LL(1) and the grammar has to be transformed into an LL(1) grammar before the method can be applied. LR(1) parsing, as we shall see in the next chapter, can be applied to an even wider class of languages and grammar transformations are rarely required. The relative merits of the two methods will be discussed in the next chapter.

We can extend the idea of LL(1) grammars to that of LL(k) grammars where k $(k > 1)$ symbols of lookahead can be used to distinguish between alternative productions for nonterminals. The parser will then have to consider lookahead strings of length k and since this may introduce many more possibilities the problem becomes that much more complex. In practice even LL(2) grammars are rarely used for parsing, though a grammar which was locally LL(2) could form the basis of an LL(1) parser which was allowed an extra symbol of lookahead when required.

The grammar at the beginning of Section 4.2 is LL(2), whereas the grammar with the following productions is LL(3):

PROGRAM → *begin DECLIST semi STATELIST end*
DECLIST → *d semi DECLIST*
          d
STATELIST → *s semi STATELIST*
          s

An equivalent LL(1) grammar is

$$PROGRAM \rightarrow begin\ d\ semi\ X\ end$$
$$X \rightarrow d\ semi\ X$$
$$X \rightarrow s\ Y$$
$$Y \rightarrow \varepsilon$$
$$Y \rightarrow semi\ s\ Y$$

Exercises

4.1 State, giving reasons, which of the following languages are deterministic:

(a) $\{\alpha c \alpha^r \mid \alpha \text{ in } \{0,1\}*\}$
(b) $\{c \alpha \alpha^r \mid \alpha \text{ in } \{a,b\}*\}$
  (α^r means α reversed)
(c) $\{0^n 1^n \mid n \geq 0\}$
(d) $\{0^n 1^{2n} \mid n \geq 0\}$
(e) $\{0^n 1^n \mid n \geq 0\} \cup \{0^n 1^{2n} \mid n \geq 0\}$

4.2 Show that the following languages are not context free:

(a) $\{a^n b^n c^n \mid n \geq 0\}$
(b) $\{a^i \mid i \text{ is prime}\}$

4.3 Write a recursive descent parser corresponding to the grammar with productions (E is the sentence symbol)

$$E \rightarrow TG$$
$$G \rightarrow + TG$$
$$\qquad \varepsilon$$
$$T \rightarrow FU$$
$$U \rightarrow \times FU$$
$$\qquad \varepsilon$$
$$F \rightarrow (E)$$
$$\qquad identifier$$

4.4 A context-free grammar is said to be a q-grammar if (and only if) it has the following properties:
  1. the right-hand side of each production either begins with a terminal or is empty,
  2. for each nonterminal appearing on the left-hand side of more than one production the sets of director symbols corresponding to the right-hand sides of alternative productions are disjoint.
  Deduce
  (a) any q-grammar is LL(1),

(b) any *s*-grammar is a *q*-grammar,

(c) any LL(1) grammar can be transformed into a *q*-grammar.

4.5 Give LL(1) grammars for each of the following languages:

1. $\{0^n a\,1^{2n} \mid n \geq 0\}$
2. $\{\alpha \mid \alpha$ is in $\{0,1\}^*$ and does not contain two consecutive *1*'s$\}$
3. $\{\alpha \mid \alpha$ consists of an equal number of *0*'s and *1*'s$\}$

4.6 Convert the grammar with the following productions into LL(1) form (E is the sentence symbol):

$$E \rightarrow E + T$$
$$E \rightarrow T$$
$$T \rightarrow T \times F$$
$$T \rightarrow F$$
$$F \rightarrow (E)$$
$$F \rightarrow x$$
$$F \rightarrow y$$

4.7 Is the grammar with the following productions LL(1) or not? Give a reason for your answer.

$$S \rightarrow AB$$
$$S \rightarrow PQx$$
$$A \rightarrow xy$$
$$A \rightarrow m$$
$$B \rightarrow bC$$
$$C \rightarrow bC$$
$$C \rightarrow \varepsilon$$
$$P \rightarrow pP$$
$$P \rightarrow \varepsilon$$
$$Q \rightarrow qQ$$
$$Q \rightarrow \varepsilon$$

(S is the sentence symbol).

4.8 Deduce that all LL(1) grammars are unambiguous.

4.9 Build an LL(1) parsing table for the language defined by the LL(1) grammar with productions

$$PROGRAM \rightarrow begin\ d\ semi\ X\ end$$
$$X \rightarrow d\ semi\ X$$
$$X \rightarrow s\ Y$$
$$Y \rightarrow \varepsilon$$
$$Y \rightarrow semi\ s\ Y$$

4.10 Build an LL(1) parsing table for the language defined by the grammar in Exercise 4.6.

Chapter 5

Bottom-Up Syntax Analysis

In this chapter we discuss bottom-up parsing methods in general and describe one method in particular (LR parsing) which can be applied to a wide class of languages and grammars. We show how a parser can be constructed automatically from an LR grammar and, in the last section, we compare the relative merits of LL and LR parsing methods.

5.1 Bottom-up parsing

As discussed earlier, bottom-up parsers work by reducing a sentence of the language to the sentence symbol of the grammar by successively applying productions of the grammar. Consider for example the language generated by the productions

(1) $S \rightarrow$ **real** *IDLIST*
(2) *IDLIST* $\rightarrow$ *IDLIST, ID*
(3) *IDLIST* $\rightarrow$ *ID*
(4) *ID* $\rightarrow A|B|C|D$

(for simplicity (4) is thought of as a single production).
The sentence

    real *A, B, C*

belongs to the language and might be parsed in a bottom-up manner as follows. Each symbol read by the parser is immediately placed on top of the parse stack. For example, **real** is read and put on the stack. The first two moves of the parser are shown diagrammatically, thus:

    real $\underset{\uparrow}{}$ *A, B, C*

real $A_\uparrow$, B, C

$$\begin{array}{|c|} \hline \\ \\ \\ A \\ \textbf{real} \\ \hline \end{array}$$

where the arrow is placed immediately after the last symbol read. The next move of the parser is to replace A using production (4). This is known as a reduction. In bottom-up parsing, productions are applied the other way round from top-down parsing, i.e. right-hand sides of productions are replaced by their corresponding left-hand side rather than vice versa. Diagrammatically, we now have

real $A_\uparrow$, B, C

$$\begin{array}{|c|} \hline \\ \\ \\ ID \\ \textbf{real} \\ \hline \end{array}$$

Production (3) is then used to perform another reduction, giving

real $A_\uparrow$, B, C

$$\begin{array}{|c|} \hline \\ \\ \\ IDLIST \\ \textbf{real} \\ \hline \end{array}$$

Now the parser reads another symbol:

real $A,_\uparrow B, C$

$$\begin{array}{|c|} \hline \\ \\ , \\ IDLIST \\ \textbf{real} \\ \hline \end{array}$$

and another:

real $A, B_\uparrow, C$

$$\begin{array}{|c|} \hline \\ B \\ , \\ IDLIST \\ \textbf{real} \\ \hline \end{array}$$

The next two moves are reductions using productions (4) and (2):

real A, B ↑ , C

> | |
> |---|
> | ID |
> | , |
> | IDLIST |
> | **real** |

real A, B ↑ , C

> | |
> |---|
> | IDLIST |
> | **real** |

followed by two more symbols being read:

real A, B, ↑ C

> | |
> |---|
> | , |
> | IDLIST |
> | **real** |

real A, B, C ↑

> | |
> |---|
> | C |
> | , |
> | IDLIST |
> | **real** |

The final three moves are all reductions using productions (4), (2), and (1):

real A, B, C ↑

> | |
> |---|
> | ID |
> | , |
> | IDLIST |
> | **real** |

real A, B, C ↑

> | |
> |---|
> | IDLIST |
> | **real** |

real *A, B, C*_↑

$$S$$

The parse is complete when the stack contains only the sentence symbol and the complete sentence has been read. The parse stack corresponds to part of a push-down automaton as described in Chapter 4.

There are two types of move which a bottom-up parser makes:

1. *Shift moves* in which a symbol is read and stacked. This corresponds to moving one place along some production of the grammar.
2. *Reduce moves* in which the top so many elements of the stack are replaced by some nonterminal of the grammar using a production of the grammar.

Bottom-up parsing methods are nearly always deterministic and the only problem the parser can have is knowing in a particular situation whether to reduce or shift or, if two different reduce moves are possible, which, if any, to perform. Of course, a necessary condition for a reduce move to take place is that the right-hand side of some production appears on the top of the stack. However, this is not necessarily a sufficient condition as can be seen from the above example where it would have been incorrect to have reduced using (1) in the situation

real *A*_↑ *, B, C*

> *IDLIST*
> **real**

though not in the situation

real *A, B, C*_↑

> *IDLIST*
> **real**

It is also possible for the right-hand side of more than one production to appear on the top of the stack, for example in the situation

real *A, B*_↑ *, C*

> *ID*
> ,
> *IDLIST*
> **real**

where it is correct to reduce using production (2) but incorrect to reduce using production (3).

A deterministic bottom-up parsing method will provide some decision criterion when these conflicts arise. For example, the decision may be made by considering one or more lookahead symbols (as in LL parsing) or from the information available in the parse stack. If we consider the sentence used in the above example to be followed by an end marker, '$\perp$', say, then when the stack contained

$$\boxed{\begin{array}{l} \\ \\ \\ \textit{IDLIST} \\ \textbf{real} \end{array}}$$

whether to shift or to reduce by (1) is determined by whether the lookahead symbol is ',' or '$\perp$'.

Some bottom-up parsing methods, such as precedence and bounded context methods (Gries [1971]), can be applied only to a relatively small subset of languages. The LR method is the most general available in that it can be applied to all languages (and grammars) which can be parsed deterministically. An LR(k) grammar is one which, when used as the basis of a bottom-up parser, all shift–reduce and reduce–reduce conflicts can be resolved by means of the text read so far and a *fixed* amount of lookahead (at most k symbols). The L in LR indicates that the strings are read from Left to right and the R that a Rightmost parse is obtained. It should now be clear why the productions used in a rightmost parse, which is usually associated with a *bottom-up method*, are listed in the *opposite* order to that which would have been obtained by starting with the sentence symbol and working in a rightmost way towards the sentence (see Section 2.4).

Knuth's original description of LR parsing (Knuth [1965]) made the method appear rather cumbersome and inefficient. However, the later work of Aho and Johnson [1974], De Remer [1971], and others have made the method more attractive from a practical point of view.

5.2 LR (1) grammars and languages

We explained in the last section what is meant by an LR(k) grammar. In practice the value of k is always 0 or 1. To consider sets of even two lookahead symbols in resolving conflicts would make the method extremely cumbersome. Moreover, it would not allow us to parse any more languages using the method, for it can be shown that any language which is LR(k) is also LR(1) (i.e. can be generated by an LR(1) grammar) and indeed LR (0), if each sentence is assumed to be followed by an end marker (Hopcroft and Ullman [1979]). So while there exist grammars which are LR(2) and not LR(1), for example

(1) $S \to F, S$
(2) $S \to F$
(3) $F \to a L$

(4) $L \rightarrow t$
(5) $L \rightarrow t, L$

there are no languages which are LR(2) and not LR(1). This is quite different from the LL case where by increasing the value of k it was always possible (though not very practicable) to parse more languages. The grammar with the above productions is not LR(1) since after reading the handle (a handle is an initial substring of a sentence)

   at

and given the lookahead symbol ',' the parser cannot tell whether to reduce using (4) or to shift. Two lookahead symbols can be used to resolve the conflict. For example the lookahead pair

   $, t$

would indicate a shift, while the pair

   $, a$

would indicate a reduction.
   However, according to the theory, these must be an LR(1) grammar generating the same language. A possible grammar is

$S \rightarrow a t F$
$F \rightarrow , ITEM F$
   ε
$ITEM \rightarrow a t$
   t

The non-LR(1)-ness of the grammar is removed by allowing the ',' to appear only once in the grammar. However, the above grammar shows that lookahead symbols alone are not always sufficient to resolve conflicts. In some cases the left context also has to be taken into account. For example, whether the sequence

   at with the lookahead symbol ','

should be reduced to $ITEM$ or not depends on whether it is the first occurrence of the sequence or not. Fortunately, as we shall see, the decision whether to reduce or not in LR parsing does not in general require a complete scan of the left context or the contents of the stack.
   As already mentioned, the LR method can be applied to all languages which can be parsed deterministically. In particular, all LL(1) grammars and languages are LR(1). This follows from the fact that the decision to apply a particular production during LL(1) parsing is based on the nonterminal in the sentential

form to be replaced, together with a single symbol of lookahead, whereas when the decision to perform a reduction in the LR(1) case is taken the complete right-hand side of the production has been put on the stack *and* a further symbol of lookahead has been read. This means that there is at least as much information available on which to base the decision to apply a particular production in the LR(1) case as there is in the LL(1) case. This can be shown diagrammatically:

LL(1) decision point   LR(1) decision point

$\downarrow$ $\downarrow$

γ $a\,\alpha$ $l\beta$

$\gamma a\,\alpha\,l\beta$ represents the sentential form, immediately after in the LL(1) case and immediately before in the LR(1) case, the production $A \rightarrow a\,\alpha$ (say) is applied.

Also there exist grammars and languages which are LR(1) and not LL(1). For example, the grammar of Section 5.1 is LR(1) and not LL(1). The fact that it contains left recursion is sufficient to prevent it being LL(1). Left recursion does not cause problems in LR parsing.

Since all languages which can be parsed deterministically possess an LR(0) grammar, we might have been expected to have confined our attention to LR(0) grammars for the rest of this chapter. However, many typical features of programming language grammars are not LR(0) while they do tend to be LR(1), so that by considering LR(1) grammars we can usually avoid the problems of grammar transformations which are nearly always required using the LL method.

This is a plus point for LR parsing, especially when one remembers the undecidable nature of the transformation problem. It seems appropriate here to mention some decidability results regarding LR grammars.

1. It is decidable whether a grammar is $LR(k)$ for a given k. In particular it is decidable whether a grammar is LR(0) or LR(1).
2. It is undecidable whether there exists a k for which a given grammar is $LR(k)$. This result is not of great practical importance from a parsing point of view since we are not generally interested in $LR(k)$ grammars where $k > 1$.

As the basis for a syntax analyser, LR(1) grammars possess some attractive features. Their greater generality and the fact that transformations are rarely required seem to give them the edge over LL grammars. In Section 5.5 we discuss how the two types of grammar compare in practice. Meanwhile, in the next two sections, we discuss how LR parsers are produced.

5.3 LR parsing tables

In Section 5.1 we saw in general terms how a bottom-up parser works. What was missing from the explanation was the method of deciding whether to perform a particular reduction when the right-hand side of a production appeared on the top of the stack. The missing piece of the jigsaw is the parsing table and it is this table which enables the correct decision to be made in each instance. In this section we describe the form of the table (which is quite different from the LL table) and how it is used, and in the next section we describe how the table is formed from the grammar. The productions of the grammar were

(1) $S \rightarrow$ **real** *IDLIST*
(2) *IDLIST* $\rightarrow$ *IDLIST, ID*
(3) *IDLIST* $\rightarrow$ *ID*
(4) *ID* $\rightarrow A|B|C|D$

The parsing table consists of a rectangular matrix with columns for each terminal and nonterminal in the grammar plus the end marker, and a row corresponding to each state in which the parser may be in. We explain later the precise significance of the states, but in the meantime note that each state corresponds to a position in a production which the parser has reached. The parsing table for the grammar of Section 5.1 would be as shown in Table 5.1. The language-independent part of the parser, or the driver as we called it in the last chapter, makes use of two stacks (though see Exercise 5.10) which may be referred to as the symbol stack and the state stack. There are four types of entry in the parsing table:

1. Shift entries of the form $S7$; meaning stack the symbol corresponding to the column on the symbol stack, stack 7 on the state stack and go to state 7. If the input symbol is a terminal, accept it.
2. Reduce entries of the form $R4$; meaning reduce by production (4), i.e. assuming n is the number of symbols on the right-hand side of production (4), remove n items from the symbol stack and n items from the state stack and goto the state on the top of the state stack. The nonterminal on the left-hand side of production (4) should be considered as the next input symbol.
3. Error entries which are blank in the table and correspond to syntax errors.

Table 5.1

State	S	*IDLIST*	*ID*	**real**	','	A B C D	' $\perp$ '
1	HALT			S2			
2		S5	S4			S3	
3					R4		R4
4					R3		R3
5					S6		R1
6			S7			S3	
7					R2		R2

4. Halt entry(ies) which, when encountered, complete the parse.

Let us consider how the string

    real $A, B, C \perp$

would be parsed using the above parsing table. At each stage we show the contents of the symbol stack and the state stack. Initially we are in state *1* which is stacked

symbol   state
stack   stack

   real $A, B, C \perp$
↑

input symbol is **real** —from the table entry (*1*, **real**),
shift to state *2*

   real $\,\, A, B, C \perp$
      ↑

symbol stack	state stack
	2
real	1

input symbol is A —shift to state *3*

   real $A \,\, , B, C \perp$
      ↑

symbol stack	state stack
	3
A	2
real	1

input symbol is ',' —reduce by production (4)

   real $A \,\, , B, C \perp$
      ↑

symbol stack	state stack
	2
real	1

input symbol is *ID*—shift to state *4*

real $A_\uparrow$, *B, C*⊥

	4
ID	*2*
real	*1*

input symbol is ',' —reduce by production (3)

real $A_\uparrow$, *B, C*⊥

	2
real	*1*

input symbol is *IDLIST*—shift to state *5*

real $A_\uparrow$, *B, C*⊥

	5
IDLIST	*2*
real	*1*

input symbol is ',' —shift to state *6*

real $A,_\uparrow$ *B, C* ⊥

	6
,	*5*
IDLIST	*2*
real	*1*

input symbol is *B*—shift to state *3*

real $A, B_\uparrow$, *C*⊥

B	*3*
,	*6*
	5
IDLIST	*2*
real	*1*

input symbol is ',' —reduce by production (4)

real $A, B_\uparrow$, *C*⊥

	6
,	*5*
IDLIST	*2*
real	*1*

input symbol is *ID*—shift to state *7*

real $A, B_{\uparrow}, C\perp$

	ID		7
			6
	,		5
	IDLIST		2
	real		1

input symbol is ','—reduce by production (2)

real $A, B_{\uparrow}, C\perp$

			2
	real		1

input symbol is *IDLIST*—shift to state *5*

real $A, B_{\uparrow}, C\perp$

			5
	IDLIST		2
	real		1

input symbol is ','—shift to state *6*

real $A, B,_{\uparrow} C\perp$

			6
	,		5
	IDLIST		2
	real		1

input symbol is *C*—shift to state *3*

real $A, B, C_{\uparrow}\perp$

	C		3
			6
	,		5
	IDLIST		2
	real		1

input symbol is '$\perp$'—reduce by production (4)

real $A, B, C_{\uparrow}\perp$

			6
	,		5
	IDLIST		2
	real		1

input symbol is *ID*—shift to state 7

real *A, B, C* ↑ ⊥

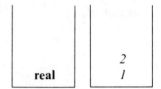

input symbol is '⊥'—reduce by production (2)

real *A, B, C* ↑ ⊥

input symbol is *IDLIST*—shift to state 5

real *A, B, C* ↑ ⊥

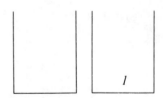

input symbol is '⊥'—reduce by production (1)

real *A, B, C* ↑ ⊥

input symbol is *S*—therefore *HALT*

The parse has been successfully completed.

Notice that after a shift action the input symbol is always the lookahead symbol whereas after a reduce action it is the symbol just reduced to.

5.4 Construction of an LR parsing table

In this section we describe how the LR parsing table is constructed from a grammar. We wish to be able to refer to a particular position in a production so we introduce the idea of a configuration. For example, given the (augmented) grammar

(1) $S \rightarrow$. **real** *IDLIST*

(2) *IDLIST* → *IDLIST* , *ID*

(3) *IDLIST → ID*
(4) *ID → A|B|C|D*

the dot corresponds to the configuration $(1,0)$ i.e. production (1) position 0—whereas the configuration $(1,1)$ would correspond to the dot appearing immediately after **real** in production (1), and $(2,0)$ would correspond to the dot appearing before *IDLIST* on the right-hand side of production (2). Configurations will be used to represent the progress of a parse. For example, the configuration $(2,2)$ would indicate that the right-hand side of production (2) had been recognized up to and including the comma. At any stage of a parse, a number of right-hand sides of productions may be partially recognized.

The states in the parsing table correspond roughly to the configurations in the grammar, the difference being that configurations which are indistinguishable to the parser are represented by the same state. For example, if $(1,0)$ is considered to correspond to state *1* and $(1, 1)$ is considered to correspond to state *2* then in the above grammar $(2,0)$, $(3,0)$, and $(4,0)$ will also correspond to state *2*. We say that the *closure* of $(1, 1)$ is the set of configurations

$$\{(1,1), (2,0), (3,0), (4,0)\}$$

From a given state not corresponding to the end of a production we can reach another state by inputing a terminal or nonterminal symbol. This state is said to be the successor state of the original state. To form the parsing table we must first find all the states in the grammar. We do this by starting at configuration $(1,0)$ and successively performing closure and successor operations until each configuration is included in some state. Where a number of configurations are contained in a single closure each of these configurations will correspond to the same state. A new configuration reached by a successor operation is referred to as a core configuration. If the configuration is followed by a nonterminal, the configurations corresponding to putting the dot at the extreme left of each right-hand side of a production for that nonterminal (and so on recursively) are all in the closure of the core configuration. Taking as an example the previous grammar, there are clearly seven states, which may be described as follows:

	core	*closure*
state *1*	$(1,0)$	$\{(1,0)\}$
state *2*	$(1,1)$	$\{(1,1), (2,0), (3,0), (4,0)\}$
state *3*	$(4,1)$	$\{(4,1)\}$
state *4*	$(3,1)$	$\{(3,1)\}$
state *5*	$\{(2,1), (1,2)\}$	$\{(2,1), (1,2)\}$
state *6*	$(2,2)$	$\{(2,2), (4,0)\}$
state *7*	$(2,3)$	$\{(2,3)\}$

The various states are located in the grammar as follows:

(1) $S \rightarrow_1 \textbf{real}\,_2 IDLIST\,_5$

(2) $IDLIST \rightarrow_2 IDLIST\,_{5,6}\ ID\,_7$

(3) $IDLIST \rightarrow_2 ID\,_4$

(4) $ID \rightarrow_{(2,6)} A\,|\,B\,|\,C\,|\,D_3$

Notice that a configuration can correspond to more than one state and there can be more than one configuration in the core since the successors of two configurations in the same closure may be indistinguishable. For example, configurations $(1,1)$ and $(2,0)$ in the above example are both followed by *IDLIST* making $(1,2)$ and $(2,1)$ indistinguishable *before* the closure operation (which yields no additional configurations in this case) has taken place. The number of states in the parser corresponds to the number of *sets* of indistinguishable configurations in the grammar. The reason for two or more states corresponding to a single configuration relates to the previous history of the parse. Thus a state can contain 'left context' information. However, only one state (state *3*) appears at the end of production (4) since we do not allow more than one state for the *same set* of configurations. Thus state *3* does not retain any left context information. From the core and closure sets above it can be seen that states *2* and *6* do *not* correspond to the same set of configurations.

Shift actions by the parser correspond to successor operations in finding the states. The shift actions in the parsing table can therefore be inserted from the above information regarding the location of the states in the grammar (Table 5.2). The position of the entries follows immediately from the grammar given above, e.g. from production (2) we have 'in state *2* on reading *IDLIST* goto state *5*' and 'in state *5* on reading *comma* goto state *6*', etc. The problem of inserting reduce actions in the table is complex. Whether a reduction takes place or not can in general depend on the current left context and the lookahead symbol. However, the only states in which reductions can possibly occur are

Table 5.2

State	S	IDLIST	ID	real	','	A B C D	'⊥'
1				S2			
2		S5	S4			S3	
3							
4							
5					S6		
6			S7			S3	
7							

Table 5.3

State	S	$IDLIST$	ID	real	','	$\begin{array}{c}A\\B\\C\\D\end{array}$	'⊥'
1				S2			
2		S5	S4				
3	R4	R4	R4	R4	R4	R4	R4
4	R3	R3	R3	R3	R3	R3	R3
5					S6		
6			S7			S3	
7	R2	R2	R2	R2	R2	R2	R2

those which can correspond to the ends of rules, in this case states *3, 4, 5,* and *7*. In the special case of an LR(0) grammar the lookahead symbol is irrelevant and reduce actions can be put in every column of the table in each state corresponding to the end of a rule. If this grammar were LR(0) we could put *R4* in every column of state *3*, *R3* in every column of state *4*, *R1* in every column of state *5*, and *R2* in every column of state *7*. However, in state *5* there is already a shift entry in one column. We cannot put a reduce entry in the same box, and we have a *shift/reduce conflict*. The LR(0) constructer algorithm does not work (since the grammar is not LR(0)) and we must try something else. The only problem concerns state *5* and we can in fact enter the other reduce actions, giving Table 5.3.

State *5* is said to be *inadequate*, and we try to resolve the problem by computing the lookahead symbols which would indicate a reduction in this state as opposed to a shift. From productions (1) and (2) it can be seen that the only possible lookahead symbols are '⊥' and ',' and a reduction is only appropriate if the lookahead symbol is '⊥' whereas the parser should shift to state *6* if the lookahead symbol is ','. We therefore insert *R1* in the 5th row in the column corresponding to '⊥'. This introduces no conflict and the inadequacy of the state has been resolved. When all inadequacies can be resolved in this way the grammar is said to be *simple* LR(1), or SLR(1).

Similarly, by considering lookahead symbols some of the reduce actions in states *3, 4,* and *7* can be removed from the table. The effect of not doing so is to delay in terms of parser steps (though not in terms of source text read) the detection of certain syntax errors. The removal of these entries and the insertion of the *HALT* entry gives Table 5.4, which we have met before.

The insertion of the *HALT* entry is facilitated by adding an extra production to the grammar:

$$S' \rightarrow {}_1 S \, HALT \perp$$

The distinction between LR(1) and SLR(1) grammars lies in the fact that in

Table 5.4

State	S	IDLIST	ID	real	','	A B C D	'⊥'
1	HALT			S2			
2		S5	S4			S3	
3					R4		R4
4					R3		R3
5					S6		R1
6			S7			S3	
7					R2		R2

computing the lookahead symbols in the SLR(1) constructer algorithm no attention was paid to left context whereas in the more general case left context may well have to be taken into account, to the extent that a given symbol may or may not be a valid follower depending on the left context. However, to remove the inadequacies for the most general LR(1) grammars it may be necessary to introduce many more states into the parsing table by redefining what we mean by a configuration to include the set of (follower) symbols which (for a particular parse history) may be lookahead symbols when a reduction by the production takes place. For example, referring to the grammar used so far throughout this section state 1 could be defined by

$$(1,0), \{`\perp'\}$$

whereas state 5 could be defined to include the two configurations

$$(1,2), \{`\perp'\}$$
$$(2,1), \{`\perp'`,'\}$$

The follower symbols are the symbols which can validly follow the nonterminal on the left-hand side of the production when a reduction takes place. When it comes to inserting reduce actions, these are only placed in the columns containing valid follower symbols for the particular configuration. In the most general LR constructer algorithm, states which correspond to identical sets of configurations (in the SLR(1) sense) but with non-identical follower symbol sets are considered distinct. This can lead to a considerable increase in the number of states in the parsing table and hence in the size of the parsing table itself. However, this algorithm allows us to parse all languages which can be generated by LR(1) grammars.

Fortunately the full generality of the LR(1) constructer algorithm is rarely required and in practice most features of programming languages turn out to

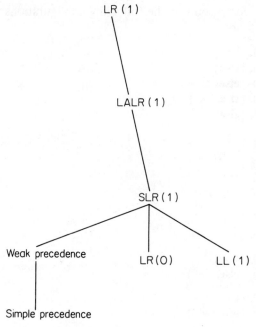

Figure 5.1   Grammar hierarchy

be SLR(1). As can be seen from Figure 5.1 the SLR(1) grammars include the weak precedence and simple precedence grammars as well as the LL(1) grammars.

Even in cases where the grammar is not SLR(1) the full LR(1) treatment is not always required. If the states which are identical apart from their follower symbol sets are merged into a single state with follower sets the unions of the various follower sets, and no inadequacies occur in forming the parsing table, the grammar is said to be LALR(1) (lookahead LR(1)). The LALR(1) parsing table has the same number of states as the SLR(1) table but the follower sets take left context into account.

Consider the grammar

(1) $S \rightarrow {}_1 T {}_2 \textbf{else} {}_3 F {}_4 ; 11$

(2) $T \rightarrow {}_1 E {}_5$

(3) $T \rightarrow {}_1 i {}_6 ; 8$

(4) $F \rightarrow {}_3 E {}_7$

(5) $E \rightarrow {}_{(1,3)} E {}_{(5,7)} + {}_9 i {}_{10}$

(6) $E \rightarrow {}_{(1,3)} i {}_{(6,12)}$

where the state numbers have been added.

The 12 states correspond to the following configurations (in the extended meaning of the term):

state *1* $(1,0), \{`\perp'\}$
    $(2,0), \{\textbf{else}\}$
    $(3,0), \{\textbf{else}\}$
    $(5,0), \{\textbf{else}, `+'\}$
    $(6,0), \{\textbf{else}, `+'\}$

state *2* $(1,1), \{`\perp'\}$

state *3* $(1,2), \{`\perp'\}$
    $(4,0), \{`;'\}$
    $(5,0), \{`;', `+'\}$
    $(6,0), \{`;', `+'\}$

state *4* $(1,3), \{`\perp'\}$

state *5* $(2,1), \{\textbf{else}\}$
    $(5,1), \{\textbf{else}, `+'\}$

state *6* $(3,1), \{\textbf{else}\}$
    $(6,1), \{\textbf{else}, `+'\}$

state *7* $(4,1), \{`;'\}$
    $(5,1), \{`;', `+'\}$

state *8* $(3,2), \{\textbf{else}\}$

state *9* $(5,2), \{`;', \textbf{else}, `+'\}$

state *10* $(5,3), \{`;', \textbf{else}, `+'\}$

state *11* $(1,4), \{`\perp'\}$

state *12* $(6,1), \{`;', `+'\}$

In determining the follower sets the following rules apply:

1. In configuration $(1,0)$ the follower set is $\{\perp\}$ since the left-hand side of the production is the sentence symbol which does not appear on the right-hand side of any production. (For a grammar in which the sentence symbol does not have this property it may be desirable to introduce a new sentence symbol S' with the property, by means of an extra production,

$$S' \rightarrow S \perp)$$

2. In performing the closure operation to identify other configurations corresponding to some core state(s) the follower sets can also be determined. For example, since configuration $(1,0)$ precedes a nonterminal, T, configurations corresponding to the extreme left of the right-hand sides of pro-

ductions for *T* are in the closure, and followers of *T in production* (1) make up the follower sets. In this way

$(2,0)$, {**else**}
$(3,0)$, {**else**}

are configurations (in the LALR (1) sense) of state *1*. $(5,0)$ and $(6,0)$ are also configurations in state *1*. In the case of $(6,0)$ **else** is in the follower set since it can follow *E* since it is a follower of *T*. $+$ is also in the follower set since *E* may have been 'called' from production '*5*'. Thus the LALR (1) configuration is

$(6,0)$, {**else**, '$+$'}

Similarly

$(5,0)$, {**else**, '$+$'}

is in state *1*.

3. Performing a successor operation on a configuration does not affect the follower set. For example, $(1,0)$ in state *1* and $(1,1)$ in state *2* have the same follower set $(\{'\perp'\})$. However, in state *9* (configuration $(5,2)$) the follower sets corresponding to configurations $(5,1)$, {**else**, '$+$'}, (state *5*) and $(5,1)$, {'$;$', '$+$'}, (state *7*) have been merged since the LALR algorithm does not allow distinct states for nondistinct sets of SLR (or LR(0)) configurations. Table 5.5 shows the parsing table with the shift entries inserted.

The grammar is not LR (0) since, for example, we cannot put reduce entries

Table 5.5

State	S	T	F	E	else	';'	'+'	i	'⊥'
1		S2		S5				S6	
2						S3			
3			S4	S7				S12	
4						S11			
5							S9		
6						S8			
7							S9		
8									
9								S10	
10									
11									
12									

Table 5.6

State	S	T	F	E	else	';'	'+'	i	'⊥'
1	HALT	S2		S5				S6	
2						S3			
3			S4	S7				S12	
4					S11				
5					R2		S9		
6					R6	S8	R6		
7					R4		S9		
8					R3				
9								S10	
10					R5	R5	R5		
11									R1
12						R6	R6		

in every column for state 5 which can correspond to the end of a rule. Nor is it SLR(1), for if so from production (6) we should have a reduce entry in the ';' column for state 6 since ';' is a valid follower of E since it is a follower of F (in the SLR(1) sense). However, to insert a reduce action in the ';' column of state 6 would conflict with the shift action already in that position. The conflict is resolved by noting from the augmented configurations corresponding to each state that **else** and '+' are the only valid follower symbols in state 6. Thus the LALR algorithm will only put an R6 action in the **else** and '+' columns in state 6. Continuing thus we can build up the complete LALR(1) parsing table (Table 5.6). The table has relatively few reduce entries and there are no conflicts. Had the LALR(1) algorithm been unable to resolve any conflicts the next step would have been to try the LR(1) algorithm. In the above case this would have involved introducing additional states. For example, state 10 would have been split into two states corresponding to

$$(5,3), \{';','+'\}$$

and

$$(5,3), \{\textbf{else},'+'\}$$

each state corresponding to the same configuration(s) apart from having different follower symbols. In this way more left context would be remembered—in this case whether the E would be reduced to an F or a T. The parser does not actually require this information since the states in which E is reduced to a T and to an F are themselves distinct. The LR(1) algorithm is rarely required, and when it is, the number of states involved is usually much larger than for the LALR(1) algorithm.

The parsing algorithm described earlier is the same whether the grammar is LR(0), SLR(1), LALR(1), or LR(1). It is only the algorithm for constructing the parsing table which becomes more complex the more general the grammar. The size of the table, i.e. the number of states, is the same whether the LR(0), SLR(1), or LALR(1) algorithm is used. It is only the LR(1) algorithm which produces a larger table. An algorithm to decide whether a grammar is LR(1) consists of trying to form the LR(0) parsing table. If this can be done without introducing any conflicts the grammar is LR(0) and therefore LR(1). If conflicts arise the SLR(1) algorithm is tried. If this is successful the grammar is SLR(1) and therefore LR(1). Otherwise the LALR(1) algorithm is tried and if this resolves all the conflicts the grammar is LALR(1), and therefore LR(1). Finally, if conflicts remain, the LR(1) algorithm is performed and the grammar is LR(1) or not according to whether any shift/reduce or reduce/reduce conflicts remain. Of course the LR(1) algorithm could have been tried in the first case, but in the vast majority of cases this would take much longer than trying the simpler algorithms first. The typical LR(1) parser generator will proceed by trying the various algorithms in order of increasing complexity. Programming language grammars are often SLR(1) and nearly always LALR(1)

A class of grammars which are not LR(1) are the ambiguous grammars (Section 2.4). The problem of whether a grammar is ambiguous or not is unsolvable. However, since no LR(1) grammars are ambiguous, the LR(1) algorithm can tell us that a grammar is unambiguous. However, it does *not* follow that the failure of the LR(1) algorithm means that the grammar is ambiguous. Otherwise we would have a definitive test for ambiguity in a grammar, contradicting the unsolvable nature of the problem.

The rectangular parsing tables which we have described are fast to access and provide good diagnostic facilities (since each blank entry could be associated with a different error message). However, they take up far too much space, possibly as much as 50K words. There are well-known techniques for storing sparse matrices, and many of these can be applied to LR parsing tables. In addition, there are other efficient methods of storing the tables which take into account their particular features (Horning [1974a]). As one might expect, something has to be paid for the increased space efficiency. This tends to be in terms of time taken to access a particular element of the parse table, but it can also mean the later detection of syntax errors, later that is in the sense that more parser actions have taken place before an error is recognized, rather than that more symbols of the program have been read.

5.5 LL versus LR parsing methods

Both LL and LR parsing methods have a good deal in their favour. Both are deterministic and have the ability to detect syntax errors at the earliest possible moment.

Both types of parsing method tend to run into difficulty when presented with an ambiguous grammar, though the YACC LALR parser generator available under the UNIX[†] operating system allows the user to include 'disambiguating' rules in his grammar. As noted in Exercise 2.5 the grammar

$S \rightarrow$ **if** b **then** S **else** S
$\rightarrow$ **if** b **then** S
$\rightarrow a$

which corresponds to the Pascal **if**-*statement* allows two parsings of the string

if b **then if** b **then** a **else** a

depending on whether the **else** is assumed to go with the first or second **then**. However, the language generated by the above grammar is not inherently ambiguous since it can be transformed into

$S \rightarrow E$
$\rightarrow T$
$E \rightarrow$ **if** b **then** E **else** E
$\rightarrow a$
$T \rightarrow$ **if** b **then** S
$\rightarrow$ **if** b **then** E **else** T

in which case the above sentence could only be parsed in one way, i.e. the **else** goes with the second **then**. Notice that E generates 'balanced' statements with equal numbers of **then**'s and **else**'s while T generates 'unbalanced' ones.

LR methods have the advantage that they apply to a wider class of grammars and languages, and that grammar transformations are not normally required. However, it is worth considering how important these theoretical advantages of LR parsers over LL ones turn out to be in practice.

If one uses a good grammar transformer to try to transform a context-free grammar for ALGOL 68 based on the Revised Report into LL(1) form, our own experience suggests that only a few parts of the grammar will be difficult to transform and will have to be dealt with manually.

We give an example of a grammar feature which has caused problems with the grammar transformer we have experience of. For further details see Hunter, McGettrick, and Patel [1977].

Suppose the grammar G_1 has productions

$S \quad \rightarrow CO|CL$
$CO \quad \rightarrow orb\ EC\ stick\ SC\ stick\ SC\ crb$
$EC \quad \rightarrow u\ semi\ EC|u$
$CL \quad \rightarrow orb\ SC\ crb$
$SC \quad \rightarrow PLU\ semi\ SC|PLU$
$PLU \rightarrow lab\ PLU|u$

[†] UNIX[TM] is a trademark of Bell Laboratories

{CO = conditional clause, CL = closed clause, EC = enquiry clause, SC = serial clause, PLU = 'possibly labelled unit', u = unit, orb = opening round bracket, etc.}

The problem arises from the fact that units cannot be labelled in an enquiry clause (occurring in a conditional clause) whereas they may be labelled in a serial clause (occurring in a closed) and the grammar transformer is not able to cope. The *language*, however, is LL(1) but is necessary to 'merge' the rules for closeds and conditionals to obtain the LL(1) grammar G_2 with productions

$$
\begin{aligned}
S &\rightarrow orb\ T \\
T &\rightarrow lab\ V\,|\,u\,W \\
V &\rightarrow lab\ V\,|\,u\,X \\
W &\rightarrow crb\,|\,semi\ T\,|\,stick\ SC\ stick\ SC\ crb \\
X &\rightarrow semi\ V\,|\,crb \\
SC &\rightarrow PLU\ Y \\
Y &\rightarrow semi\ PLU\ Y\,|\,\varepsilon \\
PLU &\rightarrow lab\ PLU\,|\,u
\end{aligned}
$$

The grammar G_2 is LL(1).

It can be shown that the original grammar, G, was not LR(1) since on reading the string

$$(u$$

and with *semi* as the lookahead symbol, it is not known whether to reduce to PLU using the second alternative for PLU or shift according to the first alternative for EC. Thus there is an unresolvable shift/reduce conflict.

This and other examples from ALGOL 68 and other languages tend to show that, where manual transformations are required to make the grammar LL(1), the grammar would still have to be transformed before it could have formed the basis of an LR parser thus suggesting that the theoretical advantage of LR parsers over LL parsers (i.e. their greater generality) is not so significant in practice. With a good grammar transformer, apart from the sort of problem mentioned above, the fact that the grammar has to be transformed does not really cause any problems for the compiler writer, and in most cases he will not even have to look at the transformed grammar. It is the relatively few cases, like the one mentioned above, where the transformer is not able to cope, and either loops or produces a misleading diagnostic, which cause the problems. Unfortunately, it appears that these parts of the grammar are often not LR(1) and difficulties arise whichever parsing method is used.

There are good reasons why we wish to avoid manual transformations if at all possible. First, the transformations may be difficult to find; and secondly, it is often difficult to ensure that they do not alter the language generated.

The two parsing methods could also be compared with respect to table size and parse time. The use of single words for the elements of the LL parsing table can keep the size of a typical parse table down to about 4K words. Using the type of LR parsing table described in Section 5.3 the corresponding size for an LR parsing table is about 50K. However, the comparison is not entirely fair, since the optimizations mentioned in the last section can be used to reduce this figure by about 90%. However, the LL method does appear to have the edge over the LR method as far as parsing table size is concerned.

Cohen and Roth [1978] have compared the maximum, minimum, and average times taken to parse sentences using LL and SLR parsers. They provide estimates for the relative efficiencies of the two methods in the context of the DEC PDP-10 machine. The results show that the LL method is faster by about 50%.

Both parsing methods are well suited to embedding actions in the syntax to perform aspects of the compilation process. We shall see how this is done in LL parsers in the next chapter. For LR parsers the actions are usually associated with reductions, and dummy rules are often introduced into the grammar where actions are required other than at the ends of rules. This does not affect the LR(1)-ness of the grammar so long as the grammar is LL(1).

Individual compiler writers tend to have a preference for one or other of the two methods described (and indeed between top-down and bottom-up parsing) and the issues are often debated. In practice, the method used often depends on the availability of a good parser generator of whatever type. There are, however, sometimes advantages in using a 'mixed' approach to parsing. For example, the C compiler for the PDP-11 includes a recursive descent parser for most of the language, though expressions are parsed using a simple bottom-up (operator precedence) method.

Exercises

5.1 Give grammars other than the ones described in the last chapter which are:

(a) LR(0)
(b) SLR(1) but not LR(0)

5.2 State, giving reasons, which of the following grammars are LR(1):

(a) $E \rightarrow E + E$
$E \rightarrow i$
(b) $S \rightarrow 0S0$
$S \rightarrow 1S1$
$S \rightarrow 0$
$S \rightarrow 1$
(c) $S \rightarrow 0S0$
$S \rightarrow 0S1$
$S \rightarrow c$

Where the grammar is not LR(1) give an equivalent LR(1) grammar if one exists.

5.3 Form the parsing table for the grammar with productions (S is the sentence symbol):

$S \rightarrow E$
$E \rightarrow E + T$
$E \rightarrow T$
$T \rightarrow T \times F$
$T \rightarrow F$
$F \rightarrow (E)$
$F \rightarrow x$
$F \rightarrow y$

Is the grammar SLR(1)?

5.4 Deduce that the following grammar is not LR(1) (*PROGRAM* is the sentence symbol):

$PROGRAM \rightarrow begin\ DECLIST\ semi\ STATELIST\ end$
$DECLIST \rightarrow d\ semi\ DECLIST$
$\qquad\qquad d$
$STATELIST \rightarrow s\ semi\ STATELIST$
$\qquad\qquad s$

Transform the grammar into an equivalent SLR(1) grammar and construct the corresponding parsing table.

5.5 Produce a parsing table for the grammar (S is the sentence symbol):

$S \rightarrow at F$
$F \rightarrow , ITEM\ F$
$\qquad \varepsilon$
$ITEM \rightarrow a\ t$
$\qquad\qquad t$

5.6 Deduce that the following grammar is not LR(1) (S is the sentence symbol):

$S \rightarrow 1 S 0$
$S \rightarrow 0 S 1$
$S \rightarrow 1 0$
$S \rightarrow 0 1$

5.7 Is (a) the grammar in Exercise 5.6
    (b) the language generated by the grammar in Exercise 5.6
LR(k) for any k?

5.8 Show that the following grammar is not LR(1) but is LR(2):

$$S \rightarrow V := E$$
$$S \rightarrow L\,S$$
$$L \rightarrow I :$$
$$V \rightarrow I$$

Suggest how the non-LR(1)-ness might be dealt with at the lexical analysis stage.

5.9 What advantage might there be in constructing an SLR(1) parsing table from a grammar which was LR(0)?

5.10 Does the LR parsing method require the use of two stacks (symbol stack and state stack) or could the two stacks be merged into one? Give a reason for your answer.

5.11 Deduce that all regular languages are LR(1).

Chapter 6

Embedding Actions in Syntax

Although it is often convenient to consider the analysis and synthesis stages of compilation as distinct processes, in many cases they will take place in parallel. Clearly this must be the case for a single-pass compiler, but even with multi-pass compilers, generation of object code, or perhaps some sort of intermediate code, will often take place along with syntax analysis. This should not be surprising when one realizes that once the syntax analyser has recognized, say, an assignment, it is natural to output code for an assignment at that point. In this chapter we discuss how a grammar may contain calls of actions not only to generate code but also to perform other compilation tasks such as building and interrogating symbol tables, etc.

6.1 Production of quadruples

As an example of how actions may be inserted in a grammar to generate code we discuss the problem of breaking down arithmetic expressions into quadruples. The expressions will be defined by a grammar with the following productions:

$$
\begin{aligned}
S &\to EXP \\
EXP &\to TERM \\
&\quad\ \ EXP + TERM \\
TERM &\to FACT \\
&\quad\ \ \ TERM \times FACT \\
FACT &\to - FACT \\
&\quad\ ID \\
&\quad\ (EXP) \\
ID &\to a \,|\, b \,|\, c \,|\, d \,|\, e
\end{aligned}
$$

where S is the sentence symbol.
Examples of expressions are

$$
\begin{aligned}
&(a + b) \times c \\
&a \times b + c \\
&a \times b + c \times d \times e
\end{aligned}
$$

The identifiers are all single letters: this avoids having to consider lexical analysis.

A grammar for quadruples has the following productions:

$$QUAD \rightarrow OPERAND \; OP1 \; OPERAND = INT$$
$$OP2 \; OPERAND = INT$$
$$OPERAND \rightarrow INT$$
$$ID$$
$$INT \rightarrow DIGIT$$
$$DIGIT \; INT$$
$$DIGIT \rightarrow 0\,|\,1\,|\,2\,|\,3\,|\,4\,|\,5\,|\,6\,|\,7\,|\,8\,|\,9$$
$$ID \rightarrow a\,|\,b\,|\,c\,|\,d\,|\,e$$
$$OP1 \rightarrow +\,|\times$$
$$OP2 \rightarrow -$$

Examples of quadruples are

$$-a = 4$$
$$a + b = 7$$
$$6 + 3 = 11$$

and the expression

$$(-a + b) \times (c + d)$$

would correspond to the following sequence of quadruples:

$$-a = 1$$
$$1 + b = 2$$
$$c + d = 3$$
$$2 \times 3 = 4$$

the integers on the left-hand sides of the equal signs referring to other quadruples. Having formed the quadruples it is not difficult to generate machine code from them, and many compilers translate into an intermediate code based on quadruples. The object of this section is to demonstrate how actions may be inserted in the expression grammar to generate the corresponding quadruples. Actions will be enclosed in angle brackets, $\langle, \rangle$ and will be named $A1, A2, \ldots$. In this case four distinct actions are required. The algorithm makes use of a stack, and quadruple numbers are allocated by means of an integer variable. The actions are

$A1$ to insert an item on the stack,

$A2$ to remove three items from the stack, print them out followed by an '=' and the next quadruple number to be allocated, and put this integer on the stack,

A3 to remove two items from the stack, print them out followed by an '=' and the next quadruple number to be allocated, and put this integer on the stack,

A4 to remove a single item from the stack.

The grammar with these actions added is

$$S \rightarrow EXP \langle A4 \rangle$$
$$EXP \rightarrow TERM$$
$$\qquad EXP + \langle A1 \rangle \ TERM \ \langle A2 \rangle$$
$$TERM \rightarrow FACT$$
$$\qquad TERM \times \langle A1 \rangle \ FACT \ \langle A2 \rangle$$
$$FACT \rightarrow - \langle A1 \rangle \ FACT \ \langle A3 \rangle$$
$$\qquad ID \ \langle A1 \rangle$$
$$\qquad (EXP)$$
$$ID \rightarrow a|b|c|d|e$$

A1 is used to stack all identifiers and operators, and *A2* and *A3* produce dyadic and monadic quadruples respectively. We can write the code for the actions in Pascal assuming the following definitions and declarations:

```
type st = array [1..20] of record case quad:boolean of
                                    true :(qno :integer);
                                    false :(idop :char)
                                  end;
var stack :st ;
    ptr, quadno, i:0..maxint ;
    in :char
```

where *stack* is an array of variant records each containing an integer or character value, *ptr* is the stack pointer, and *quadno* is a variable whose value is the last quadruple allocated.

Initially *ptr* and *quadno* are set to zero. *in* is assumed to have the value of the last character (or symbol) read. The actions are then

```
⟨A1⟩
begin ptr := ptr + 1 ;
      stack[ptr].quad := false ;
      stack[ptr].idop := in
end

⟨A2⟩
begin for i := ptr-2 to ptr do
      if stack[i].quad
      then write (stack[i].qno)
```

```
        else write (stack[i].idop);
        quadno := quadno + 1 ;
        writeln ('=', quadno);
        ptr := ptr-2 ;
        stack[ptr].quad := true ;
        stack[ptr].qno := quadno
    end
```

⟨A3⟩

```
begin for i := ptr-1 to ptr do
        if stack[i].quad
        then write (stack[i].qno)
        else write (stack[i].idop);
        quadno := quadno + 1 ;
        writeln('=', quadno);
        ptr := ptr-1 ;
        stack[ptr].quad := true ;
        stack[ptr].qno := quadno
    end
```

⟨A4⟩

```
ptr := ptr-1
```

As an example we follow through the conversion of

$$(-a + b) \times (c + d)$$

into quadruples. Action *A1* will take place after each identifier and each operator has been recognized, action *A2* after the second operand of each dyadic operator, and action *A3* after the first (and only) operand of each monadic operator. *A4* will be executed once only when the complete expression has been read.

Last character read	Action	Output
(	—	
− (minus)	*A1*, stack '−'	
a	*A1*, stack *a*	
	A3, unstack 2 elements, stack '*1*'	$-a = 1$
+	*A1*, stack '+'	
b	*A1*, stack *b*	
	A2, unstack 3 elements, stack '*2*'	$1 + b = 2$

Last character read	Action	Output
)	—	
×	*A1*, stack ' × '	
(	—	
c	*A1*, stack *c*	
+	*A1*, stack ' + '	
d	*A1*, stack *d*	
	A2, unstack *3* elements, stack '*3*'	$c + d = 3$
)	*A2*, unstack *3* elements, stack '*4*' *A4*, unstack *1* element	$2 \times 3 = 4$

The following points should be noted:

1. In the above example we never had to compare the priorities of two operators since this information was contained in the grammar.
2. The method could easily be extended to cope with languages with many different operator priorities.
3. The grammar was left recursive since rules of the form

$$TERM \rightarrow FACT \times TERM$$

imply a different order of evaluation: $(A \times (B \times C))$, for example, rather than $((A \times B) \times C)$. However, we can transform the left recursive rules into equivalent right recursive ones with actions in the corresponding places by the introduction of new nonterminals, e.g.

$$TERM \rightarrow FACT$$
$$TERM \rightarrow TERM \times \langle A1 \rangle FACT \langle A2 \rangle$$

is equivalent to

$$TERM \rightarrow FACT\ NEW$$
$$NEW \rightarrow \varepsilon$$
$$\times \langle A1 \rangle\ FACT \langle A2 \rangle\ NEW$$

Moreover, the transformation can be done automatically so that, for simplicity, it is preferable to think in terms of the original (left recursive) rules.

The idea of an (LL) syntax analyser generator can be extended to include actions embedded in the syntax. Just as one can 'call' a rule from within another rule so one could call an action when it appears in the grammar.

The amount of 'code' in the above example is remarkably small and, as will be seen from other examples using this technique, the most difficult part of the exercise often lies in determining where the actions should appear in the grammar rather than in writing the code for the actions.

6.2 Symbol table manipulation

Since the grammar used by the syntax analyser is normally context free, some method must be found of specifying the non-context-free parts of the language. For example, in many languages identifiers may not be used unless they have been declared, and there are restrictions on the ways in which values of different types may be used in a program. Most compilers use a symbol table to keep track of the identifiers that have been declared and their types.

When an identifier is declared, e.g.

var *a* : *integer*

we say that we have a *defining occurrence* of *a*. However, *a* may occur in a different context, e.g.

$a := 4$ or $a + b$ or   *read*(*a*)

and these would be *applied occurrences* of *a*.

The compiler action concerned with a defining occurrence of an identifier is to put the object in the symbol table, whereas the action associated with an applied occurrence of an identifier, etc., is to search the symbol table to find the entry corresponding to the defining occurrence of the object and so obtain its type and (possibly) other compile-time properties.

In many languages the same identifier may be used to represent different objects in different parts of the program, the program structure being used to distinguish between the different objects represented by the same identifier, e.g.

```
program demo (input, output);
var i : integer;
procedure one;
var i : char;
begin
  :
end;
procedure two;
var i : real;
begin
  :
end;
```

begin

:

end.

Just as the program has a structure, so the symbol table must have a structure to distinguish between the different uses of the same identifier.

Let us consider an ALGOL 60 type language with the following properties:

1. The defining occurrence of an identifier must occur (textually) before any applied occurrences.
2. All declarations in a block must occur immediately after the **begin**, i.e. before any statements.
3. Given an applied occurrence of an identifier, the corresponding defining occurrence is in the smallest enclosing block containing a declaration of that identifier.
4. An identifier cannot be declared more than once in the same block.

(3) and (4) are common to virtually all block-structured languages, while (2) is true for ALGOL 60 and (1) is a restriction occurring in some implementations of ALGOL 60.

We will assume that the syntax of identifier declarations is given by the rules

$DEC \rightarrow$ **real** $IDS|$**integer** $IDS|$**boolean** IDS
$IDS \rightarrow id$
$IDS \rightarrow IDS, id$

and a block is defined as

$BLOCK \rightarrow$ **begin** $DECS$; $STATS$ **end**

where

$DECS \rightarrow DECS$; DEC
$DECS \rightarrow DEC$
$STATS \rightarrow STATS$; s
$STATS \rightarrow s$

The symbol table might have the structure shown in Figure 6.1.

At any point in the parse the blocks in the chain would be those currently entered, and those identifiers which had already been declared would be in the identifier list for the block in which they had been declared.

The following structure might be used to represent the symbol table:

type $btab =$ **record** $levno : integer$;
      $idl : \uparrow idlist$;
      $next : \uparrow btab$
   end ;

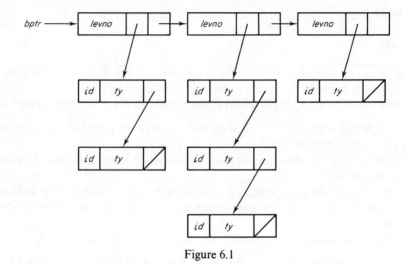

Figure 6.1

where
type *idlist* = **record** *id, ty*: *integer*;
　　　　　　　nextid: ↑*idlist*
　　　end

in which we assume that identifiers and types are represented by integers.

There would be a pointer to the symbol table element corresponding to the smallest enclosing block. It would be declared as

　　var *bptr*: ↑*btab*

and would always point to the symbol table element corresponding to the smallest enclosing block and would have the value **nil** initially; *temp* would be a variable of the same type as *bptr*.

There would be actions associated with block entry and block exit which would appear in the grammar thus:

　　BLOCK → **begin** ⟨*A1*⟩ *DECS*; *STATS* ⟨*A2*⟩ **end**

where

　　⟨*A1*⟩
　　begin *new*(*temp*);
　　　　temp↑.*next*: = *bptr*;
　　　　ln: = *ln* + *1*;
　　　　temp↑.*levno*: = *ln*;
　　　　temp↑.*idl*: = **nil**;
　　　　bptr: = *temp*
　　end

where *ln* is the current level number (i.e. the depth of nesting) and is initially zero

⟨A2⟩
begin *ln* := *ln* − *1* ;
    bptr := *bptr* ↑ *.next*
end

There would also be an action for each defining occurrence of an identifier. The action would appear in the grammar as follows:

IDS → *id* ⟨A3⟩
    IDS, id⟨A3⟩

(Notice that the left recursion would allow us to specify a special action associated with the first identifier in the list. Similarly, right recursion would allow us to specify a particular action for the last identifier.)
The action would be as follows:

⟨A3⟩
begin *ptr* := *bptr* ↑ *.idl* ;
    error := *false* ;
    while *ptr* < > **nil do**
    begin if *ptr* ↑ *.id* = *iden*
            then begin *error* := *true* ;
                        ptr := **nil**
                end ;
            else *ptr* := *ptr* ↑ *.nextid*
    end ;
    if *error*
    then *writeln* ('*identifier*', *iden*, '*already declared*')
    else begin *new* (*itemp*) ;
                itemp ↑ *.id* := *iden* ;
                itemp ↑ *.ty* := *itype* ;
                itemp ↑ *.nextid* := *bptr* ↑ *.idl* ;
                bptr ↑ *.idl* := *itemp*
        end
    end   .

where *ptr*, *itemp* and *error* are identifiers corresponding to variables of appropriate types. *iden* is the name of the identifier and *itype* its type. Notice that a check is made to see if the identifier has already been declared in the block.
Associated with an applied occurrence of an identifier would be the action *A4* which would discover the type of the identifier from the symbol table.

⟨A4⟩
begin *found* := *false* ;
    b := *bptr* ;

```
            while(b < > nil) and not found do
            begin ptr := b↑.idl;
                    while (ptr < > nil) and not found do
                    begin if ptr↑.id = iden
                            then begin itype := ptr↑.ty;
                                        found := true
                                  end;
                            ptr := ptr↑.nextid
                    end;
                    b := b↑.next
            end;
            if not found
            then begin writeln ('identifier not declared');
                        new (itemp);
                        itemp↑.id := iden;
                        itemp↑.ty := deftype;
                        itemp↑.nextid := bptr↑.idl;
                        bptr↑.idl := itemp
                  end
      end
```

where *found*, *b*, and *itemp* are identifiers corresponding to variables of appropriate types.

Notice that if an identifier has not been declared it is inserted in the symbol table and given a suitable default value for its type. This avoids an avalanche of error messages when an identifier has mistakenly not been declared.

This then completes our description of the symbol table operations required for our simple language. In an actual compiler the symbol table could contain other compile-time information about the identifier such as its run-time address or, in the case of a constant, its value. Later we will discuss how these algorithms are generalized to deal with more complex languages. However, before leaving the topic for the moment, we would like to point out the existence of simpler symbol table maintenance algorithms for the sort of language discussed in this section. The disadvantage of these simple algorithms is that they are not easily generalized to deal with more complex languages.

For a language with the properties described earlier in this section a suitable data structure for the symbol table would be a stack, each element of which was a symbol table entry.

On encountering a declaration the corresponding symbol table entry would be put on top of the stack and on leaving a block all the symbol table entries corresponding to declarations in that block would be removed from the stack, and the stack pointer lowered to its position on entering the block. The result would be that at any time during the parse the symbol table entries corresponding to all the current identifiers would be on the stack and relating applied and defining occurrences of identifiers would involve searching the stack from the top downwards. The use of a stack for a symbol table in place of the more complex linked structure would save a great deal of space required for pointers in the case of the linked structure. The following example indicates how the method would work.

outline program

———————————

begin integer a, b
.
.
.

  begin integer c, d
  .
  .
  .
  end;
  begin integer e, f
  .
  .
  .
  end
end

symbol table

———————————

f	integer
e	integer
b	integer
a	integer

The symbol table is shown after **begin integer** e, f has been encountered

6.3 Other applications

The previous examples have shown that the idea of embedding actions in a grammar gives rise to a compiler design which is simple and elegant and leads to actions being performed at the appropriate level in the grammar. The compiler writer should be able to consider each level independently and the grammar provides the framework for the complete compiler.

It has been said before that a compiler is simply a program which takes as its input a program in a particular language and produces as output the corresponding program in some machine code. The fact that the output is machine code is not particularly relevant so far as the syntax analyser is concerned and the idea of a 'syntax analyser' which produces some other type of output is worth some consideration. The technique of embedding actions in a grammar can be extended to produce almost any program whose input can be defined by a grammar. We illustrate the idea with some examples.

1 Layout program (pretty printer)

The idea of a program which accepts as input any program in a language such as Pascal or Ada and outputs the program neatly laid out according to some convention is not new. Many such programs have been written, and one approach is to use a syntax analyser for the language concerned, augmented by suitable actions to perform the laying out. After all, the layout conventions are almost certainly closely related to the syntactic structure of the program and this approach is therefore natural and simple. Also, it should not be difficult to alter the layout convention merely by adding, deleting, or altering some of the actions. Of course a layout program based on a parser would normally fail for input which was not syntactically correct. A good pretty printer, however, would 'recover' from most syntax errors and attempt to lay out the rest of the program in a sensible manner.

An extension of the idea of a pretty printer would be a 'zoom' lister, a utility which could be used to list part of a program in a level of detail specified by the user and to 'zoom' in and out giving a more detailed or a wider view of the program at the user's request.

2. Program analysers

The following tasks, each of which analyses programs in a particular way, can also be treated in a similar manner:

(a) Listing of the identifiers used in each block.
(b) Counting the number of occurrences of various types of clauses, statements, etc.
(c) Optimization of source code. Here the output is another version of the program in the *same* language.

The input to the analyser need not even be in a programming language as long as its format can be defined by a grammar. A program which reads in a football league table, together with a set of results, and updates the table could be written naturally in this way. It is not even necessary to specify the input precisely; spaces and newlines, for example, could be ignored by the input procedure.

Exercises

6.1 Show how the example of Section 6.1 can be amended to produce postfix notation in place of quadruples. (In postfix notation each operator appears immediately after its operands. For example, the (infix) expression

$$(a + b) \times (c + d)$$

would become

$$ab + cd + \times$$

in postfix notation.)

6.2 Give an example to show that the insertion of an action in a grammar may prevent it being converted into LL(1) form.

6.3 In the example in Section 6.1 is it necessary to stack the operator if there is only one operator with each priority?

6.4 In some languages the priority of an operator can be declared by the programmer. How would you expect the syntax analyser to cope with this facility?

6.5 Give examples of inputs (other than programs) which might be processed by a syntax analyser.

6.6 What problems do you see in writing a completely satisfactory 'layout' program?

6.7 Explain how the values of integer constants could be determined during lexical analysis by means of inserting actions in an appropriate grammar.

6.8 What form would you expect the symbol table to take in BASIC or FORTRAN?

6.9 What are the arguments in favour of allowing declarations to appear almost anywhere within a block?

6.10 In this chapter we have introduced the idea of the parsing table being able to 'call' compile-time actions. How will the parse table elements and the LL(1) driver described in Section 4.5 have to be modified as a result?

Chapter 7

Compiler Design

In this chapter we discuss in more detail the issues involved in designing a compiler. In Chapter 6 we chose examples where lexical analysis was not necessary and where compile-time information such as types was always available when required. By so doing we avoided considering some aspects of the problem. Actual programming languages are usually more complex and it is the particular features of the language to be compiled which to some extent dictate the overall design of the compiler. Other factors include the environment in which the compiler is to be used, whether compile-time or run-time efficiency is more important, and what emphasis is to be placed on good diagnostic and error recovery capabilities.

7.1 Number of passes

Many compiler writers find the idea of a single-pass compiler attractive, partly no doubt because there is no need to worry about inter-pass communication, intermediate languages, and so on. It is also not difficult to associate program errors with the original source text, nor do problems exist as to how one pass should patch up an error in order to hand over something sensible to the following pass. Single-pass compilers are usually faster than multi-pass compilers, unless they become unduly involved in backtracking or lookahead to resolve problems which could have been better dealt with by adding another pass. However, they may produce slower object code since they are unlikely to be able to perform extensive optimizations.

Some languages, such as FORTRAN and Pascal, can be fully compiled in one pass, and in many cases where a language cannot be compiled in a single pass, one-pass compilers have been written for subsets or dialects of the language. The usual restriction which such compilers require is that all identifiers, etc., are declared (textually) before they are used. In some cases a language extension has to be introduced so that, for example in the case of mutually recursive types or procedures, an object can be 'declared' before it is fully defined. Some ALGOL 60 compilers, for instance, have required labels to be declared and the ALGOL 68R compiler written at the Royal Signals and Radar Establishment at Malvern, England, has a 'declaration' of the form

mode abc

to indicate that the bold tag **abc** is a mode to be fully defined later and not a user-defined operator (also denoted by a bold tag in ALGOL 68). The 'forward' directive in Pascal allows mutually recursive procedures to be dealt with in a single pass in a similar manner.

As well as one-pass compilers for dialects of languages which require two or more pass compilers to compile the full language, there are also multi-pass compilers written for dialects of languages which would require extra passes to compile programs in the full language. However, for the rest of this section we will confine ourselves to the problem of determining the minimum number of passes required to be able to compile all programs in a particular language, and will not allow ourselves the luxury of restricting the language or adding super-language features to it to assist the compiler writer.

It is first necessary to consider in a little more detail what we mean by a compiler pass. If a certain phase (or group of phases) of the compilation process involves reading the source text, or a translation of it into some intermediate language, then it is usually regarded as a pass. For the purpose of determining the minimum number of passes required to compile a language we shall not allow a pass to perform an arbitrary amount of lookahead (though a fixed amount of lookahead may be required by the syntax analyser) since then it could be argued that almost any language could be compiled in a single pass. Not all the work performed by a compiler is necessarily part of one of the passes. Some compilers may reorganize tables or sort types in between passes. If a compilation phase does not involve reading the source code (or a version of it) then it should not be regarded as a pass. Suppose, however, a phase of the compiler has to read a skeleton of the source text which merely gives the structure of the source program but is devoid of most of the detail. Does this constitute a pass or not? We would probably say yes since, even though certain details of the program may be missing, from a structural point of view the complete program is read and the length of the skeleton will be approximately proportional to the length of the program.

Passes may be forward or backward, i.e. a pass may read the source from left to right (as is most usual) or from right to left. The minimum number of passes required to compile a language may depend on whether all the passes are forward or whether some are backward and some forward. The idea of a backward pass may be appealing from an aesthetic point of view but with some operating systems and filing systems may not be trivial to implement.

The need for more than one pass usually arises because some information required by the compiler is not available at the appropriate time. For example, to compile

$$x + y$$

in many languages it is necessary to know the types of x and y in order to identify the operator $+$ which could mean the addition of two integers, or two real numbers, or a real and an integer, and so on. If the defining occurrences of *x* and *y* are allowed to follow their applied occurrences code cannot, in general, be generated in a single pass. In ALGOL 60 this precise problem does not arise but in the case of mutually recursive procedures one procedure has inevitably to be declared before the other one. Suppose, for example, the body of procedure *A* contains a call or calls of procedure *B* and procedure *B* contains a call or calls of procedure *A*. If procedure *A* is declared first the compiler will not be able to generate code for a call of *B* within *A* without knowing the types of the parameters (if any) of *B* and, in the case of a procedure returning a result (function), the type of the result may be required to identify an operator, say. The only reasonable solution to this problem is to allow the compiler to have an extra pass before code generation in order to determine the types of identifiers, etc., and enter them in the symbol table for use by subsequent passes. ALGOL 60 could theoretically be compiled in two passes using this approach, though many of the early ALGOL 60 compilers (Naur [1964]) had many more passes, often around seven or eight. The reason was probably to keep the maximum amount of space required by the compiler at any time as small as possible, but there are also conceptual reasons for separating the distinct aspects of the compilation process into separate passes.

In an Ada module declarations may be imported from other precompiled modules, otherwise declarations of variables etc. must appear textually before their use. Mutually recursive procedures are accommodated by separating one of the procedure specifications from its full declaration. For example:

```
procedure F(...);
procedure G(...) is
begin
   .
   .
   F(...);
   .
   .
end G;
procedure F(...) is
begin
   .
   .
   G(...);
   .
   .
end F;
```

where the two specifications of *F* have to be the same.

Similarly two types can be defined in terms of each other:

```
type node;
type list is access node;
type node is record value: integer;
                     next: list;
          end record;
```

For the main part therefore information about types of items is always known when a particular part of an Ada program is being analysed. Complications can, however, occur when analysing expressions because of *overloading*.

Operators are overloaded in many languages. For example, in ALGOL 60 or Pascal the meaning of '+' in

$x + y$

depends on the types of the variables (or possibly constants in Pascal) x and y. It could mean the addition of two integer values, two reals, or an integer and a real. In Ada literals, aggregates and subprograms can also be overloaded. The type of the literal

2

for example is not necessarily obvious. Some examples of overloading in Ada are

1. **type** *colour* **is** (*red, blue, green*);
   type *sky* **is** (*blue, grey, black*);

   The literal *blue* can then be of type *colour* or type *sky*. To distinguish we can, however, write

   colour' (*blue*)

   or

   sky' (*blue*)

2. **type** *new_int* **is** *new integer* ;
   i :*integer* ;
   n :*new_int* ;

   i and *n* or *not* of the same type. The operator '+' is further overloaded by the introduction of the type *new_int* so that two values of this type could be added. However, the expression

   $i + n$

   would be illegal since '+' has not been defined for an operand of each type. The literal *4* (for example) is now also overloaded since it could be of type *integer* or *new_int*.

3. **function** " *+* " (*m* : *integer* ; *p* : *new_int*) **return** *new_int* **is** ...

   The above declaration would further overload '+' (and make $i + n$ legal).

The following example illustrates that the type of an expression (and its components) may not be determined without one or more traversals of the corresponding expression tree. The definitions and declarations in (2) and (3) above are assumed.

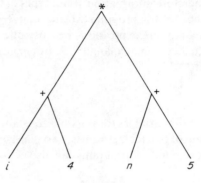

Figure 7.1

Consider the expression

$$(i+4)*(n+5)$$

whose tree representation is shown in Figure 7.1. Variables cannot be overloaded and their types can be determined from the relevant declarations. In this case
  i is of type *integer*
  n is of type *new_int*

We can now deduce the following
  4 is of type *integer* or *new_int*
  5 is of type *integer* or *new_int*

The first '+' is either of type

  $(integer, new\_int) \rightarrow new\_int$
or
  $(integer, integer) \rightarrow integer$

in an obvious notation.
  The second '+' can only be of type

  $(new\_int, new\_int) \rightarrow new\_int$

This means that the first operand of ∗ must also be of type *new_int* (assuming ∗ has not been overloaded to include $(integer, new\_int)$). Thus the '+' in

  i + 4

has to be of type

$(integer,\ new\_int) \rightarrow new\_int$

Thus *4* is of type *new*_*int* and the complete expression is of type *new*_*int*. Thus to find the types of all the components of the expression (including the expression itself) we have performed a bottom-up followed by a top-down traversal of the expression tree.

It is interesting to note that had the overloading of '+' in

function *" + "* (*m : integer* ; *p : new*_*int*) **return** *new*_*int* **is** . . .

not existed the expression would have been illegal, while if " + " had been further overloaded by

function *" + "* (*m : new*_*int* ; *p : integer*) **return** *new*_*int* **is** . . .

the second '+' would have been ambiguous and therefore the expression would have been illegal. In this case the ambiguity could have been resolved by replacing *5* in the expression by

integer' (*5*)

or

*new*_*int'* (*5*)

as appropriate.

We have demonstrated that in Ada, unlike in most other languages, it is not always a straightforward matter to determine the types of the items at the terminal nodes of the syntax tree. Fortunately (unlike ALGOL 68) Ada is not an expression-oriented language and expression trees tend to be relatively simple. The determination of types therefore does not require additional passes over the complete source text. For a detailed discussion of overload resolution in Ada expressions see Baker [1982].

Many languages, for reasons similar to that of ALGOL 60, require at least two passes. Full ALGOL 68 compilers seem typically to have between four and eight passes and it is interesting to consider how many passes are strictly necessary to compile the language. As in ALGOL 60, in order to generate code the mode (or type) of each identifier, constant, etc. is required, and since declarations of identifiers may appear after their use at least two passes are certainly needed. One might then imagine a pass which scanned the program, noting the modes of all the identifiers and putting this information in a symbol table for use during the following pass which would generate the code. However, it is not possible for the first pass to recognize all declarations since the sequence

abc *abc*

could be a declaration of an identifier *abc* of mode **ref abc** or an expression of the form

monadic operator "**abc**" *identifier* "*abc*"

To resolve the ambiguity it is necessary to determine whether **abc** is a user-defined mode or a user-defined operator. In either case there will be a corresponding declaration of **abc**, though not necessarily before its applied occurrence in

abc *abc*

The problem requires another pass for its solution. In ALGOL 68 terminology **abc** is a bold tag, and bold tags may be used to represent user-defined modes or user-defined operators. The information about whether a bold tag represents a mode or an operator may occur textually after it is required by the pass which inserts mode information in the symbol table, and a previous pass is required to set up tables containing information about how bold tags are used in the various blocks of the program.

It now appears that compiling ALGOL 68 requires at least three passes. One reason why ALGOL 68 may require more than three passes is connected with the overloading of the opening bracket symbol '('. The symbol may be used to start a conditional clause, a case clause, a routine, a collateral, or a closed clause as well as being used in place of an opening square bracket when subscripting arrays, etc. The meaning of

(**real** x, y, **int** a, b) **real**

cannot be determined until the closing bracket has been read. Up till that point the fragment could either be the start of a routine or a closed clause (or a conditional or case clause). We have seen in Section 5.5 that the grammars for a closed clause and a conditional can be merged so that they can be expressed in LL(1) form, and it is not difficult to see that the same can be done for a closed clause and a routine (or even for all the four possibilities mentioned above). The effect of this is that the parser will not be aware whether it is dealing with a closed clause or a routine until the difference becomes apparent (at the closing bracket in the above example). It appears therefore from a parsing point of view that this overloading of the opening bracket symbol causes no problems. However, if the parser is to have actions embedded in it to generate code or update tables then problems do arise. One would expect different actions to be performed after

real x

had been read, depending on whether it formed part of a closed clause or a routine. If it occurred in a closed clause it would be an identifier declaration, and appropriate insertions would be made in the symbol table, whereas if the same fragment occurred in a routine the corresponding action would be to note the mode of one of the parameters which would in turn contribute to the mode of the routine itself.

Does the opening bracket in a routine require an extra pass for compilation? One way of avoiding it might be to perform an action which effectively combined the actions described above wherever there was any doubt whether an identifier declaration or a formal parameter was involved. This approach, however, would require table entries to be removed once the ambiguity had been resolved. Alternatively the lexical analyser might be allowed some lookahead in order to recognize routine opening brackets which it could replace by some distinct symbol. Although, since a routine may have an arbitrarily large number of parameters, the amount of lookahead could be arbitrarily large, in practice it would probably be quite small. The problem is essentially one of transmitting information back along the source text and, apart from using lookahead or a backward pass, one approach would be to adopt the same solution as was used to solve the problem of applied occurrences of identifiers occurring before the corresponding defining occurrences; that is to set up a table containing the necessary information during an early pass for the use of later passes. There could be a table entry for every opening bracket in the program and once its type had been determined the table could be updated to show this information.

The following example illustrates a typical program fragment in which opening brackets appear:

$$(square := (\textbf{int } q) \textbf{ int } : q \uparrow 2 ;$$
$$a := (b|c|d) \ldots$$

The opening brackets represent **begin**, the start of a routine, and **if**, respectively.

An algorithm to fill the bracket table would proceed as follows. Each time an opening bracket was encountered a new table entry would be allocated and its address put on a stack. In the case of a conditional clause or a case clause the type of the opening bracket would be recognized at the second stick ($|$), if any, or the closing bracket (case clauses have at least two elements). The table entry corresponding to the address on top of the stack would be updated and on encountering the closing bracket the address on top of the stack would be removed. If on reaching the closing bracket the construction was clearly not a conditional or a case then a decision would be delayed until a colon (indicating a routine) was encountered or not, and then the appropriate table entry would be updated and the stack decremented by one. This phase can be combined with other ones and, if the meanings of bold tags are known when it is executed, closed clauses and routines can be distinguished by the time the closing bracket has been read since the last element of a closed clause cannot be a declaration.

From a code generation point of view it is not essential to be able to distinguish between conditional clauses and closed clauses on reading the opening bracket.

However, for diagnostic purposes (and possibly to keep the parsing table as small as possible) it can be useful. Consider the following example

$$(a := b; L: c := d; a = c|x|y)$$

The above fragment contains a syntax error since labels are not allowed between the **if** (represented by an opening bracket) and the **then** (represented by |) in a conditional clause. However, if the opening bracket has not been recognized as an **if**, an error message cannot be given until the | is encountered.

An alternative to introducing a bracket table is to have an extra backward pass immediately prior to syntax analysis. This pass would use a stack as described earlier but instead of inserting information in a table would actually amend the source text, replacing opening brackets by distinct symbols indicating their meaning. A single forward pass could also be used if the source text was held in some form of direct access store and a stack was used to remember the addresses of the opening brackets until their meaning was clear, at which stage the source text would be amended to include this information.

A bracket pass may also be used to do some checking of the source text. In ALGOL 68 an **if** must be matched by a **fi** and an opening bracket by a closing bracket, i.e. the sequences

if ....)

or

(.................... **fi**

are illegal (and similarly for cases, etc.). A bracket pass can check for consistency in this respect and simply replace opening and closing brackets by **if**, **fi**, **case**, etc. as appropriate which will help to reduce the size of the grammar (and hence the parsing table).

The analysis stage of compilation may consist of several passes over the source text (or a translation of it), each of which may perform one or more phases of the compilation process. For example, in a typical ALGOL 68 compiler, the lexical analysis phase and an identification of bold tags phase may take place in parallel within the same pass. In a well-constructed compiler, however, the two phases would appear as separate as possible from the compiler writer's point of view even though they would be executed in parrallel at compile time. One way of achieving this would be for the lexical analyser to be written as a procedure for the bold tag phase to call whenever a new symbol was to be read. In this way the bold tag phase would effectively see the source text as if lexical analysis had taken place in a previous pass, and the lexical analysis phase would know nothing about the workings of the bold tag phase. From the point of view of modularity, documentation, and maintenance, as well as of reliability, such an approach is almost essential.

Each pass of the analysis stage may be syntax directed, i.e. based on a grammar. However, the grammar may be different for each pass. For example, if the pass was only concerned with declarations in order to determine types, priorities of operators would be irrelevant. However, the final analysis pass would require to be able to form a full syntax tree for code generation, and would require to be based on the full context-free grammar. The grammar used in the earlier pass would correspond to a superset of the language generated by the grammar used in the later pass. The more permissive grammar of the earlier pass would tend to be smaller, and to have a correspondingly smaller parsing table than that of the later pass.

Non-context-free requirements of the language would normally be represented by actions embedded in a context-free grammar. These actions might be to insert information in the symbol table, or to search tables for type or other information. The actions would correspond to attributes in an attribute grammar or meta-notions in a two-level grammar. Corresponding to each attribute or meta-notion in the grammar there would appear an action in one or other of the passes of the analysis stage. For example, the pass which recognized identifier declarations would include actions to insert type information in the symbol table, whereas a subsequent pass would include actions to search the symbol table for this information. The checking of the non-context-free aspects of the language can be thought of as being spread over a number of compilation passes in a similar way to that in which the context-free aspects are dealt with. There is an algorithm to determine the minimum number of passes required to analyse a given attribute grammar (Bochmann [1973]).

Further reasons why compilers may have additional passes are associated with the model for machine code generation used, what optimizations are required, and whether portability is an aim. Some of these points will be discussed in Chapters 10 and 11.

We have seen that a compiler may require at least three passes if it is to be able to analyse all programs in a language. However, not every program may require all three passes for analysis. For example, a program in the language may not have any applied occurrences of identifiers occurring before their defining occurrences and may not contain any user-defined modes or operators. In this case the program *could* be compiled in a single pass. It would seem wasteful for such a program to have to be processed by three compilation passes when only one was really required. The compiler, however, is not going to know (unless the user is expected to tell it) at the start of compilation whether passes are required to build up the symbol tables, etc., before analysis can be completed, or whether a single pass could be used instead. A solution adopted by the Manchester ALGOL 68 compiler for the MU5 (Barringer and Lindsey [1977]) is to assume that analysis can be completed in a single pass until this is found to be impossible.

Consider the following example:

```
begin int p;
begin proc q = void:
```

begin ... p; ...
end;
proc $p =$ **void**:
.
.
.

The compiler could try to complete the analysis of the above program in a single pass. Information would be inserted in the tables as it is encountered and compilation would proceed under the assumption that everything was declared before use until this was found not to be the case. In the above example, the applied occurrence of p within the body of procedure of q would be assumed initially to refer to the p declared in the outer block. However, when a declaration of p was encountered within the *same* block it would then be realized that a wrong assumption had been made, and the attempt to complete analysis in one pass would be abandoned. However, the compiler would continue to read the source text in order to accumulate as much symbol table information as possible for use by the following pass which would again try to analyse the program fully, this time with the aid of some symbol table information. It is obvious that spurious error messages could appear due to a wrong assumption in an early pass, but these would not be communicated to the user in the first instance.

The benefit of such a scheme is that programs would be analysed in as few passes as possible—often in a single pass—whereas only those programs which require them will use the maximum number of passes.

In the ALGOL 68 compiler project at the University of Strathclyde lexical analysis alone was performed in the first pass. This meant that at the end of the first pass it was known whether either of the symbols **op** or **mode** appeared in the program. If **op** did not appear then bold tags in the program (apart from language words such as **begin**, **for**, etc.) must have corresponded to user-defined modes, whereas if **mode** did not appear then any bold tags must have corresponded to user-defined operators. With this information available the pass for identifying bold tags could often be omitted when compiling programs.

We have confined our discussion mainly to Ada and ALGOL 68. However, the same sort of analysis could be used to determine the minimum number of passes required to compile other languages. It turns out, as we have mentioned, that many compilers contain more passes than the minimum number theoretically required to compile programs in the source language.

7.2 Intermediate languages

One penalty for writing a compiler containing more than one pass is that there is usually a need to design intermediate languages in which to represent the source text between passes (i.e. as the output from one pass and the input to the following pass). This problem can be approached at two levels. First there is the source text after lexical analysis. As we saw in Chapter 3, one of the main actions performed by lexical analysis is to replace variable length objects such as identifiers, constants, etc. by fixed length symbols. The simplest form that these symbols may take is integers. The source text after lexical analysis, therefore, might consist of a sequence of integers, some of which corresponded to language words while others represented pointers into the identifier table or the constant table and so on. This intermediate form of the program would not itself contain all the information in the original source text, but together with the tables formed during lexical analysis would contain essentially the same information.

In contrast, the sort of intermediate language produced by one of the final passes would be much closer to machine code, e.g. quadruples, and will be discussed in the next section.

What about the code output by passes 2 or 3 of a typical five-pass compiler? Would it resemble more the first type of intermediate code or the second? The answer is probably the first. In fact, the intermediate language output by the first few passes may be the same. After all, the earlier passes are used largely to build tables for the later passes to use, and several passes may actually read the same version of the source text though the information they will find in the tables will be different. Alternatively, the intermediate *language* may be the same but successive passes will enrich the source text by inserting additional information in it (e.g. meanings of brackets, etc.) required by the parser.

One way of looking at a multi-pass compiler is that it consists of a number of preliminary passes to set up the symbols tables, etc., and (possibly) to enrich the source text so that analysis (and possibly code generation) can be completed in a single pass.

7.3 Target language

It is sometimes possible to separate the machine-independent and machine-dependent parts of a compiler. This is obviously desirable if the compiler is to be portable and one method is to define a language, sometimes known as the target language or intermediate language which acts as an interface between the two parts, the machine-independent part of the compiler translating the source code into the target language and the machine-dependent part translating from the target language into the particular machine code. If the *same* target language (and a common implementation language) could be used the problem of implementing m languages on n machines would essentially involve writing $m + n$ pieces of software, i.e. m machine-independent 'front ends' of compilers and n machine-dependent 'back ends' of compilers, rather than $m \times n$ complete compilers. The target language could also be thought of as a machine, usually called an abstract machine, since the front end of a compiler will see it like an object machine. There are a number of examples of such universal target languages or abstract machines, e.g. JANUS (Poole [1974]), but the idea does not seem to work out as well as one might have hoped. It would appear that, to accommodate a wide range of languages, the target language has to be at too low a level to be implemented efficiently on all the machines. It seems better to design a target language for translating a *particular* high-level language into or for implementing on a *particular* machine. For example, CTL (common target language) is used by most of the compilers on the MU5 machine as a target language. On the other hand, BCPL (Richards [1971]) has been implemented on many machines using OCODE or INTCODE as a target language and Branquart *et al.* [1976] have designed a target language for ALGOL 68 which could be implemented on many machines. In the latter case some knowledge of the object machine is required by the front end of the compiler but this only amounts to knowing how much space is required for an integer value, a real value, and so on. This is necessary since storage allocation is performed prior to production of the target language. It would be possible to allocate space without this machine-dependent information but it would make the handling of run-time addresses unduly complicated.

Most implementations of Pascal use an intermediate language called *P-code* or 'pseudo-code'. Compilers generate P-code which is then usually interpreted. P-code has also been an aid in transporting Pascal to new environments.

P-code essentially simulates a stack machine with most instructions taking their data from and returning their results to the top of the stack. P-code reflects the design of Pascal in a number of ways. Pascal procedures map on to P-code procedures and instructions are provided corresponding to procedure entry and exit. Addresses of array elements can be computed from array base addresses in a single instruction. P-code allows the implementor to set up constants corresponding to the space allocated for the standard data types.

A number of variations of P-code exist. The original P-code (Ammann [1974]), referred to as P-2 P-code, was later replaced by P-4 P-code which is now considered the standard. At the University of California at San Diego a derivative of P-2 P-code known as UCSD P-code has been used to implement a complete Pascal programming system on micro-computers. The P-code generated is extremely compact and is not produced in text form. Under the UCSD P-system other programming languages such as FORTRAN are also available.

The language MODEL (Morris [1976]) developed at the Los Alamos Scientific Laboratory, and based on Pascal, has been implemented using a variation of P-4 P-code known as LASL P-code. The implementation was on a CRAY-1 computer with the P-code being translated rather than interpreted. Not surprisingly LASL P-code contains features of the CRAY-1, thus decreasing the portability of the MODEL implementation.

For a comparison of the various P-codes see Nelson [1979]. Further details of P-code are discussed in later chapters.

Another intermediate language which has been used in implementing Pascal is Tanenbaum *et al.*'s [1980] EM, an intermediate language designed for implementing a range of high-level languages such as Pascal, C, Ada, ALGOL 68, BCPL, etc., on a variety of machines. The instruction set is designed to store programs compactly and to reduce the time required to transmit the programs over communication lines. The language is intended for interpretation or translation into machine code and particularly for use with cross compilers. The language is stack-based (like P-code) and has been used to implement the Pascal-VU compiler written at the Vrie Universteit in Amsterdam.

DIANA (Goos [1983]) seems to be emerging as a 'standard' intermediate language for Ada. DIANA programs are represented by trees, essentially the syntax trees of the original Ada programs together with attributes computed by semantic analysis. The DIANA interface is therefore at a relatively high level and does not relate to any particular implementation of Ada. DIANA also provides a convenient representation of Ada programs on which software tools such as syntax-directed editors can be based.

In this chapter we have discussed some aspects of the design of compilers, especially how they are split up into phases and passes and the design of intermediate languages. In the next few chapters we will be concerned with the design of symbol and type tables and models for storage allocation.

Exercises

7.1 Give reasons why languages are not always designed so that they can be compiled in a single pass.

7.2 Give reasons why it might be desirable to include more passes in a compiler than are strictly necessary to compile the language concerned.

7.3 Comment on the statement that a one-pass compiler is likely to be more helpful from a diagnostic point view.

7.4 Mention a language feature which would be well suited to a backward compiler pass.

7.5 Give arguments for and against 'readable' intermediate languages.

7.6 Do you think the compiler should give an indication of the pass in which it discovers a programming error?

7.7 The MU5 ALGOL 68 compiler has a 'variable' number of passes. Give arguments against this approach.

7.8 In what ways might the design of a compiler be influenced by the machine on which it is to run?

7.9 If the chief design aim for a compiler was portability how might this affect its overall structure?

7.10 If the chief design aim for a compiler was reliability how might this affect its overall structure?

Chapter 8

Symbol and Type Tables

Symbol tables are used by the syntax analyser for storing type information about identifiers, etc., and (possibly) by the code generator for storing compile-time addresses of values. The type information may consist simply of an integer, representing a type, in languages containing only a finite number of types or, in languages containing potentially an infinite number of types, such as Pascal or Ada, may consist of a pointer to a type table whose entries are structures representing the type. In this chapter we consider first symbol tables and later type tables.

8.1 Symbol tables

For languages such as FORTRAN or BASIC the symbol table can take a fairly simple form. FORTRAN, for example, has only a finite (and small) number of types and each type can be represented by an integer. For example, the type 'integer' might be represented by 1 and the type 'real' by 2. The symbol table might then be an array of entries of the form

   identifier, type

Identifiers in FORTRAN cannot be more than six (two in BASIC) characters long so that the actual identifiers can be stored in the symbol table rather than some post lexical analysis representation of them.

The following actions can be associated with the symbol table:

1. When an identifier is encountered for the first time (i.e. it does not already appear in the table) it will be entered in the table along with its type. If an identifier is not introduced by an explicit declaration such as

   REAL X

   its type can be deduced from its initial letter (I to N inclusive imply integer, otherwise real).
2. When an identifier is encountered which has already been entered in the table its type is determined by the appropriate entry.

152

Using this model the identifiers will appear in the table in the same order as they first occurred in the program. Each time the analyser comes across an identifier it will check to see if the identifier is in the table and, if it is not, an appropriate entry will be inserted at the end of the table. In those cases in which the identifier is *not* in the table this will involve searching the complete table element by element; and even in those cases in which the identifier is in the table, half the table on average will be searched. The type of search involved is usually referred to as a *linear search*, and performing linear searches on large tables can be very time consuming. If the identifiers were arranged in alphabetical order, then the search could be performed much faster by successively halving the table until the identifier was either found or shown to be absent (binary search method). However, the time involved in sorting the entries into order each time a new entry was added would be likely to more than outweigh the gains (unless of course there were many more searches than insertions). Another solution is to use a *hashing* method.

To introduce the idea of hashing, suppose for a moment that FORTRAN allowed only identifiers consisting of a single letter so that there would be 26 possible identifiers and the symbol table could consist of an array with 26 entries, one for each possible identifier. This would mean that no searching would be required to find if a table entry existed for a particular identifier since any entry for the identifier *A* would be in the first element, and so on. This sort of approach might just about be feasible for a version of BASIC in which all identifiers are of one of the forms

> *letter*
> *letter digit*
> *letter dollar*

or

> *letter percent*

allowing only 338 possible identifiers. However, for FORTRAN the number of possible identifiers, though finite, is very large and for ALGOL 60, Ada or Pascal the number of possible identifiers is infinite.

A generalization of the scheme described above is to use an array with more elements than the maximum number of identifiers expected to appear in a program and to define a mapping (called the *hash function*) from each *possible* identifier on to an element of the array. The mapping of course, will not be one-to-one as we had previously, but many (possibly an infinite number of) identifiers will map on to the same array element. Each time a FORTRAN identifier is encountered the corresponding array element will be examined to see if it contains an entry. If not, the identifier is not already in the symbol table and an appropriate entry can be made. If the element is non-empty it is examined to see if the entry corresponds to the identifier in question. If not, the next entry is examined in the same way and so on until an empty element or an entry corresponding to the identifier is found. The symbol table is thus searched (linearly) from the entry given by applying the mapping function to the identifier, until either the identifier is found or a blank element indicating that no entry exists for that identifier. In the latter case a suitable entry is inserted in the empty element. The array is normally referred to as a *hash table* and the mapping function is called the *hash function*. The array is treated in a circular manner in the sense that, if a search has not been completed on reaching the end of the table, it will continue from the start of the table.

A simple hash function would be to use the first letter of each identifier to map the identifier on to an element of a 26 element array, identifiers beginning with *A* mapping on to the first element, those beginning with *B* on to the second element and so on. After the following identifiers had been encountered

CAR   DOG   CAB   ASS   EGG

the table would look as shown in Table 8.1, the positions of the various identifiers in the table depending on the order in which they had been inserted. When an identifier cannot be inserted in the position given by the hash function a *clash* is said to occur. The larger the table (and the fewer identifiers mapping on to each entry) the fewer clashes would be expected to occur. If a program contained only the above identifiers and the hash function described were used then the hash table would not be filled at all evenly and *clustering* would be said to occur. Programmers might tend to use identifiers beginning with certain letters of the alphabet, in which case the above function would tend to produce clashes and is, therefore, a little too simple-minded. A function which depended on the last character of an identifier might be less likely to cause clustering. Alternatively, the hash function might use all the characters in the identifier to compute the appropriate element of the table. Of course, the more complex the function the more time would be required to evaluate it each time an identifier had to be inserted in the table or the table had to be searched for a particular identifier, and this would have to be offset against the time saved by having shorter searches due to there being less clustering.

Table 8.1

1	ASS	
2		
3	CAR	
4	DOG	
5	CAB	
6	EGG	
7		
8		
9		
.		
.		

Up till now we have dealt with clashes by simply trying the next element of the table (in a cyclic manner) until the identifier or an empty element is found. Other methods could also be used to find another element in the table when the one indicated by the hash function was already full. We require a rule which will take us from one entry in the table to another in such a way that successive applications of the rule will (if necessary) lead to all the entries of the table before any entry is encountered for the second time. The action performed by the hash function is usually referred to as *primary hashing* and the calculation of further addresses in the table is known as *secondary hashing* or *rehashing*. The rehash function considered so far consists merely of adding one (cyclically) to the table address. This rehash function has the property, along with all rehash functions, that if n is some address in the table and p is the number of entries in the table,

$$n, rehash\ (n), rehash^2\ (n) \ldots. rehash^{p-1}\ (n)$$

are all distinct addresses and

$$rehash^p\ (n) = n$$

The following function defines the rehash function described above:

function *rehash* (n:*integer*):*integer*;
begin if $n < p$
    then *rehash* := $n + 1$
    else *rehash* := 1
end

This rehash function tends to cause clusters in the table as any chance occurrence of a cluster tends to grow due to rehashing. It would be preferable if the rehash function were to find an address well away from the one it started with. If the number of elements in the table were prime then instead of the rehash function adding one to an address it could add any positive integer, h, such that $h < p$; giving the rehash function

function *rehash 1* (n:*integer*):*integer*;
began if $n + h <= p$
    then *rehash1* := $n + h$
    else *rehash1* := $n + h - p$
end

A suitable value of h will tend to minimize clustering. Since p is prime the rehash function will successively deliver all the addresses in the table before repeating itself. For this property to hold it is not actually necessary that p is prime but h and p must be relatively prime, i.e. have no common factors other than one.

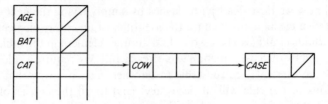

Figure 8.1

There is a great deal more that could be said about hashing and rehashing and the reader is referred to Hall [1975] for further information. We hope the principle is clear and we now consider other approaches to the problem. For example, we could avoid rehashing completely by linking together items which overflowed the table (see Figure 8.1), the only cost apparently involved being the space for the pointers.

An alternative structure for holding ordered items is a *binary tree*. The binary tree in Figure 8.2 can be considered as five items (or nodes), each of which consists of an identifier and its type, etc., and two pointers to other nodes or nil pointers in the case of the nodes containing *BUS*, *HADDOCK*, and *MOUSE*.

A binary tree is defined to consist of a finite set of nodes which is either empty or consists of a root (the node containing *LEMON*) and two disjoint binary trees called the left and right subtrees of the root. A binary tree consisting of zero nodes is referred to as the empty binary tree and is denoted by

in the diagram. Otherwise, the subtree of a node is indicated by means of a pointer.

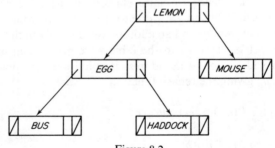

Figure 8.2

The binary tree in Figure 8.2 is said to be of depth 2 and the node containing *BUS* is said to be at distance 2 from the one containing *LEMON*. The node containing *EGG* is said to be a descendant of the node containing *LEMON*.

The binary tree above is ordered (alphabetically) from left to right or, more precisely, the nodes are in alphabetical order when the tree is traversed in inorder. Knuth [1973] gives the following (recursive) algorithm for traversing a binary tree in *inorder*:

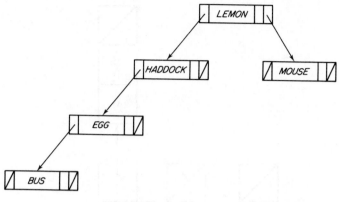

Figure 8.3

traverse the left subtree in inorder
visit the root
traverse the right subtree in inorder.

It is always possible to add a new node to the binary tree in its appropriate place in the ordering and the time taken to search for a node depends only on the depth of the tree. This time will be a minimum (on average) for a tree containing a given number of nodes if the tree is balanced, i.e. the distances of all the terminal nodes (nodes with no descendants) from the root differ by no more than one. The tree pictured in Figure 8.2 is balanced whereas that in Figure 8.3 is not.

A binary tree can be built up by adding nodes one at a time, the first node being the root and the next one being inserted to its right or left as appropriate, and so on. Whether the final tree is balanced or not will depend on the order in which the nodes are inserted. If the tree is not balanced there will exist a binary tree with the same inorder order of nodes which is balanced. Reasonably efficient algorithms exist for balancing trees (replacing a tree by a corresponding balanced one) and in some circumstances it may be worthwhile rebalancing a tree after each insertion. This will depend mainly on the relative frequency of searches and insertions.

The cost of using a binary tree as a symbol table or dictionary is largely the extra space required for the pointers. However, in comparing binary trees and hash tables for use as symbol tables, it should be remembered that in order to work efficiently and avoid too much clustering a hash table should be significantly (possibly 50%) larger than the maximum number of entries it is likely to contain.

Symbol Tables for particular languages

The sort of symbol table required by a Pascal compiler to accommodate function and procedure declarations is similar to that described in Chapter 6

158

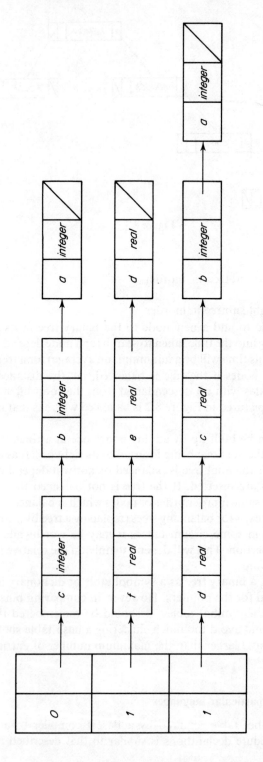

Figure 8.4

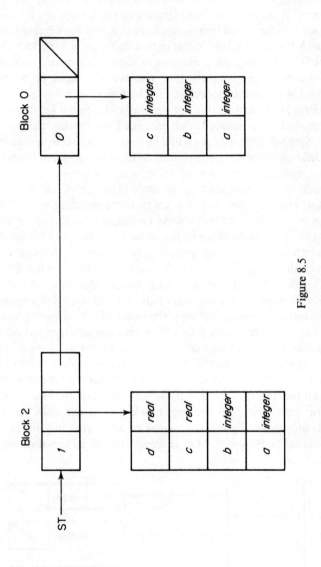

Figure 8.5

though the use of hash tables or binary trees would avoid the linear searching described there. Some implementations of Pascal (e.g. Pascal S), however, do not release a section of the symbol table on function or procedure exit but keep all symbol table information for run-time diagnostics.

For some languages (ALGOL 68 is an example) setting up the symbol table and searching it occur in different passes of the compiler. To describe what happens we will refer to the two passes as Pass A and Pass B respectively. At the end of Pass A a symbol table similar to that in Figure 8.4 might be formed. The symbol table is an array, each element of which is a record consisting of two fields, an integer value giving the level number of a block or procedure and a pointer to a list of variables declared in the block.

During Pass B relevant sections of the symbol table can be read in each time a block or procedure is entered and discarded on leaving the same block or procedure. Symbol table sections could be linked together as shown in Figure 8.5 to ensure that appropriate declarations of each variable are found.

When an applied occurrence of an identifier is encountered in pass *B* the symbol table is searched starting at the beginning of the list and working towards the end. In this way the entry corresponding to the appropriate declaration of the identifier will always be found first. (It can be assumed that if an identifier is declared twice in the same block this will be detected in pass *A*.) This method of searching implies a linear search through (possibly all) the entries in the symbol table. An alternative would be to use a hash table to hold all the identifiers declared in each block. However, this might not be any great improvement if the number of identifiers declared in a block was small. If the assumption is made that only the outer block of a program contains a large number of declarations then a compromise solution would be to use a hash table only for identifiers declared in the outermost block of a program.

Another approach would be to replace the complete symbol table by a hash table in which each element was a list containing type information, etc., regarding all the declarations of a particular identifier in the current and outer blocks. For example, after entering block 0 in a program the table might appear as shown in Figure 8.6, whereas after entering block 2 it might appear as shown in Figure 8.7. On entering a block an identifier which has not

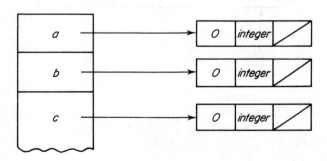

Figure 8.6

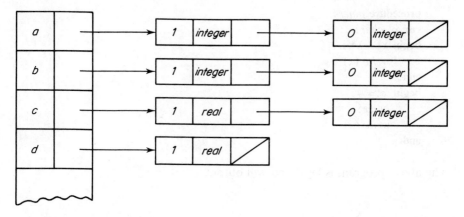

Figure 8.7

been declared in previous blocks is allocated a new entry in the hash table according to the hashing functions, and its properties (level number and type) are inserted in a single list element corresponding to that entry. However, an identifier which *has* been declared in a previous block (whether the block has been left or not) will already have an entry in the hash table. It is then a matter of adding to the front of its list of properties (or if it has none since all the blocks containing declarations of that identifier have been left a new list element is generated) the properties corresponding to the declaration in the current block. On leaving a block the first element of each property list is deleted for each identifier declared in that block. This can be done, knowing the current level number, by scanning the complete hash table or, more efficiently, with the aid of a stack as follows. On entering a block the names of all the identifiers declared in the block are put on the top of a stack and on leaving the block the appropriate amendments are made to the hash table entries corresponding to these identifiers, and the identifiers are removed from the stack. Notice that an entry is never removed from the hash table as otherwise the rehashing function might terminate too soon on finding an empty entry and prevent the search process from working. If an identifier has not been declared in any of the current blocks it will remain in the table but will have a null property list. This means that the hash table must have space for all the identifiers declared in the program and, for efficiency, some more. Pass A should be able to provide the information to make the hash table of the correct size.

Ada requires a much more general symbol table structure than Pascal. In Pascal the declaration of an identifier x in a procedure or function will hide any declaration of x at an outer level, e.g.

    program *sample* (*output*);
    var x : *integer* ;

```
procedure inner;
var x: char;
begin x: = 'A';
      write (x)
end;
begin x: = 4;
      inner;
      write (x)
end.
```

The above program is legal and will output

A 4

The character variable *x* declared in inner is said to hide the global variable *x* of type integer and there is no way that the integer variable can be accessed within inner. The symbol table structure we have discussed will ensure this.

In Ada the situation is slightly different, We could have

```
procedure main is
x:integer;
   procedure inner is
   x:character;
   begin x: = 'A';
         put (x);
         put (main.x);
   end inner;
begin x: = 4;
      inner;
      put (x);
end main;
```

A call of the procedure *main* would output

A 4 4

showing that the integer variable *x* declared in *main* is not completely hidden but may be accessed by writing

main.x

Clearly the symbol table for an Ada implementation would need to reflect this, presumably by naming sections of the symbol table.

Ada has one or two other interesting features as far as symbol table design is concerned. An Ada package is a program module containing declarations which are local to the package together with declarations which can be used outside the package. These can be made directly visible by means of a **use** clause, e.g.

    use *stack* ;

where *stack* is the name of a package which might allow procedures for adding items to and deleting items from a stack to be made visible without allowing access to any other identifiers declared in the package. When compiling a package a symbol table segment will be created for all the identifiers declared in the package and the compile-time implementation of a **use** clause would seem to consist of copying part of this symbol table segment and placing it just in front of the symbol table section for the current scope. However, the following points should be observed.

1. An identifier is made directly visible by a **use** clause only if it would not already be directly visible if the **use** clause were not present.
2. An identifier made directly visible by a **use** clause must be declared in one and only one package named in the **use** clause. If necessary any clashing identifiers must be removed from the symbol table.

It is, however, possible for a symbol in a **use** clause to overload a symbol already visible.

A **use** clause is equivalent to a set of declarations and the symbol table segment corresponding to these declarations should be discarded when the scope of the **use** clause is left.

8.2 Type Tables

In languages with a finite number of possible types (e.g. FORTRAN) each type which occurs in a program can be represented by a distinct integer. In many languages such as Pascal, ALGOL 68, and Ada, however, there are an infinite number of possible types which may occur in a program. In these cases a type table whose elements are structures can be used to hold the various types present in a particular program. The symbol table field representing the type of a user-defined identifier can then consist of a pointer to an entry in the type table.

We illustrate the idea of a type table with reference to Pascal. The situation in ALGOL 68 and Ada is similar but more complex.

In Pascal types come in seven varieties:

    scalar
    subrange
    pointer
    set
    array
    record
    file.

It may also be convenient to think of functions and procedures as types. Scalar types include the standard types *integer, real, boolean,* and *char* which may be represented by integers rather than pointers to the type table. All other types could be represented by structures of various forms. If the implementation language was Pascal variant records could form the basis of the structures (Ammann [1974]).

In designing the structures attention should be paid to the sort of operations which will be performed on types at compile time. These include:

1. finding the type of a field of a record,
2. finding the type of a component of an array,
3. finding the type of an element of a file,
4. checking the types of the parameters of procedures and functions.

Each structure (or record) representing a type could contain an initial field denoting whether the type was an array, record, pointer, etc., together with further fields which would depend on the value of the first field. For example an array type would have pointers to its component type and its index type, a subrange type might have three further fields giving the lower and upper limits of the subrange and the base type, while a record type might contain a pointer field to the types and selectors of the various fields of the record.

As an example the type

> **array** [1 .. 5] **of record** *no* : *integer* ;
> *letter* : *char*
> **end**

could be represented as in Figure 8.8.

Two-dimensional arrays would be represented as arrays of arrays and records which contained fields that were records to any depth could be accommodated.

Pointer, set, and file types would be represented by one field containing pointer, set, or file as appropriate and a second field pointing to another type, for example the base type of the set type.

In the Pascal Report (Jensen and Wirth [1978]) there was some doubt as to whether name or structural equivalence would be used to determine whether two Pascal types were the same. Given the declarations

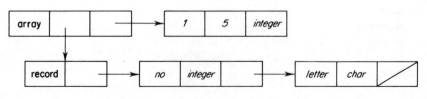

Figure 8.8

var P: **array** [$1..10$] **of** *integer*;
Q: **array** [$1..10$] **of** *integer*;

the types of P and Q are the same as far as structural equivalence is concerned but different with regard to name equivalence.

The assignment

$$P := Q$$

would be legal in the program body (assuming Q had a value) assuming structural equivalence but would be illegal with name equivalence. However, if the declarations had been replaced by

var P,Q :**array** [$1..10$] **of** *integer*

the assignment would have been legal in either case.

In ALGOL 68 two types are equal if they are structurally equivalent. This makes type checking a complex process for an ALGOL 68 analyser since different 'spellings' of the same type have to be recognized as being equivalent.

In Ada name equivalence is used giving added security to programmers in some cases but occasionally producing some surprising results.

The current Pascal Standard uses name equivalence for the main part. In

type *arr10* = **array** [$1..10$] **of** *integer*;
var P, Q: **array** [$1..10$] **of** *integer*;
R :**array** [$1..10$] **of** *integer*;
S, T :*arr10*

P and Q are variables of the same type, as are S and T. Otherwise the variables are all of distinct types.

The use of name equivalence will affect the type table. Possibly types that are structurally equivalent will be represented more than once in the table. Alternatively the type table might be seen as containing type templates each of which might correspond to more than one program type. In this case an identifier's type field in the symbol table would point indirectly to the type table via a 'type name' table.

with *Statement*

The **with** statement is used in Pascal so that the field selectors of record variables can be used as variables on their own. For example

$$john.age := 14$$

where john is a record variable, could be written

with *john* **do**
      age := *14*

The implementation of a **with** statement will cause some compile-time action to make the field selectors and their types visible. The type tables can be used to append this information to the symbol table during the scope of the **with** statement.

Pointer types

In Pascal a list type can be defined as follows:

> **type** *list* = ↑ *listel* ;
>   *listel* = **record** *no* : *integer* ;
>   *next* : *list*
> **end**

The two types defined are mutually recursive. A one-pass compiler can, however, set up the two entries in the type table though it has to read the complete text of the second type definition before it can complete the entry for the first type definition.

Exercises

8.1   What are (a) the advantages and (b) the disadvantages of the restricted form that BASIC identifiers may take?

8.2   In FORTRAN the type of an identifier can usually be deduced from its first letter. Does this make a symbol table unnecessary? Give a reason for your answer.

8.3   How would the problem of inserting identifiers in a hash table be simplified if a lexical analysis pass had already taken place?

8.4   Certain languages have standard identifiers such as *SIN* and *COS*. Describe how these identifiers might be inserted
      (a) in a simple hash table,
      (b) in a block structured symbol table.

8.5   Discuss the pros and cons of using pointers in a hash table as described in Section 8.1.

8.6   Identifiers are stored in alphabetical order in a one-dimensional array of strings. How would you set up a balanced binary tree with these identifiers as nodes such that on traversing the tree in inorder the identifiers would appear in alphabetical order?

8.7   What advantages do you see from the user's point of view of being able to use identifiers before they have been declared?

8.8   'In an ALGOL 68 compiler the mode table should have exactly one representation of each mode in the program.' Discuss this statement.

8.9 For Pascal experts!

Can a **with** statement hide any identifiers which would otherwise be visible?
Give a reason for your answer.

8.10 Assuming name equivalence in Pascal, are *A* and *B* of the same type?

> **type** *arr10* = **array** [*1 . . 10*] **of** *integer* ;
>
> **var** *A* : **array** [*1..5*] **of** *arr10* ;
>
> *B* : **array**[*1..5*] **of** *arr10*

Chapter 9

Storage Allocation

Having recognized the structure (and the meaning) of a program it is necessary to allocate space for values of variables, etc. and to put the corresponding addresses, where appropriate, in the symbol table. The storage allocation phase is relatively language and machine independent, and would be fairly similar for a great many block-structured languages being implemented on most typical machines. It essentially consists of mapping the values which appear in a program on to the memory of the machine. If we assume we are implementing a typical block-structured language, and the machine has a linear store, then a stack or last-in-first-out store seems to be the most appropriate device on which to base our storage allocation. In this chapter we describe the classical run-time stack structure for local storage allocation, and also consider how global space can be allocated in a separate area called the heap.

9.1 The run-time stack

Almost every program will require some space in which to store values of variables and intermediate values of expressions. For example, if an identifier is declared as

   var x : *integer*

indicating that x can take on values (one at a time) of type integer then the compiler will need to allocate space for values of x, i.e. sufficient space to store any integer within a certain range ($-maxint$ to $maxint$), the exact limits in the size of the integer being dependent on the particular implementation. Similarly, if y is declared as

   var y : **record** *number* : *integer* ;
                       size : *real* ;
                       n : *boolean*
          end

then the compiler will have to allocate space for the value of y, in this case sufficient space to store an integer value, a real value and a boolean value. In both the above cases the compiler would have no difficulty in calculating the amount of space required to store the value. Similarly, if z was declared as

z : **array**[$1..10$] **of** *integer*

then the space required for all the *elements* of z would be ten times the space required to store a single integer value.

As well as space being required for values corresponding to identifiers, space may also be required for intermediate results and constants. For example, in evaluating the expression

$a + c \times d$

$c \times d$ is evaluated first, the value is stored in the machine, and then the addition is performed. Space required for intermediate results is known as *working space* or *working storage*.

Each compiler will have a scheme for allocating storage which will, to some extent, depend on the language being compiled. In FORTRAN, space once allocated for values of variables may never be released, so that a one-dimensional array would be a suitable structure from which space could be allocated. If the array is assumed to have a left end and a right end, space could be allocated from the left to the right, a pointer being used to indicate the first free cell in the array, e.g. the effect of the declaration

INTEGER A, B, X, Y

would be to allocate space as shown in Figure 9.1. This simple scheme is very inefficient (in terms of space usage) for a block-structured language.

In a block-structured language space is normally released on leaving the block in which it is allocated. A suitable storage allocation mechanism would be to allow the pointer in the above example to move back to the left when space is released. This is equivalent to having a run-time stack or last-in-first-out store, though it is customary to show a stack growing from the bottom up. (Some authors, however, prefer a downward-pointing stack.)

The storage allocation scheme required for Pascal is not quite so general as that required for other block-structured languages. Pascal has two simplifying aspects:

1. Blocks always correspond to procedures and functions.

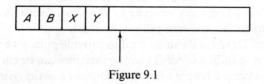

Figure 9.1

2. All storage is static, i.e. the amount of space required to store a value is always known at compile time.

The storage required for a block is known as a data segment (Ammann [1981]). The size of each segment is known at compile time, as is the position of each value, including array elements, within the segment.

The compile-time nesting of blocks is referred to as the static structure of a program while the way in which calls of blocks are nested at run time is referred to as the dynamic structure of a program. The absolute addresses of values at run time will depend on the dynamic structure of the program. At run time space will be allocated on the stack for segments corresponding to the currently active procedures or functions.

Consider the following Pascal program

```
program demo (output):
var x,y:real;
        procedure first;
        var c,d:integer;
        begin
        .

        .

        end;
        procedure second;
        var p,q:char;
        begin
        .

        .

        end;
    begin
        first;
        second
    end.
```

Immediately after entering the program the run-time stack might appear as in (1) of Figure 9.2. On calling procedure *first* it will appear as in (2) while on calling procedure *second* it might appear as in (3). Neither of the procedures has any parameters or they might also, depending on the method of call, be allocated space on the stack.

In the figure x, y, etc. indicate the space occupied by the values of these variables at run time and we have assumed that a real value occupies twice as much space as an integer or character one. The section of the stack corresponding to a particular block is usually referred to as a stack *frame*. A *stack pointer* is assumed to point to the first free cell on the stack.

An array called *DISPLAY* can be used to provide pointers to the foot of the stack frames corresponding to blocks whose variables can be currently accessed. *DISPLAY* will be updated every time a procedure or function is entered or left. A

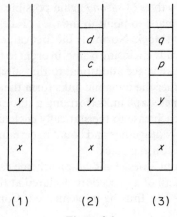

Figure 9.2

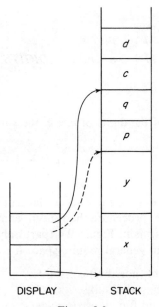

Figure 9.3

procedure or function which is declared at level 2 (for example) will always have its variables accessed via the second element of the *DISPLAY*. It is possible, however, at run time to have a procedure which has been entered (but not left) whose variables are not accessible at a particular instant. For example, if, in the previous example, *second* had contained a call of *first* a snapshot of the run-time stack during execution could look like figure 9.3 (ignore the dashed line for the moment).

On leaving *first* the *DISPLAY* would be reset as shown by the dashed line, making access to the variables of *second* again possible. That is, the top element of *DISPLAY* would be made to point to the foot of the frame corresponding to the *dynamically* enclosing block. Normally the first value in a frame is a pointer to the foot of the 'dynamically enclosing frame' in order to facilitate this action. This pointer, which will require space additional to that already shown, is known as the dynamic link. Together the dynamic links form the dynamic chain. In some storage allocation schemes static links (forming a static chain) are also stored in each frame pointing in each case to the statically enclosing frame. This obviates the need for a *DISPLAY* altogether and could in certain situations lead to more efficient access to values on the stack.

We have shown that our storage allocation scheme can deal with a procedure whose body contains a call of a procedure declared at the same level. Recursive procedures or functions can thus be implemented. Consider the function

```
function DIGITS (n:integer):integer;
var m:integer;
begin   if n < 10
        then DIGITS:= n
        else begin m:= n div 10;
                    DIGITS:= n - m*10 + DIGITS (m)
             end
end
```

whose value is the sum of the digits of n, e.g. the value of

$$DIGITS\ (315)$$

would be 9.

Space would be allocated for m and n at each level of entry of the function. The run-time stack after the procedure had been entered for the third time (recursively) would appear as in Figure 9.4 (part only shown).

Each stack frame will in general require space for

(a) values of variables and (possibly) constants,
(b) dynamic (and possibly static) links,
(c) values of procedure and function parameters,
(d) a result, if the frame corresponds to a function.

The storage allocation phase of a compiler will allocate stack addresses for variables, etc., of the form:

   block level number, offset

and, where appropriate, insert these addresses in the symbol table for use during code generation.

The addresses of array elements will have to be calculated at run time. The

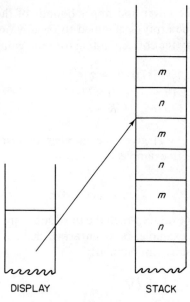

DISPLAY STACK

Figure 9.4

address of the first element of the array will be known at compile time and a displacement, unknown in general until run time, must be added to this base address to access any other element.

Consider the array

var *table* : **array** $[1..10, -5..5]$ **of** *integer*

We will assume that the elements are stored in lexicographic order of the indices or what is sometimes referred to as storage by rows, i.e. the elements of *table* would be stored in the following order:

table $[1, -5]$, *table* $[1, -4]$ .... *table* $[1, 5]$,
table $[2, -5]$, *table* $[2, -4]$ .... *table* $[2, 5]$,

.
.
.

table $[10, -5]$ .... *table* $[10, 5]$

The address of a particular element is calculated as a displacement from the base address (address of the first element) of the array

$$ADDR\ (table\ [I, J]) = ADDR\ (table\ [l_1, l_2])$$
$$+ (u_2 - l_2 + 1) \times (I - l_1) + (J - l_2)$$

where l_1 and u_1 are the lower and upper bounds of the first dimension, etc., and each element of the array is assumed to occupy one unit of space. For a three-dimensional array the corresponding formula would be

$$ADDR\,(AR\,[I,J,K]) = ADDR\,(AR\,[l_1, l_2, l_3])$$
$$+\,(u_2 - l_2 + 1) \times (u_3 - l_3 + 1) \times (I - l_1)$$
$$+\,(u_3 - l_3 + 1) \times (J - l_2) + K - l_3$$

The expression $(u_i - l_i + 1)$ gives the number of distinct values which the ith subscript can take. For example

$$u_3 - l_3 + 1$$

is the number of distinct values which the third subscript can take and hence the distance in the above example, between array elements which differ only by one unit in the second subscript. Similarly

$$(u_2 - l_2 + 1) \times (u_3 - l_3 + 1)$$

represents the number of distinct pairs of values which the second and third subscripts can take and also the distance between array elements which differ only by one unit in the first subscript. The distance between elements which only differ by one unit in the ith subscript is known as the *ith stride*. Thus in the above example the first stride is

$$(u_2 - l_2 + 1) \times (u_3 - l_3 + 1)$$

and will be denoted by s_1, the second stride is

$$u_3 - l_3 + 1$$

and will be denoted by s_2 and the third stride is 1 denoted by s_3. Figure 9.5 shows the strides for the array

var N: **array** $[1..5,\ 1..5,\ 1..5]$ **of** *integer*

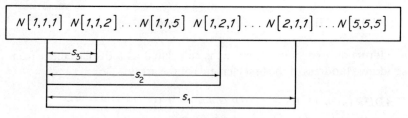

Figure 9.5

If each array element had occupied an amount of space r then the strides would have been obtained by multiplying each of the above quantities by r.

Clearly the calculation of addresses of array elements can be a time-consuming process at run time. This is a reason for advising programmers to avoid array accesses as far as possible, especially when many-dimensional arrays are involved. However, the various strides can be calculated once only (at compile time in Pascal) and stored along with the bounds. The lower and upper bounds will be required for checking that subscripts are within the array bounds, and the strides and the lower bounds will be required for accessing particular array elements.

Working storage may be required for evaluating expressions such as

$$(a + b) * (c + d)$$

so the values of $a + b$ and $c + d$ may be stored in the current frame. Working storage (unlike variable space) can be re-used within a particular stack frame. The compiler will be able to work out the total working storage required in each frame and allocate addresses for code generation. If, however, Pascal is being implemented via P-code, the P-code machine will provide the working storage.

As we have seen the amount of space allocated for a record variable is merely the sum of that required by its various fields. In the case of a variable of type variant record in Pascal the maximum space required by any of the variants is allocated.

Many block structured languages are more complex than Pascal as far as storage allocation is concerned. For example, in ALGOLs 60 and 68 and Ada variables may be declared in blocks which do not correspond to functions or procedures but are more equivalent to compound statements in Pascal. We refer to such blocks as static (rather than dynamic) blocks. The following might be the outline of an ALGOL 60 program:

begin integer a ;
.
.
.
    begin integer b ;
    .
    .
    end ;
.
.
end

At run time each active static block will correspond to a stack frame as for procedure or function blocks. The action on entering a static block will be to assign the value of the stack pointer (which always points to the first free element of the run-time stack) to the next element of the DISPLAY, and on leaving a block to reverse the process by assigning the top value on the DISPLAY to the stack pointer. There is no need with static blocks to follow the dynamic link.

An alternative method of implementing blocks in ALGOL 60, for example, is not to create a new stack frame for every block but only for procedure (dynamic) blocks. This avoids the run-time overheads (which have not all been described) associated with block entry and exit. The disadvantage of this approach is that space is required throughout the execution of each procedure for all the variables declared in it. Either method of implementing blocks is a compromise and perhaps this is a situation where the compiler writer can appeal to the original design aims of his compiler to determine whether saving space or time should be given greater priority.

An extreme case which illustrates how execution time can be saved with minimal cost in terms of space concerns the scope of the control variable in a loop in Ada or ALGOL 68. In either language the control variable is implicitly declared by its occurrence after the word **for** and its scope is the loop itself. An implementation might raise a new stack frame simply for this variable. However, it now seems to be generally accepted that this is not required.

Throughout computing there are examples of space/time trade-offs. In a compiler the user might be given the option of optimizing on the size or the execution time of the object code produced. Presumably he could indicate his preference by means of a pragma in Ada (or pragmat in ALGOL 68).

Another complication which Pascal avoids is the allocation of space for dynamic arrays—arrays whose size is not known at compile time. For example, in ALGOL 60 we can have

begin integer array $A[1:n]$

where the value of n is not known until run time.

Space which cannot be allocated at compile time is known as dynamic space. Code has to be generated (at compile time) to allocate such space at run time. Although the compiler (in general) does not know the actual size of the array it does know some facts about it:

(a) the number of bounds it has ($2 \times$ number of dimensions),
(b) the type of the elements of the array (and hence the amount of space each element will occupy).

In addition the number of strides are known (though not their values). Space can therefore be allocated for the bounds and the strides at compile time. This information is sometimes referred to as the array descriptor and is of static size. Space can therefore be allocated at compile time for the array descriptor and a pointer to the start of the array elements.

Each frame of the run-time stack will have (in general) a static part where space is allocated at compile time and a dynamic part, where space is allocated at run time. In many implementations the dynamic part of the stack frame is assumed to sit on top of the static part of the frame at run time (see Figure 9.6).

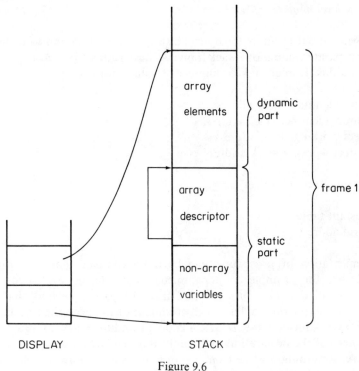

Figure 9.6

Array elements are accessed, as we have seen, from the base address of the array. In languages with dynamic arrays this base address will not be known at compile time. However, space will be allocated at compile time alongside the array descriptor for this address, which will be filled in when the space for the array elements is allocated at run time. As a general rule any value on the dynamic part of a frame must be accessible from the static part.

The price paid for dynamic arrays is the extra indirection involved in accessing their elements via the pointer stored with the descriptor. To this extent languages like FORTRAN and Pascal which do not have dynamic arrays could be said to produce more efficient code.

ALGOL 68 is one of the few languages in which declarations and statements may occur in (almost) any order in a block. This complicates the allocation of working storage since it cannot necessarily be allocated after all the variable storage has been allocated for a block. Static working storage, however, can still be allocated in a separate section of the frame from static variable storage as long as addresses are allocated from the start of each section of the frame and only later (during another pass perhaps) be made to refer to the start of the frame. This can be done once the size of variable section is known.

The simple run-time addresses required for Pascal of the form *block level number, offset*

can be generalized to allow for dynamic storage allocation and to distinguish between separate sections of a stack frame. A third field called *address type* can be used to do this. It might take a number of values, for example:

> direct identifier stack address
> indirect identifier stack address
> direct working stack address
> indirect working stack address

and for non-stack addresses

> constant table address
> literal address.

Implementation of procedures can be more complex than in Pascal. In ALGOL 68, for example, any parameters have to be evaluated in the environment of the procedure call and then the procedure body has to be executed in the (possibly different) environment of the procedure declaration. This involves adjusting the *DISPLAY* on procedure entry to simulate the environment of the declaration and readjusting the *DISPLAY* on leaving the procedure. Returning a value from a procedure is also more complex than in Pascal where only simple types may be results of functions.

Methods of passing parameters of procedures vary from language to language and will usually involve the run-time stack in some way. The more common methods are:

Call by value (value parameters in Pascal)

The actual parameter (which may be an expression) is evaluated and its value copied into space allocated for the formal parameter. This is one of the methods available in ALGOL 60 and Pascal where the formal parameter may also behave like a local variable and can be assigned to within the procedure body. However, such an assignment does not affect the value of the actual parameter and this method of call cannot be used to deliver a result from a procedure. Call by value is an efficient method of passing information into a procedure where large arrays do not make the copying process expensive.

Call by name

This is the alternative method available in ALGOL 60. It involves textually replacing the formal parameter in the procedure body by the actual parameter *before* executing the procedure body. Where the actual parameter is an expression, the expression will have to be evaluated each time the corresponding formal parameter appears in the procedure body. This tends to be expensive but can be useful in certain circumstances. Call by name is not usually provided in more modern languages than ALGOL 60 since the same effect can usually be obtained by using a procedure as a parameter of a procedure, and this approach should make the programmer more aware of the cost involved. From an implementation point of view, the effect of textual substitution can be obtained by providing a special run-time routine to evaluate the expression corresponding to the actual parameter, a call of the routine effectively replacing each occurrence of the formal parameter in the procedure body.

Call by result

As in call by value, space is allocated for the value of the formal parameter on entering the procedure. However, *no* initial value is assigned to the formal parameter. The procedure body may (and almost certainly does) assign to the formal parameter and, on leaving the procedure, the value currently held by the formal parameter is copied into the actual parameter. This method is useful for communicating a result from a procedure and is available in ALGOL W.

Call by value and result

The method, also available in ALGOL W, is a combination of call by value and call by result and involves copying on entering and leaving the procedure.

Call by reference (*variable parameters in Pascal*)

In this method the address of the formal parameter is assumed to be the address of the actual parameter, unless the actual parameter is an expression in which case the expression is evaluated and its value put in an address allocated to the formal parameter. The effect is, therefore, similar to call by value for expressions and, otherwise, similar to call by name and is a good compromise method available in many languages.

In Ada there are three methods of passing parameters:

in　　　–like call by value, but a formal parameter cannot be used as a local variable. Arrays and records may not actually be copied but any program whose effect depends on whether copying takes place or not is said to be erroneous (illegal).

in out　–like call by reference and call by value and result. Any program whose effect depends on which of these methods is used is erroneous.

out　　　–like call by result. Again arrays and records may not actually be copied and any program whose effect depends on whether copying takes place or not is erroneous.

In ALGOL 68 it is possible to simulate parameter passing mechanisms similar to the in and in out mechanisms in Ada.

Parallel processing

If parallel processing may occur in the language being implemented, i.e. a number of processes may be active simultaneously or merged in some arbitrary way, then a stack becomes unsuitable as a model for storage allocation, since space is no longer necessarily released in the order opposite to that in which it was allocated. (The last-in-first-out principle no longer applies.) However, a suitable generalization of a stack can be used, namely to allow the stack to have branches like a tree, each branch corresponding to one of the concurrent processes. For example, the implementation of the parallel clause

par (A, B, C)

where A, B, and C are processes to be executed in parallel would involve allocating space on the run-time 'stack' shown in Figure 9.7.

9.2 The heap

So far we have considered only local storage, which is well suited to a stack-based allocation system. The conventional block structure associated with most programming languages ensures that space is normally released in the opposite order to that in which it was originally allocated. There are situations, however, in which space has to be retained after the block or procedure in which it was allocated has been left. This occurs in two types of situation:

1. Space for own variables.
2. Space accessed by pointers.

1. Storage allocation for own variables

Own variables first appeared in ALGOL 60. Such variables, although local in scope to the block or procedure in which they are declared, retain their values

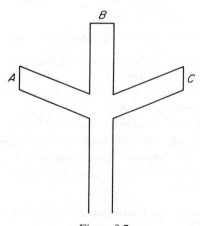

Figure 9.7

from one block or procedure entry until the next. Space for such variables cannot be allocated on a stack and ALGOL 60 implementations maintain a separate (static) area for the values of own variables. ALGOL 60 also allowed own arrays, even dynamic ones, though dynamic own arrays are excluded from most implementations. A PL/1 variable with the attributes static/internal behaves similarly to an own variable in ALGOL 60. In FORTRAN the fact that space can be allocated statically suggests that variables local to a subprogram would retain their values from one call of the subprogram to another. In many implementations of FORTRAN this is indeed the case. However, the FORTRAN standards insist that programmers should *not* assume that local variables have the 'own' property and should expect them to be 'undefined' on each entry to a subprogram. In FORTRAN 77 the *SAVE* statement has been introduced in order that the values of variables can be explicitly *SAVE*d between calls of subprograms.

Many modern languages such as Pascal, Ada, and ALGOL 68 have nothing equivalent to own variables as language designers now seem to feel the idea was ill-conceived and not very useful.

2. Space accessed by pointers

In many languages space for anonymous variables can be allocated dynamically at run time. Such space can be accessed by means of pointers and is not de-allocated on leaving the block or procedure in which it is allocated. In this way linked data structures can be built within a procedure without being destroyed when the procedure is left.

As an example, consider how a list of characters might be set up in Pascal. A suitable type definition would be

```
type list = ↑ listel;
     listel = record next : list;
                     case point : boolean
                     of true : (sub : list);
                        false : (letter : char)
              end
```

A typical list could be shown diagrammatically as in Figure 9.8, where A represents the character '*A*', and so on. Each element consists of a head, which is a character or a pointer to another list, and a tail, which is a pointer to another list or the null list represented by

The same list could be written as

$(A,(B,C,D),E)$

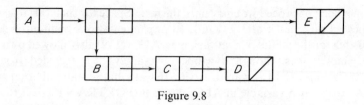

Figure 9.8

where the brackets are used to delimit lists and sublists.

The following procedure could be used to read * as data and set up the corresponding list:

```
procedure readl (var lst : list);
var ls, l : list;
    in : char;
begin if (input ↑ = '(') or (input ↑ = ',')
    then read (in);
    if input ↑ = ')'
    then begin read (in);
               l := nil
         end
    else begin new (l);
               if input ↑ = '('
               then begin l↑. point := true;
                          readl (ls);
                          l↑. sub := ls
                    end
               else begin l↑. point := false;
                          read (in);
                          l↑. letter := in
                    end;
               readl (ls);
               l↑. next := ls
         end;
    lst := l
end
```

The procedure is entered recursively for each field of a *listel* which is itself a list. Space for each list element is allocated globally (i.e. for the duration of the program) by means of a generator of the form

new (l)

There would be no point in using a procedure to set up a list if on leaving the procedure all the space for the elements of the list were to be de-allocated. Consider, however, the following fragment of program:

readl (*l*);
process (*l*);
l: = *nil*

(*l* is a 'pointer' to a list). Global space will be allocated by *readl* and, this space can be accessed via the identifier *l*. However, after the assignment the space may no longer be accessible. While the normal interpretation of the term global space is that such space is allocated for the duration of the program, it would seem a sensible economy to recover space which can no longer be accessed by the program. In Pascal the procedure *dispose* can be used in a similar way to *new* to de-allocate space referenced by a pointer. For example

   dispose (*l*)

would de-allocate (and make available for some other purpose) the space pointed to directly by *l*. The philosophy of Pascal seems to be that the programmer by using *dispose* should take responsibility for de-allocating any global space no longer required. An alternative approach is that the run-time system should be responsible for recovering any space that is no longer accessible from the program.

If such a strategy seems somewhat against the spirit of global space allocation in languages such as Pascal, it can hardly be criticized if it does not alter the meaning of any program, i.e. the space recovery process is invisible to the programmer. As long as there is no method of accessing a particular piece of storage, then there is no way the programmer can tell if it is subsequently re-allocated for some other purpose.

Global storage can also become inaccessible due to the block structure of a program, e.g. in Pascal if *c* is a local variable

   new (*c*)

generates global space for an appropriate value and associates the name of the space with the identifier *c*. This association will only exist during the current block and, unless something is done to prevent it, the space for the value of *c* will be inaccessible once the current block is left. One method of avoiding this would be to assign *c* to a variable of the same type, say *d*, declared in an outer block

   d: = *c*

After leaving the block in which *c* was declared the space could still be accessed via *d*.

Since its allocation and de-allocation do not conform to the last-in-first-out principle global space cannot be stack oriented. Normally a special area of store is set aside for global storage, sometimes referred to as the heap. A compiler may allocate space both from a stack and a heap, in which case it

184

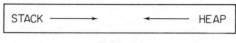

Figure 9.9

is sensible to make the two areas grow towards one another from opposite ends of the available store (Figure 9.9). This means that space can be allocated from either region until the two meet, and makes better use of the available space than by dividing it in some arbitrary way between the two regions and so constraining both the stack and the heap to lie within their allocated areas.

The size of the stack will rise and fall in an orderly way as blocks are entered and left. However, apart from holes which may appear due to storage which has been reclaimed, the heap can only increase in size. There are two distinct philosophies for controlling the heap. One uses what are usually called *reference counters* and the other goes by the picturesque name of *garbage collection*. We discuss each in turn.

Reference counters

When reference counters are used, space is reclaimed immediately it can no longer be accessed by the program. The heap is considered as a sequence of consecutive cells each of which contains a field (the reference counter), invisible to the programmer, which contains a count of the number of other cells or values on the stack which point to it. Reference counters are updated during the execution of the program and, when a particular counter becomes zero, the corresponding space can be recovered. The algorithm for updating reference counters is not trivial, as can be seen from the following example.

Suppose, for simplicity, that each cell has three fields, the first field being the reference counter. This will allow us to demonstrate how the reference counter technique can be used to control list storage. The idea can be generalized to deal with more complex structures. If X is an identifier which points to a list its value could be as shown in Figure 9.10.

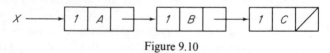

Figure 9.10

$Y := X\uparrow.next$

The effect of the assignment would be as shown in Figure 9.11.

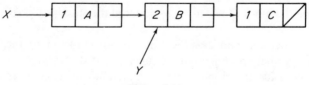

Figure 9.11

$$X := Z$$

The next assignment gives Figure 9.12.

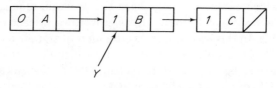

Figure 9.12

Not only has the reference counter of the cell pointed to by X been decremented by 1 but so has the cell pointed to by that cell. The algorithm for decrementing the reference counters after an assignment is: decrement the reference counter of the cell previously pointed to by the identifier on the right-hand side of the assignment by one. If the reference counter is now zero, follow all pointers from this cell decrementing reference counters until (for each path) on decrementing a reference counter a nonzero value is obtained or the end of the path is reached. Assuming two or more paths cannot be followed in parallel a stack is required to store pointers that have still to be followed.

The reference counters do not actually need to be stored in the cells themselves but could be stored elsewhere as long as there was a one-to-one correspondence between the address of each cell and its reference counter.

The reference counter method of controlling heap storage has two chief disadvantages:

1. The space allocated to certain structures will *not* be recovered using the algorithm described above, even once none of the space can be accessed. Consider, for example, the circular list shown in Figure 9.13 Its reference counters are all nonzero, even though no external pointers point to it so that the space will not be recovered.
2. Updating the reference counters is a significant overhead which has to be borne by all programs, even those with modest space requirements. This is contrary to the Bauer principle which asserts that 'simple programs' should not have to pay for expensive language facilities which they do not use.

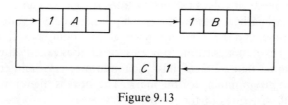

Figure 9.13

Garbage collection

A completely different approach to reclaiming heap storage is the method known as *garbage collection*. In this method storage is not reclaimed as soon as it becomes inaccessible but only when the program requires heap storage (or possibly stack storage if the two areas grow towards each other) and there is none available. In this way programs with modest storage requirements may never have to reclaim storage, whereas those which do ever run out of heap storage will have to be suspended, to reclaim inaccessible storage, before they can continue. Of course, it may happen that a program is suspended to reclaim storage and there is none to reclaim. In these circumstances the program will be forced to terminate because of lack of space.

The process which reclaims the storage when the program is suspended is known as the garbage collector. It has two phases:

1. *Marking phase* in which all the addresses (or cells) which can be accessed (directly or indirectly) by identifiers in the program are marked either by altering a bit in the cell itself or in a storage map elsewhere.
2. *Compaction phase* in which all the marked cells are moved to one end of the heap (the end furthest away from the stack if the two areas grow towards one another).

The compaction phase is not trivial since it may involve changing pointers. In this section, however, we confine our attention to the marking phase and discuss some of the possible algorithms for performing it. A critical factor of course is the amount of working space available for the garbage collector. Since it is shortage of space which has caused the garbage collector to be called in the first place, it would not be sensible for the garbage collector itself to require a large (let alone an unpredictable) amount of space. It is also of course desirable that the garbage collector should be efficient from a time point of view, so that programs will spend as small a proportion of their time as possible performing (unproductive) garbage collection.

Whatever the process involved it is rarely possible to optimize both space and time and often some compromise between the two aims has to be accepted. Garbage collection is no exception to this principle, and it is the choice of such compromises which makes the study of algorithms to perform the marking phase of garbage collection of such interest.

It should be apparent that finding the cells that can be accessed from a program, in general, involves traversing trees since cells can contain pointers to other cells. All paths represented by such pointers must be followed, presumably one at a time, and the 'obvious' place to store pointers still to be followed is on a stack. The first algorithm to be described does exactly this. For simplicity, it is assumed that each cell has a maximum of two pointers and a field, invisible to the programmer, for the mark. The store is, therefore, represented by an array of structures of the form

```
    record left, right :integer;
           mark :boolean
    end
```

the *left* and *right* fields being integer pointers to other cells, with zero being used to represent the null pointer. For the purposes of the algorithm we are only concerned with the pointer fields and the *mark*, and other (possible) fields are not shown.

The algorithm is represented by procedure *MARK 1* in which *STACK* is the stack used by the garbage collector to store pointers and *T* is the stack pointer which points to the top element. *A* is an array of structures, indexed from 1, representing the heap. After having set all the marks to *false*, the cells referred to directly by identifiers in the program or other values on the run-time stack are marked and their addresses put on *STACK*. The algorithm proceeds by taking the top element from *STACK*, marking any unmarked cells to which the cell at that address points, and putting their addresses on *STACK*. The algorithm terminates when *STACK* is empty.

```
    procedure MARK1;
    var k :integer;
    begin while T < > 0 do
          begin k := STACK[T];
                T := T - 1;
                if (A[k].left < > 0) and
                   not A[A[k].left].mark
                then begin A[A[k].left].mark := true;
                           T := T + 1;
                           STACK[T] := A[k].left
                     end;
                if (A[k].right < > 0) and
                   not A[A[k].right].mark
                then begin A[A[k].right].mark := true;
                           T := T + l;
                           STACK[T] := A[k].right
                     end
          end
    end
```

Before the procedure was called, the heap might be as shown in Table 9.1, with only *A*[3] marked because it is referred to directly by an identifier in the program. The effect of the algorithm would be to mark *A*[5], *A*[1], and *A*[2] in that order.

The algorithm is very fast (it would be difficult to write a faster or simpler one) but is extremely unsatisfactory due to the fact that it could require a large amount of space for the stack, and because the amount of storage required

Table 9.1

A	left	right	mark
5	2	1	false
4	1	2	false
3	5	1	true
2	3	0	false
1	5	0	false

is unpredictable. It thus follows that the garbage collector itself might fail, due to there being insufficient space in which it could operate.

At the other extreme, if one was looking for an algorithm which required a small fixed amount of space and was prepared to accept inefficiency from a time point of view, it is difficult to improve on the algorithm given by procedure *MARK2*, which requires working space for only three integers, k, $k1$, and $k2$. It operates by scanning the whole heap for pointers from marked cells to unmarked cells, marking these unmarked cells and remembering the smallest address of a cell so marked. It then repeats this process, but starting at the smallest address marked last time, until during a complete scan no new cells are marked. It may be necessary to scan the heap many times, and the algorithm will be particularly inefficient if there are a lot of backward pointers in the heap.

As in the previous algorithm, it is assumed that cells referred to directly by identifiers in the program or other values on the run-time stack are already marked. The cells in the heap are represented by the array A with bounds $1..M$:

```
procedure MARK2;
var k, k1, k2: integer;
begin k1 = 1;
    repeat k2:= k1;
          k1:= M + 1;
          for k:= k2 to M do
          if A[k].mark
          then begin if (A[k].left < > 0) and
                         not A[A[k].left].mark
                      then begin A[A[k].left].mark:= true;
                                 k1:= min (A[k].left, k1)
                           end;
                      if (A[k].right < > 0) and
                         not A [A[k].right].mark
                      then begin A[A[k].right].mark:= true;
                                 k1:= min (A[k].right, k1)
                           end
               end
    until k1 = M + 1
end
```

min is a function whose value is the minimum of its two parameters.

If the algorithm is applied to the example discussed in connection with the previous algorithm, *MARK1*, the cells are marked in the same order (5, 1, 2).

Both the algorithms described so far are rather unsatisfactory (though for different reasons). It is, however, possible to combine the two algorithms in such a way as to attempt to obtain the benefits (but not the drawbacks) of them both. The resultant algorithm is described in detail in Knuth [1968 b], p. 415, and is outlined as follows.

Instead of using an arbitrary sized stack as in *MARK1* a fixed size stack is used. The larger it can be, the less time the algorithm is likely to take. For a sufficiently large stack the algorithm proceeds exactly like *MARK1*. Since, however, the stack cannot be extended, the algorithm has to be able to deal with stack overflow, should it occur. What happens is as follows. If the stack becomes full, one value is removed to leave space for another to be added, and an integer variable is used to remember the *lowest* address removed from the stack in this way (similar to what happens in *MARK2*). The stack is used in a circular manner with two pointers, one to the top and one to the bottom, thus avoiding having to move all the elements of the stack when one element is removed (see Figure 9.14). The algorithm proceeds for the most part like *MARK1* and when the stack is empty it terminates, unless some elements have been removed from the stack due to overflow. If this has happened, the lowest address which has 'dropped out' of the stack is known and the heap must be scanned from this address in a process similar to that performed by procedure *MARK2*. Any further addresses which are required to be marked are put on the stack and, if at the end of the scan the stack is empty, the algorithm terminates. Otherwise, it behaves like *MARK1* again and so alternating between the two modes until it (necessarily) terminates.

To summarize, the algorithm (call it *MARK3*) behaves like *MARK1* when the stack is large enough, and otherwise like a mixture of *MARK1* and *MARK2*. It is a good compromise between the algorithms given by *MARK1* and *MARK2* which (for a large enough stack) will work efficiently most of the time and, otherwise, will at least not fail.

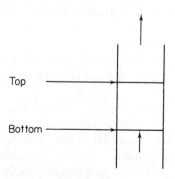

Figure 9.14

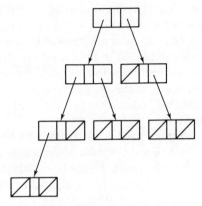

Figure 9.15

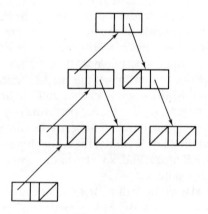

Figure 9.16

Another approach is due to Schorr and Waite and is also fully described in Knuth [1968b]. It differs from the previous algorithms in that during the marking phase of garbage collection the structures which have to be traversed are temporarily altered, to provide return routes so that all paths may be followed. This avoids using an arbitrary sized stack. For example, suppose the binary tree shown in Figure 9.15 had to be traversed then, when the marking phase had reached the bottom left-hand cell, the tree would look as shown in Figure 9.16.

Of course, once marking is complete, the structure will have been restored to its original form. The algorithm requires one extra field associated with each cell to keep track of which paths have been followed, and several pointer variables to be used when pointers are being manipulated. As with *MARK1*, the time taken by the algorithm is proportional to the number of cells to be marked but the constant of proportionality is larger.

Exercises

9.1 In a conventional block-structured language how might a programmer take advantage of the fact that storage is re-usable?

9.2 What cost is involved in accessing values via a *DISPLAY* mechanism? How might this be avoided for static values in a language which did not have procedures?

9.3 Rather than each stack frame containing space for working storage a separate stack could be used. Discuss the advantages and disadvantages of this alternative.

9.4 In a certain language values are either defined globally or are local to a particular procedure, a procedure body cannot contain a procedure call, and procedure calls cannot be nested. How would these restrictions simplify the organization of the run-time stack?

9.5 One of the design aims of Pascal was that it should lead to efficient object code on 'present day' computers. What aspect of the language mentioned in this chapter is consistent with the above design aim?

9.6 In many cases the effect of calling a parameter of a procedure by reference and by value and result is the same. Explain how a program might be written to illustrate the difference between the two methods.

9.7 Suggest a reason why own variables do not tend to appear in 'modern languages'.

9.8 Discuss whether reference counter or garbage collection management of the heap would be preferable in a real-time environment.

9.9 Suggest how algorithm *MARK2*, to perform the marking phase of garbage collection, might be speeded up with the aid of a preliminary scan over the heap.

9.10 Schorr and Waite's algorithm could be used simply to traverse a binary tree in preorder (see Section 10.1). What advantages would it offer over more conventional methods?

Chapter 10

Code Generation

We have already noted that the compilation process can be thought of as consisting of two stages called analysis and synthesis. Chapters 10 and 11 (and to a large extent Chapter 9) deal with the synthesis stage. Having analysed the program and tabulated the information required for code generation, the compiler should then proceed to build the appropriate machine code program.

Code is generated by traversing the parse tree built by the analyser. This is normally done in parallel with building the tree but could also be done in a later pass. If two separate passes are involved then a representation of the complete parse tree will require to be passed between the two passes.

In the next two chapters we assume that the actual production of machine code involves two distinct passes:

1. production of a machine-independent intermediate code (or target language),
2. production of machine code (or assembly code) for a specific machine.

In many compilers only one pass would be involved.

10.1 Intermediate code

Intermediate codes can be designed at different levels. On the one hand, the intermediate code may be produced by simply breaking down the complex structures of the source language into more manageable units, while on the other hand, the intermediate code (often referred to as a target language in this case) may be a sort of generalized machine code readily translatable into code for an actual machine. Generation of intermediate code may come before or after storage allocation. In the former case the code will use the program identifiers (or their post-lexical analysis representations) and compiler-assigned identifiers as operands, while in the latter case run-time addresses may be used.

Quadruples (see Chapter 6) are one type of intermediate code. For example, the expression

$$(-a+b) \times (c+d)$$

might be represented in quadruples as

$$- a = 1$$
$$1 + b = 2$$
$$c + d = 3$$
$$2 \times 3 = 4$$

in which the integers correspond to compiler-assigned identifiers. Quadruples can be thought of as a high-level intermediate code. Such a code is often referred to as a three-address code, two addresses being for the operands (except where monadic operators are involved) and one for the result. An alternative to quadruples is triples (two-address code), each triple consisting of two operand addresses and an operator. Where an operand is itself a triple the position of the triple is used thus avoiding the need for a result address in each triple.

The expression

$$a + b + c \times d$$

could be represented in quadruples as

$$a + b = 1$$
$$c \times d = 2$$
$$1 + 2 = 3$$

and in triples as

$$a + b$$
$$c \times d$$
$$1 + 2$$

Triples are more compact than quadruples but their use causes complications if the compiler has an optimizing phase which moves intermediate code statements around. The best solution to this problem is to use indirect triples, i.e. an operand which refers to a previously evaluated triple points to an entry in a table of pointers to triples, rather than to the triple itself.

Both triples and quadruples can be extended to deal with language constructs other than expressions. For example, the assignment

$$a := b$$

could be expressed as

$$a := b = 1$$

as a quadruple, and

$$a := b$$

as a triple.

Other popular types of intermediate code are *prefix* notation and *postfix* notation. In prefix notation each operator appears before its operands and in postfix notation each operator appears after its operands. This is in contrast to the more usual (*infix*) notation where (dyadic) operators appear between their operands, e.g. the infix expression

$$a + b$$

would appear as

$$+ ab$$

in prefix notation and

$$ab +$$

in postfix notation.

Prefix notation is also known as *Polish notation* after the country of its originator, Lukasiewicz, and postfix notation is also known as *reverse Polish notation*. More complex expressions can be expressed in these notations in a similar way, e.g.

$$(a + b) \times (c + d)$$

becomes in prefix form

$$\times + ab + cd$$

and in postfix form

$$ab + cd + \times$$

each operator coming immediately before, in the case of prefix notation, and after, in the case of postfix notation, its operands.

Brackets are no longer required in prefix and postfix notations since there is never any doubt as to which operands belong to a particular operator. There is no such thing as operator precedence in these notations, though clearly this must be taken into account in transforming infix expressions into prefix or postfix expressions.

The rearrangement involved in transforming

$$(a + b) \times (c + d)$$

into

$$ab + cd + \times$$

can be performed using a stack and the algorithm involved is well known (see, for example, Rohl [1975]). Alternatively the transformation can be based on a grammar for infix expressions and involves three actions:

1. print an identifier when it is encountered on reading the infix expression from left to right,
2. stack an operator when it is encountered,
3. print out the operator which is on top of the stack on encountering the end of an expression (or sub-expression).

The method is very similar to the one described in Chapter 6 to produce quadruples and the reader is invited to code the actions.

   Prefix and postfix expressions can also be obtained from the binary tree representation of an expression. For example, the expression

$$(a + b) \times c + d$$

could be represented by the binary tree in Figure 10.1. To obtain the prefix representation of the expression the tree is traversed in preorder, defined by Knuth [1973] as

   visit the root
   traverse the left subtree in preorder
   traverse the right subtree in preorder
which gives

$$+ \times + abcd$$

To obtain the postfix representation the tree is traversed in postorder, defined by Knuth as

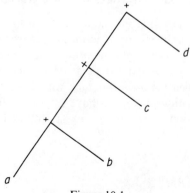

Figure 10.1

traverse the left subtree in postorder
traverse the right subtree in postorder
visit the root
which gives

$$ab + c \times d +$$

Postfix notation is well suited for generating code for a stack machine. On reading a postfix expression from left to right the following actions should be performed.

1. On encountering a variable, generate code to put its value on top of the stack.
2. On encountering a dyadic operator, generate code to apply the operator to the top two values on the stack replacing them with the result.
3. On encountering a monadic operator generate code to apply it to the value on top of the stack replacing that value by the result of applying the operator.

The above actions assume that we can distinguish between monadic and dyadic operators. The code to put the value of a variable on top of the stack will involve calculation of the actual run-time address of the variable from its compile-time address of the form

   (*block level number, offset*)

which is stored in the symbol table at compile time.

Pascal P-code contains instructions to load an address or a value on to the top of the stack, to apply an operator to the top two elements on the stack, to store the value on top of the stack in an address, and so on. The stack referred to is the 'hardware' stack of the P-machine which will be referred to as *the stack* throughout the rest of this chapter to avoid confusion with any other compile-time or run-time stacks.

10.2 Data Structures for code generation

Most Pascal compilers generate P-code direct from Pascal expressions (rather than via postfix notation) by means of actions in the recursive descent compiler. An alternative (and cleaner) way of generating code is by inserting actions in the grammar used to form the context-free parser. This method requires the use of a compile-time stack called the *operator stack* which is used to delay the action of an operator until both its operands have been identified.

Assume an expression is generated by a grammar with the following productions

$$EXP \rightarrow TERM\,|$$
$$EXP + TERM\,|$$
$$EXP - TERM$$

$$TERM \to FACT|$$
$$TERM * FACT|$$
$$TERM/FACT$$

$$FACT \to variable|$$
$$constant|$$
$$(EXP)$$

Actions are required after reading a constant or a variable, after an operator, and after the second operand of each operator.

The grammar becomes (with action names added)

$$EXP \quad \to TERM|$$
$$EXP + \langle E2 \rangle TERM \langle E3 \rangle|$$
$$EXP - \langle E2 \rangle TERM \langle E3 \rangle$$

$$TERM \to FACT|$$
$$TERM * \langle E2 \rangle FACT \langle E3 \rangle|$$
$$TERM/\langle E2 \rangle FACT \langle E3 \rangle$$

$$FACT \to variable \langle E1 \rangle|$$
$$constant \langle E1 \rangle|$$
$$(EXP)$$

If the variables and constants can be of various types (e.g. real, integer) and the operator symbols can have more than one meaning then a *type stack* will be required at compile time to assist in the identification of operators. The type stack will be used effectively to transfer type information up the syntax tree and is similar to Branquart's [1976] *bottom stack* which was used more generally to transfer compile-time information up the syntax tree in his ALGOL 68 implementation. The use of the type stack assumes that the types of the values at the terminal nodes of the syntax tree are readily determined (usually from the symbol table). We have already seen in Chapter 7 that this information may not be so readily available for Ada programs.

The actions E1 to E3 might be

E1. Put the type of the variable or constant on the type stack. Generate code to put the value of the variable or constant on top of the stack.
E2. Put the operator symbol on the operator stack.
E3. Remove the operator symbol from the top of the operator stack. Identify the operator uniquely from the types on top of the type stack. Replace these two types on the type stack by the type obtained by applying the operator. Generate code to apply the operator to the top two values on the stack, replacing them by the result.

The effect of the type stack is to perform what is sometimes called the compile time evaluation of the expression. Although the value of the expression cannot in general be obtained at compile time (since the values of variables are unknown) the type of the expression can be evaluated. The actions performed on the type stack at compile time almost exactly mirror the actions performed on the stack at run time.

A slight complication arises with action E3 if a type change is required. In Pascal, for example, the operator symbol '+' is used for addition of two integer values and for the addition of two real values. However, it is not defined for the addition of a real value and an integer value. Nonetheless

$$4 + 6.3$$

is a legal expression in Pascal and implies the addition of two real values by virtue of the rule that an integer may appear anywhere in a Pascal program where a real would be expected and is converted to type real where appropriate. Thus if in trying to identify an operator, the top two values in the type stack are integer and real (in either order) the integer value should be changed to real and code should be generated to perform the corresponding change to the run-time value at run time.

We can illustrate the actions by means of an example. Suppose the variables a, b, x, and y have been declared as

    var a, b : *integer* ;
      x, y : *real*

and we wish to generate code for the expression

    $a*b + x*y$

then we can rewrite the expression showing where each of the actions would be called during its compilation

$$a\langle E1\rangle * \langle E2\rangle b\langle E1\rangle \langle E3\rangle + \langle E2\rangle x\langle E1\rangle * \langle E2\rangle y\langle E1\rangle \langle E3\rangle \langle E3\rangle$$

The detailed actions would be

E1. Put the type of a (integer) on the type stack. Generate code to put the value of a on the stack.
E2. Put $*$ on the operator stack.
E1. Put the type of b (integer) on the type stack. Generate code to put the value of b on the stack.
E3. Remove $*$ from the operator stack. Identify $*$ as multiplication of two integer values from the top two elements of the type stack. Replace these two values by the type integer. Generate code to perform integer multiplication on the top two values on the stack and replace them by the result.
E2. Put $+$ on the operator stack.

E1. Put the type of *x* (real) on the type stack. Generate code to put the value of *x* on the stack.

E2. Put * on the operator stack.

E1. Put the type of *y* (real) on the type stack. Generate code to put the value of *y* on the stack.

E3. Remove * from the operator stack. Identify * as multiplication of two real values from the top two elements of the type stack. Replace these two values by the single value real. Generate code to perform real multiplication on the top two values on the stack and replace them by the result.

E3. Remove + from the operator stack. Try to identify + from the top two elements of the type stack. Change integer to real and generate code to change the type of the corresponding value on the stack from integer to real. Identify + as addition of two reals. Replace the top two values on the type stack by the single value real. Generate code to perform real addition on the top two values on the stack and replace them by the result.

In many implementations real values occupy more (possibly twice as much) space than integer values. The above actions do not assume that integers and reals occupy the same amount of space but would be more complicated to implement if this were not the case.

The type stack could also be used to pass other compile-time information, such as scope and diagnostic information, up the syntax tree. In addition a *top stack* might be used to pass information down the syntax tree. This might allow the code generator to use some context information to produce more optimal code.

To summarize, a number of data structures are required by the code generator. Typically these might be

Operator stack
Type stack
Top stack.

In addition the code generator would require access to

Symbol table
Type table

set up by other phases.

10.3 Generating code for some typical constructs

In this section we discuss the generation of code for some constructs typical of high-level programming languages.

1. Defining occurrence of a variable

Consider the variable declaration

var *number* : *integer*

There are compile-time actions associated with this declaration but no code is generated for execution at run time. The compile-time actions are

1. Insert the type of the variable in a new symbol table entry.
2. Allocate an address of the form

   (*block level number, offset*)

   for the value of the variable. The offset is given by the value of a compile-time integer variable used to point to the first free space on the variable part of the current stack frame. After the address has been allocated the value of this variable is incremented by the number of stack elements required for the value of the program variable.
3. Insert the 'address' of the variable in the symbol table.

2. Applied occurrence of a variable

An applied occurrence of a variable may occur

in an expression, or
on the left-hand side of an assignment statement.

The actions are

1. The type of the variable should be found from the symbol table and put on the type stack.
2. (a) In the case of a variable occurring in an expression code should be generated to put its value on top of the stack at run time.
   (b) In the case of a variable appearing on the left-hand side of an assignment statement code should be generated to put the address of the variable on top of the stack at run time.

3. Assignment statement

An assignment statement is of the form

   destination : = *source*

and two sets of actions should be inserted in the syntax

   destination $\langle A1 \rangle$: = *source* $\langle A2 \rangle$

where the actions *A1* are described in 2(b) above and *A2* consist of

1. The types of the top two elements on the type stack are compared for compatibility. Apart from the possibility of assigning an integer value to a real variable the types should be the same.
2. An integer to real conversion is performed on the top element of the stack if necessary and code is generated to perform the corresponding type conversion at run time.

3. If appropriate, code is generated to perform range checking.
4. The type of the destination is noted and the top two elements are removed from the type stack.
5. Code is generated to move the value of the top element on the stack to the address given by the second top element of the stack and to remove the top two elements from the stack.

(In the case of a value which is not 'simple', i.e. an array or record, the address of the value on the right-hand side of the assignment statement will be stacked rather than the value itself.)

4. Loops

The implementation of loops and other control structures involves generating code for tests and jumps and placing compiler-defined labels. These labels must be distinct from any user-defined labels and we will assume they are of the form

Li

where i is an integer. When a new label is allocated the value of i will be determined by incrementing a label number set initially to zero. Because of the nesting of program statements a label stack will be required to relate applied and defining occurrences of compiler-defined labels. In many cases the operator stack defined earlier and the label stack can be merged into one.

There are four types of loop in Pascal:

1. **while** b **do** S
2. **repeat** S **until** b
3. **for** $i := k$ **to** l **do** S
4. **for** $i := k$ **downto** l **do** S

where S is a single statement in (1), (3), (4) and a sequence of statements in (2).

1. Three sets of actions are required to implement the **while** loop

while $\langle W1 \rangle b \langle W2 \rangle$ **do** $S \langle W3 \rangle$

where

$W1$ increment label number;
      generate code to set label;
      stack label number.

$W2$ increment label number;
      generate code to jump to label if b false;
      stack label number.

$W3$ unstack label number, j say;
      unstack label number, k say;

generate code to jump unconditionally to Lk;
generate code to set label, Lj.

Notice that the applied and defining occurrences of the two labels involved do not 'nest' in the usual way so care has to be taken in unstacking the labels in $W3$.

2. Two sets of actions are required

> **repeat** $< R1 > S$ **until** $b < R2 >$

where

$R1$ increment label number;
generate code to set label;
stack label number.

$R2$ unstack label number, j say;
generate code to jump to Lj if b false.

3. There are four sets of actions

> **for** $i \langle T1 \rangle := k \langle T2 \rangle$ **to** $l \langle T3 \rangle$ **do** $S \langle T4 \rangle$

$T1$ perform compile-time actions and generate code to perform run-time actions as for the left-hand side of an assignment.

$T2$ perform compile-time actions and generate code to perform run-time actions to assign k to i, leaving the value of i on the stack.

$T3$ increment label number;
generate code to set label;
increment label number;
generate code to jump to label if $i > l$;
stack two label numbers used—second one first.

$T4$ generate code to increment i by 1;
unstack label number, j say;
generate code to jump to Lj;
unstack label number, m say;
generate code to set Lm;
generate code to remove the values of i and l from the stack.

4. The actions are similar to (3)

> **for** $i \langle D1 \rangle := k \langle D2 \rangle$ **downto** $l \langle D3 \rangle$ **do** $S \langle D4 \rangle$

where

$D1$ is $T1$;
$D2$ is $T2$;

D3 is *T3* except $'i < l'$; replaces $'i > l'$;
D4 is *T4* except *i* is decremented by 1.

5. Conditional statements

There are two types of **if** statements in Pascal;

1. **if** *b* **then** *S*
2. **if** *b* **then** *S1* **else** *S2*

1. Two sets of actions are required

> **if** *b* $\langle I1 \rangle$ **then** *S* $\langle I2 \rangle$

where

I1 increment label number;
  generate code to jump to label if *b* is false;
  stack label number.

I2 unstack label number (*k* say);
  generate code to set *Lk*.

2. Three sets of actions are required

> **if** $b \langle E1 \rangle$ **then** $S1 \langle E2 \rangle$ **else** $S2 \langle E3 \rangle$

where

E1 increment label number;
  generate code to jump to label if *b* is false;
  stack label number.

E2 increment label number;
  generate code to jump to label;
  unstack label number, *k* say;
  generate code to set *Lk*;
  stack label number used in unconditional jump above.

E3 unstack label number, *k* say;
  generate code to set *Lk*.

Notice the order of the subactions in *E2*. The new label number is used to generate a jump instruction but is not stacked until the label number stacked by *E1* has been unstacked.

6. Procedure (and function) declarations

There are a number of compile-time actions associated with procedure (and function) declarations. These include:

1. Enter the type of the procedure including the types of its parameters, and result if a function, in the symbol table.
2. Put an entry in a procedure table associating the procedure with a compiler-defined label. Generate code to set this label.
3. Initialize the variable stack pointer prior to allocating local storage.
4. Compile the procedure body.
5. Generate code to jump back to the instruction after the procedure was called. The label of this instruction might have been stored on the run-time stack.

7. Procedure (and function) calls

Actions include

1. Generate code to assign an appropriate value to the dynamic link of a new stack frame.
2. Generate code to amend *DISPLAY* so that its top element points to the new stack frame. If the procedure called is at the same level as the calling procedure the top value of *DISPLAY* is overwritten; otherwise a new element is added to the top of *DISPLAY*.
3. Check the types of the parameters with the entry in the symbol table and generate code to evaluate the parameters storing each parameter or its address on the new stack frame.
4. Allocate a label for returning and store it in the stack frame.
5. Generate code to jump to the label given in the procedure table.
6. Generate code to set the label allocated in 4.
7. Generate code to reinstate the *DISPLAY*.

10.4 P-code

P-code has been widely used as an intermediate language for implementing Pascal and is based on a stack machine.

P-code instructions have the following format:

FPQ

where *F* is a function code and *P* or *Q* (or both) may be absent depending on the function code. If present, *P* can specify a type or a block level number while *Q* can denote an immediate operand or the offset of an address.

Instructions then may have zero, one, or two parameters. The simplest instructions have zero parameters and take their operands from the stack, for example:

ADI – Add the values of the top two elements of the stack and replace them by their (integer) sum (decreasing the height of the stack by one).
ADR – As *ADI* but for real values.

AND – Applies the boolean *AND* operator to the top two elements of the stack leaving the result in their place.

DIF – Set difference.

NGI – Change the sign of the integer value on the top of the stack.

FLT – Convert the value of the top of the stack from integer to real.

FLO – Convert the value on second top position on the stack from integer to real.

INN – Test set membership leaving *true* or *false* on top of the stack.

Other instructions are used to load a value on to the top of the stack or to store the value on the top of the stack in an address, for example:

LDCI		4	Load integer constant *4*
LODI	0	5	Load integer value in address (*0, 5*)
LDA	0	6	Load address (*0, 6*)
STRI	1	4	Store integer in address (*1, 4*).

P-code also includes jump instructions, for example.

UJP	*L7*	Unconditional jump to label *7*
FJP	*L8*	Jump to label *8* if the value on top of the stack is false (top element is removed from the stack).

Labels may also be set in code, for example:

L4

Single instructions are used to call standard procedures or function, for example:

CSP	*ATAN*	Applies *arctan* function to the value on the top of the stack.
CSP	*WLN*	Performs a *writeln* on the file specified on the top of the stack.

We can now give examples showing the P-code produced for some of the language features discussed in the last section. We assume that expressions leave their value on top of the stack.

1. **if** *b* **then** *S1* **else** *S2*

```
        code for b
        FJP     L1
        code for S1
        UJP     L2
    L1
        code for S2
    L2
```

2. **while** *b* **do** *S*

> *L1*
>> code for *b*
>> *FJP*   *L2*
>> code for *S*
>> *UJP*   *L1*
> *L2*

3. *An applied occurrence of a variable*

In the case of a simple variable either the address of the variable or the value is loaded on the stack, for example

> *LDA* *1* *7*

will load the address represented at compile time as $(1, 7)$ on to the stack whereas

> *LODI* *1* *7*

will load the integer value in address $(1, 7)$ on to the stack.

If the variable is an array element the address of the element will be computed at run time by adding the displacement to the base address of the array.

4. $r := s$

There are two cases to consider:

(a) *A 'simple' assignment*

The value of the expression on the right-hand side of the assignment will already be on top of the stack and the address of the variable to which it is to be assigned will be in the second top position. An indirect store, for example

> *STOI*

will 'perform' the assignment and adjust the stack appropriately.

(b) *An assignment involving an array or a record*

The addresses of the source and the destination will be on top of the stack and a *MOV* instruction of the form

> *MOV m*

will be generated to copy *m* values starting at the source address to addresses starting at the destination address and adjust the stack appropriately.

10.5 Compile time versus run time

We have seen from examples that the code generator performs some actions at compile time such as manipulating the type stack, etc., as well as generating code for other actions to be performed at run time. Exactly what can be done at compile time and what has to be left until run time depends to some extent on the language being compiled. For example, in POP-2, in which the types of identifiers are dynamic (i.e. may change dynamically at run time), all type checking has to be done at run time and code has to be generated to perform it. In Pascal, however, types are static (i.e. known at compile time) and type checking can be performed during compilation.

However, while the language is the main determining factor in deciding what is done at compile time and what is done at run time the compiler writer does have some discretion in the matter. In Pascal some range checking can be done at compile time—for example when a subscript is a constant. This will involve extra work at compile time but will avoid generating code to do the checking at run time.

It may be desirable to perform additional work at compile time to improve the efficiency of the code produced. This is usually known as optimization and can involve removing code from loops where this does not affect the meaning of the program, not evaluating identical expressions more than once, etc. A description of some well-known optimizing techniques can be found in Gries [1971]. In addition, in ALGOL 68, for example, copying of complex data structures at run time can sometimes be avoided by careful analysis at compile time (Simpson [1976]).

Compilers which perform extensive optimizations will almost certainly take longer to compile programs than those which do not. It depends on the design aims of the compiler what optimizations are included. According to Horning [1974b], some local optimizations (e.g. peep-hole optimizations—see Section 11.3) are so inexpensive at compile time as to be almost always worth including, whereas most global optimization techniques are only appropriate where the need for run-time efficiency predominates over all else.

Exercises

10.1 Express the following expression:
   (a) in triples,
   (b) in quadruples.

$$(a + b + c) \times (d + e + f)$$

10.2 Why are indirect triples used?

10.3 What problems are involved in converting expressions involving monadic operators into reverse Polish notation?

10.4 In some early compilers expressions were first converted into fully parenthesized form before code was generated, e.g.

$$a + b \times c$$

was replaced by

$$(a + (b \times c))$$

What are the advantages and disadvantages of this approach?

10.5 In some languages all operators have the same priority but are evaluated strictly from left to right, i.e.

$$a + b \times c$$

is evaluated as

$$(a + b) \times c$$

Comment on this design feature from an implementation point of view.

10.6 In APL all operators have the same priority but expressions are evaluated from right to left, i.e.

$$a + b \times c$$

is evaluated as

$$a + (b \times c)$$

How does this affect implementation?

10.7 In some early compilers the type of each identifier was inserted in the source text adjacent to the identifier itself. What advantages and disadvantages do you see in this approach?

10.8 Outline how a *case* or *switch* statement in a language with which you are familiar might be implemented.

10.9 Outline how a *goto* statement might be implemented.

10.10 Comment on the use of P-code from an efficiency point of view.

Chapter 11

Generation of Machine Code

In this chapter we discuss the final task of the compiler, namely to produce machine code for a specific machine. For the purpose of description it is simpler to assume that assembly code is produced (as indeed may be the case). The Intermediate Code (or Target Code) from which the assembly code is produced is assumed to be machine (though not necessarily language) independent. In general each intermediate code instruction will give rise to a sequence of assembly code instructions including, possibly, calls of assembly code sub-routines. The translation of each intermediate code instruction is assumed to be independent of the translation of the preceding or succeeding intermediate code instructions except, possibly, through its effect on compile-time global variables.

We will sometimes refer to the task of producing code from the intermediate code as translation, to distinguish it from the process of generating intermediate code which we have referred to as code generation.

11.1 General outline

We will begin by showing how some of the P-code instructions introduced in Chapter 10 can be used to generate assembly code for a non-stack-based machine. For simplicity (and efficiency) we will assume that each distinct P-code instruction type is represented by an integer rather than a string. The general form of the translator could be

```
    declarations (including functions and procedures)
    begin while true do
            begin read (n);
                case n of
                1:...
                2:...

                  .

                  .

                  .

                end
            end;
999:    end
```

so that each P-code instruction would lead to an element of the case statement which would read in parameters, as appropriate, and generate the relevant code. The translation would be terminated by reading a special value for n which would lead to a jump out of the loop.

At this stage it is convenient to think of P-code instructions as having up to three parameters. In addition to the P and Q parameters mentioned earlier some P-code instructions would have a C parameter (which would come first) denoting a type. For example, instead of

ADI

being used for integer addition and

ADR

being used for real addition the code 28 might be used for both types of addition and the C parameter would be an integer value used to indicate whether integer or real addition was involved. In the case of relational instructions in P-code the single parameter is really a C parameter giving the types of the operands. In most cases the P and Q parameters denote an address P being the level number and Q the offset.

11.2 Examples of Machine Code Generation

Nearly all P-code instructions involve the stack in some way. A few examples will illustrate how assembly code for a hypothetical machine might be produced.

1. $AD(I)$
   We assume that the machine has registers numbered 1 to 3, each of which can hold an integer value. Register 1 will hold the value of the stack pointer which will always point to the top element on the 'stack'. A Pascal segment to generate code for AD, when C is integer, is

   ```
   writeln ('LDX    2   0(1)');
   writeln ('SUBN   1   1');
   writeln ('ADX    2   0(1)');
   writeln ('STO    2   0(1)')
   ```

   where

LDX	means load in register
$SUBN$	means subtract literal from the value in the register
ADX	means add into the register
STO	means store from the register.

The first parameter in the assembly code is always a register and the second an address. *0(1)* is an example of indexed addressing, i.e. address *0* plus the integer value in register *1*. Throughout the examples registers *2* and *3* are used as working registers.

The code generated would be

```
LDX    2   0(1)
SUBN   1   1
ADX    2   0(1)
STO    2   0(1)
```

2. *GEQ* (*greater than or equal to*)
   The code generated might be

```
        LDX    2   0(1)
        SUBN   1   1
        SUBX   2   0(1)
        BNG    2   T23
        LDN    2   1
        BRN        T24
T23     NULL
        LDN    2   0
T24     NULL
        STO    2   0(1)
```

where

```
SUBX   means subtract from register
BNG    means branch if negative
BRN    means branch unconditionally
LDN    means load literal
NULL   is the null statement (which does nothing).
```

T labels are labels generated by the translator.

3. *LOD*
   Here we have to load the contents of an address on to the top of the stack. There are three parameters:

   C – the type of the value in the address
   P – the level number of the address
   Q – the offset of the address.

First the parameters will have to be read by the action for *LOD*:

readln (C, P, Q)

Assuming *C* is integer and that integer values occupy one stack element the code generated for *P* = 2 and *Q* = 4 would be

```
LDX   2   DISPLAY + 2
ADN   2   4
LDX   2   0(2)
ADN   1   1
STO   2   0(1)
```

where

> *DISPLAY*   is the address of the zeroth element of the display
> *ADN*   means add literal to the value in the register.

The effect of

```
LDX   2   0(2)
```

is to put in register 2 the value to which it points.

4. *STR*

This is the complement of *LOD*. Again there will be *C*, *P*, and *Q* parameters. If *C* is integer, *P* = 2, and *Q* = 4 the code would be

```
LDX    2   0(1)
SUBN   1   1
LDX    3   DISPLAY + 2
ADN    3   4
STO    2   0(3)
```

5. *UJP*

UJP has one parameter, a label. This has to be read by the action for *UJP*. If the label was *L7* the code generated might be

```
BRN        L7
```

6. *FJP*

FJP will also have a label parameter to jump to if the value on the top of the stack is false. The code generated might be

```
LDX    2   0(1)
SUBN   1   1
BZE    2   L7
```

7. *MOV*

We have to generate code to perform a block move. The start address of the block to be copied is on top of the stack and the start address of the area to be copied to occupies the second top position on the stack. *MOV* has a single parameter giving the number of values to be moved. Code may be generated to copy the two addresses into registers and then a block move instruction can be generated in assembly code if this is available. Alternatively a loop will have to be set up in assembly code containing a simple move instruction.

The above examples show how some typical P-code instructions could be translated into assembly code for a fairly conventional machine. Implementation on a stack-based architecture or a machine with a more sophisticated assembly code would, if anything, be more straightforward. The production of native machine code and the linkage process are beyond the scope of this book.

Application to ALGOL 68

The implementation of Branquart *et al*'s [1976] *Intermediate Code Instructions* for ALGOL 68 follows similar lines to that described for P-code. The main differences are:

(a) The ICIs may contain a number of addresses as parameters since the intermediate language is not stack based.
(b) The computation of stack addresses is more complex since ALGOL 68 arrays may be dynamic.
(c) Moving values may involve mode (type) scanning at translation time.

11.3 Object code optimization

As discussed at the end of Chapter 10, compilers vary in the extent to which they attempt to optimize the object code produced to make the program run in as short a time as possible. Certain local optimizations, referred to as peep-hole optimizations, are nearly always worth doing and are described briefly in this section. Consider the following three sequences of object code:

1.   *LDX   1   2*
        LDX   2   1

Having loaded the contents of register *2* into register *1* there is clearly no point in then loading the contents of register *1* into register *2* in the very next instruction. The second instruction (as long as it is unlabelled) is clearly redundant and can be removed.

2.   *BRN   L23*
        unlabelled instructions

where *BRN* denotes unconditional branch. There is no way in which a series of unlabelled instructions following an unconditional branch can be executed and they can therefore be removed.

3.
```
      BRN    L2
  L2  BRN    L1
```

In this case the same effect may be obtained by replacing the first instruction by

```
      BRN    L1
```

Such optimizations can be performed as the code is generated, are easily implemented, and are inexpensive as far as compile time is concerned.

Exercises

11.1 Suggest advantages and disadvantages of compiling into assembly code rather than direct into machine code.

11.2 Show how assembly code could be generated for the *LDA* instruction of P-code.

11.3 Show how assembly code could be generated for the *NGI* instruction of P-code.

11.4 What advantage might there be in interpreting P-code rather than translating it?

11.5 When a Pascal program is compiled labels may appear in the resultant assembly code. What are three stages at which these labels may have been introduced?

11.6 In what circumstances would you expect the translator to generate calls of assembly code routines?

11.7 Why do you think 'mode scanning' is involved in moving ALGOL 68 values?

11.8 Suggest how the translator could have made use of more registers than appeared in the examples shown.

11.9 Indicate what would be involved in implementing the peep-hole optimizations described in Section 11.3.

11.10 The third optimization in Section 11.3 assumes that the two unconditional branches occur in consecutive instructions. Outline how the more general case might be dealt with.

Chapter 12

Error Recovery and Diagnostics

In this chapter we consider, perhaps rather belatedly, how a compiler should deal with programs containing programming errors. The compiler writer should plan from the outset how his compiler will deal with programs containing errors, since many (if not the majority of) programs submitted to the compiler will contain at least one error. Having avoided, up till now, the complications involved in detecting and recovering from errors we now wish to emphasize the importance of dealing with errors properly in a practical and useful compiler.

We shall, however, only consider errors which can be detected by the compiler, or which will lead to an error situation at run time. We will not be concerned with formal techniques of program verification, and programming errors which do not affect the validity of the program (perhaps writing a ' − ' instead of a ' + ') will not be detected at compile time or run time.

If a program submitted to the compiler is, strictly speaking, not in the source language an unfriendly compiler might simply inform the user of this fact without giving any indication as to where an error may have been made. Most users, quite rightly, would find this approach unsatisfactory and would expect the compiler

(a) to indicate exactly where the (first) programming error lay,
(b) to continue compiling (or at least analysing) the program after the first error was found in order to detect any further errors.

We shall see later (Sections 12.3 and 12.4) that it is not always possible to achieve (a) since the effect of a programming error is not necessarily to invalidate the program stream *at the point where the error was made*. As far as (b) is concerned this too is not a simple problem. If the program stream has become invalid it is not clear what action the compiler should take in order to continue analysing the program. Possibilities include the insertion, deletion, or replacement of symbols in the program stream; various techniques of error recovery (as it is called) are discussed in Section 12.4.

12.1 Types of error

There are a number of ways in which errors may arise in a program:

1. The programmer does not fully understand the language in which he is writing and uses an invalid program construction.

2. The programmer is not sufficiently careful in his use of a construction in the language and forgets to declare an identifier or to match an opening bracket with a closing bracket, or something similar.
3. The programmer makes a slip in writing or typing the program and misspells a language word or some other symbol in the program.

The three types of error would be detected in different ways by the compiler. Type-1 errors would probably be caught by the parser and a message pinpointing the symbol at which the program stream became illegal would be generated. Type-2 errors fall into two distinct categories. Those which relate to non-context-free features of the language, such as not declaring an identifier, would be detected by one of the routines for accessing the symbol table called by the parser during syntax analysis. Other errors such as missing brackets might be detected by the parser itself or, in the case of bracket matching, might be detected by a special bracket-matching phase or pass (see Section 7.1). Type-3 errors would normally be detected during lexical analysis though, in the case of a mis-spelt identifier, one of the symbol table actions would again be involved.

There is one other type of error which can occur. This corresponds to a program trying to divide by zero or read past the end of a file, or something similar. Such errors are known as run-time errors and cannot, in general, be detected at compile time.

In the rest of this chapter we discuss how the various types of error—lexical, bracket matching, syntax, non-context-free and run-time—are detected and reported in terms meaningful to the programmer. We also discuss error recovery techniques for each type of error.

12.2 Lexical errors

The job of the lexical analyser is to assemble sequences of characters into symbols of the source language. In so doing it has to work solely on local information. It has very little memory and no lookahead. It follows that the only errors which will be detected during lexical analysis will be caused by the lexical analyser being unable to assemble some sequence of characters into symbols. Lexical errors can occur in a number of ways:

1. One of the characters may be illegal, i.e. it cannot occur within any symbol, in which case the lexical analyser may either ignore the character or replace it by some other character.
2. In attempting to assemble a language word, for example a bold word in ALGOL 60, it may be discovered that the sequence of letters does not correspond to any such word. In this case it may be possible to use a word-matching algorithm to identify a language word with a slightly different spelling. If this does not work then, assuming language words are delimited by quotes, as in

'BEGIN'

it may be worth checking if the sequence of letters starts with a language word. If so the insertion of one or two quotes may make the sequence legal. For example, in ALGOL 60 the lexical analyser would have difficulty with

(a) *'BEGIN INTEGER'*

or

(b) *'REALAB'*

However the insertion of two quotes in (a) and a single quote in (b) giving

(a) *'BEGIN' 'INTEGER'*

and

(b) *'REAL' AB*

solves the problem.

In Pascal a mis-spelt language word would simply be treated as some other identifier by the lexical analyser.

3. In assembling numbers the lexical analyser would have difficulty in dealing with a sequence such as

42.34.41

One possibility would be to assume, whatever mistake had been made, that a single number had been intended and warn the programmer that a particular default value had been taken for the number.

4. The effect of a missing character in a program is often that the lexical analyser is unable to separate one symbol from another. In some cases two symbols will appear as one to the lexical analyser. For example, if the $+$ was omitted in

$A + B$

the lexical analyser would simply pass on the identifier AB without signalling any error at that stage. The omission of $+$ in

$1 + A$

however would cause an error though it might be difficult for the lexical analyser to know whether to categorize

1A

as an illegal identifier, an illegal number, or what. In some cases it may be best to break up illegal sequences into shorter legal ones. Thus *1A* would be number *1* followed by the identifier *A*. An error would then be discovered by the syntax analyser.

5. A common problem for the lexical analyser occurs when a string quote is missing, as in, for example,

$$message := 'hello$$

which may mean that for the rest of the program opening quotes and closing quotes are confused with the effect that what is inside quotes is thought to be outside quotes and vice versa, and almost certainly an avalanche of error messages is produced. A similar problem occurs with comments in ALGOL 60 and with formats in ALGOL 68. These difficulties are much less severe when language designers use *different* symbols for opening and closing comments, etc., as for example with comments in Pascal.

There are some compilers which do not proceed beyond the first pass in which an error is discovered. However, if the aim is to discover the maximum number of errors, it is desirable to proceed further if at all possible. The lexical analyser must therefore hand over to the following pass (or phase) a sequence of valid symbols (not necessarily a valid sequence of symbols). For lexically correct programs this presents no problem. For lexically incorrect programs, sequences of characters may have to be ignored or inserted, spelling may have to be altered, or strings may have to be split into valid symbols. Ignoring sequences of characters would seem to be the simplest expedient but is almost certain to lead to syntax errors later. The methods used by the lexical analyser to recover from illegal input tend to be rather *ad hoc* and in practice will almost certainly depend on the language being compiled and the way in which programmers are expected to use it. One possibility which might be worth exploring is that, where the lexical analyser is unable to recognize any valid symbol or symbols from a string of characters, it should return a special 'don't know' symbol which the syntax analyser, which normally has a list of valid continuation symbols, can interpret as it thinks appropriate.

12.3 Bracket errors

Bracket errors are relatively easy to detect and some compilers have a bracket matching (and bracket identification) phase prior to full syntax analysis. If only one type of brackets is involved (e.g. '(' and ')') then checking can be done by means of an integer counter set initially to zero, incremented by one for each opening bracket, and decremented by one for each closing bracket. The bracket sequence is legal unless

1. the counter is ever negative, or
2. the counter is nonzero on completion.

The following bracket structures would be legal:

```
((      )  (      )  (        ))
(       )  ((((   ))))
```

whereas the following would not:

```
(    )  (   ))  ((
```

since the counter goes negative and

```
(    )  ((        )
```

since the counter is nonzero on completion.

In most programming languages a number of types of bracket can occur, e.g.

It is not sufficient to apply the above algorithm treating all opening brackets like '(' and all closing brackets like ')' since the sequence

```
[(          ])
```

should not be considered legal. It is necessary to match each closing bracket with a corresponding opening bracket. The algorithm uses a stack and proceeds by reading the bracket structure from left to right, placing each opening bracket on top of the stack. When a closing bracket is encountered the corresponding opening bracket is removed from the stack. The bracket sequence is legal unless:

1. On reading a closing bracket it does not correspond to the opening bracket on top of the stack, or the stack is empty.
2. The stack is non-empty on completion.

A bracket error should result in a clear message from the compiler such as

BRACKET MISMATCH

If the error resulted from a missing closing bracket then the type of the missing bracket could be deduced from the bracket on the top of the stack. A possible recovery when a bracket error occurs is to assume a missing closing bracket, remove the opening bracket from the top of the stack, and output a message suggesting the source of the error such as (assuming [had been on the top of the stack)

MISSING]?

The diagnostic, however, will not normally appear at the point where the omission occurred since the error will go un-noted until another closing bracket (of a different type) is encountered. Assuming syntax analysis is to follow, it is desirable that the bracket structure is repaired. Consider the (illegal) assignment

$$B := A[(p + q * r]$$

A closing ')' has been omitted. This fact will not be discovered until the ']' is encountered. However, it is not clear whether the ')' should have occurred after r or after q or, less likely, after p. There is no way of knowing what the programmer intended and the easiest 'correction' is to insert the closing bracket immediately before the ']'. This should at least allow syntax analysis to continue without generating another error message due to the missing bracket. More sophisticated repair algorithms exist and are discussed in Backhouse [1979]. Where compilers do not require a separate bracket identification pass the parser will recognize bracket errors 'automatically'.

12.4 Syntax errors

The term syntax error is used to denote an error which would be detected by a context-free parser. LL(1) and LR(1) parsers have the desirable feature that they are both able to detect a syntactically incorrect program at the first inadmissible symbol, i.e. a message can be generated on reading a symbol which cannot follow the symbol sequence read so far, in any legal program. Some parsers (e.g. operator procedence parsers) do not have this property. In this section we shall assume that syntax errors are detected at the earliest possible opportunity.

In describing error recovery methods we will tend to think in terms of LL(1) parsers, though most of the ideas could readily be extended to LR(1) parsers. Unfortunately, syntax errors are not necessarily discovered close to the point where the programmer made a mistake. The error point (where the error is detected) may relate to an error of omission or commission earlier in the program. The bracket errors discussed in the last section illustrate this point. In ALGOL 68 the problem can occur in more complex situations.

Consider the loop

while $x > y$ **do** *something* **od**

The syntax of the language does not allow a semi-colon before the **do**. However, we show that the parser would be unable to indicate an error *at that point* if a semi-colon was present.

In ALGOL 68 an infinite loop (one which would cause the program to loop an infinite number of times unless halted by a construction such as a **goto**) may be written as follows:

> **do**
> *something else*
> **od**

In a program we could have two loops nested as follows:

> **while** $x := 1$; **do** *something else* **od** ; $x > y$
>   **do** *something* **od**

where the **while** part of the outer loop is a serial clause (more correctly an enquiry clause) containing a unit which is an infinite loop. The point of interest is that the program fragment contains the sequence

> ; **do**

So if we had written

> **while** $x > y$; **do** *something* **od**

no syntax error should be reported at the semi-colon or at the **do** since the syntax analyser could not at that stage exclude the possibility that the **do** was the start of an infinite loop rather than being associated with the preceding **while**. Of course another **do** would be expected to go with the **while** and this before any bracket structures which had been opened prior to the **while** had been closed. The error (assuming there was one) would be detected on reading some closing bracket and a message would be output—possibly many lines of program after the illegal semi-colon had occurred.

Having indicated a syntax error the parser will in most cases try to continue parsing. To do so it may have to delete symbols, insert symbols, or change symbols (delete and insert symbols). There are a number of error recovery strategies and some of the simpler ones are described here. Virtually all of them work well in some cases and badly in others. The aim of a good strategy is to detect as many syntax errors as possible and to generate as few error messages as possible due to each syntax error. The best methods are usually language dependent, i.e. they depend on a knowledge of the source language *and* how it is used.

1. *Panic mode*
   One of the most common methods of recovering from syntax errors is what is referred to as *panic mode*. When an inadmissible symbol is encountered all subsequent source text is ignored until a suitable delimiter such as a semi-colon or **end** is encountered. This delimiter will terminate some cons-

truction in the language and items are removed from the parse stack until the return address from which this construction was called is encountered. This item is also removed from the stack and parsing continues from that address in the parsing table with the next input symbol. The method is fairly easy to implement but suffers from the disadvantage that possibly-long sequences of code corresponding to the symbols which were ignored are not analysed.

2. *Deletion of symbols*

This method is also easy to implement and does not involve altering the parse stack at all. When an inadmissible symbol is read this symbol and subsequent symbols from the source string are deleted until an admissible symbol is found. Although this could involve the deletion of a long sequence of symbols it works quite well in certain cases, for example in Pascal

if $x > y$ **then** $a := b$; **else**

where the semi-colon is illegal, the recovery would be ideal. Deletion of brackets, however, will usually upset the bracket structure of the program and lead to further syntax errors.

3. *Insertion of symbols*

An LL(1) parser should always have available a set of valid continuation symbols at any stage of the parse. It may be sensible in some cases to repair the program by inserting one of these symbols in front of the inadmissible symbol causing the error. For example, the sequence

end begin

is *never* legal in Pascal. However the insertion of a semi-colon between **end** and **begin** may allow the parser to continue.

4. *Error rules*

One way of recovering from certain types of syntax error is to extend the syntax of the language to include programs containing these errors. This does not mean that the errors would go undetected, since actions could be inserted in the grammar to report them, but the parser would not consider the input illegal and would not require to recover in any way. Examples of errors which might be dealt with in this way include semi-colons before **end**, as in ALGOL 68, or the omission of a semi-colon before the sequence

L : **end**

in Pascal. The extra rules inserted in the grammar are usually referred to as 'error rules'. Inevitably they make the grammar (and the parser) larger and it is not practical to include them other than for the most common programming errors. Care must also be taken that the inclusion of these extra rules does not make the grammar ambiguous.

Warnings

As well as indicating syntax errors the parser can also issue warnings when it encounters a legal, but unlikely, sequence of symbols, e.g.

do;

which implies that the body of the Pascal loop following the **do** consists of an empty statement only. This is unlikely (though legal) and can be detected by the parser. A warning message can therefore be emitted each time this sequence is encountered.

Warnings are useful in certain cases but do involve overheads since compile-time actions are required to check for warning situations.

Syntax error messages

Each time a syntax error is detected by the parser an appropriate message should be printed. For example, a message such as

SYNTAX ERROR IN LINE 22

might be given or the location of the error might be described more fully as being at

LINE 22 SYMBOL 4

In either case the user is likely to complain that the message is not very explicit in that there is no indication of what the programmer did wrong. As we have seen, the actual programming error may have occurred much earlier in the program and the parser can only indicate an error when it comes across an inadmissible symbol. If a programmer submits a program supposed to be written in PL/1, but with a syntax error, there is no way in which the compiler can decide which PL/1 program the programmer should have written. What a compiler might be able to do however is to deduce the minimum distance repair, i.e. the repair involving the minimum number of insertions of symbols to and deletions of symbols from the program text, which would result in a syntactically correct program. Notice that we use the term minimum distance repair and not (as some authors) minimum distance correction, as there is no guarantee that the repair actually produces the program originally intended. The purpose of the repair is to allow the parser to continue analysing the program. For a discussion of algorithms to perform minimum distance repairs see Backhouse [1979].

While minimum distance repairs seem attractive from a theoretical point of view they are inefficient to perform, since it is often necessary to backtrack over parts of programs already analysed and to undo compiler actions already performed. Most compilers do not attempt this type of repair and the only type of recovery which they perform is the insertion, deletion, or alteration of symbols *at the point where an error is detected*. This being the case, there is not much more information the compiler can give the user other than a clear identification of where an error was detected. One further piece of information which may be available to the compiler is the context in which the error was discovered; for example it may have been within an assignment or an array bound or a procedure call. This information may not always be a great help to the user but it does indicate what type of construction the parser was trying to recognize when the error was discovered and this may be helpful in finding the actual programming error. It may also be possible to indicate to the user what symbols would have been admissible when the inadmissible symbol was encountered and this too may assist the user to correct the program. Where the parser is able (in certain limited cases) to make an intelligent guess as to what was the actual programming error, it may correct the program (for the benefit of subsequent passes) as long as it is made clear to the user what action has been taken.

The problem of correcting a program (rather than repairing it in the sense described above) requires a knowledge of what the programmer really intended. A classical Computer Science examination question takes the form 'Correct the following program. . . .' However, what is the student expected to do? Is he to deduce the minimum distance correction (which may not be unique) required to produce a syntactically correct program, or is he to alter the text to produce the program he imagines the programmer (or examiner) intended to write? The problem does not seem to be well defined.

12.5 Non-context-free errors

We have already seen that certain language features occurring in typical programming languages cannot be described by means of a context-free grammar. The parser therefore is generally based on a context-free grammar which generates a superset of the language being compiled. As far as the parsing table is concerned, therefore, programs with undeclared identifiers, etc., will be syntactically correct. However, any such non-context-free errors will be detected by actions embedded in the context-free grammar, and called by the parser, which interrogate the symbol table, etc. Assuming the identifier table created during lexical analysis is still available, clear messages can usually be output corresponding to this type of error, for example

IDENTIFIER xyz NOT DECLARED
TYPES NOT COMPATIBLE IN ASSIGNMENT

Since the parser itself has not detected an error no recovery is necessary. However, unless some action is taken one error may give rise to an avalanche of messages. For example, if an identifier is mis-spelt in a declaration, e.g.

var *wedensday* : *integer*

every applied occurrence of

wednesday

could result in the error message

IDENTIFIER wednesday NOT DECLARED

To avoid this the identifier *wednesday* should be inserted in the symbol table the first time an undeclared identifier of that name is discovered. A type will also have to be put in the table corresponding to the undeclared identifier. There may not be much information on which to deduce the intended type of the identifier and many compilers assume a default type of *integer* or *real*. A better strategy is to have a special type, say *sptype* to be associated with such identifiers. As far as the compiler is concerned *sptype* will have the following properties:

1. It can be assigned to a variable of any type.
2. If a value of type *sptype* occurs as an operand, the operator is identified by means of the other operand if there is one, any ambiguity being resolved in an arbitrary manner.
3. As far as the analyser is concerned a value of type *sptype* may be selected from or subscripted, etc., though of course it may not be possible to produce appropriate code.

Another error which can arise is that an identifier may be declared twice in the same block. Each time an identifier is declared a check should be made to see if the same identifier name has been declared within the current block. If so, a message such as

IDENTIFIER blank ALREADY DECLARED IN BLOCK

should be generated. To avoid ambiguities only one entry for each identifier should appear in the symbol table at each block level. What action should the compiler take when it encounters a second or subsequent declaration of an identifier within a block? For a one-pass compiler it is best to retain the existing entry since it may already have been used by the analyser, and replacing it by information obtained from a later declaration might make the compiler appear to behave inconsistently. A more optimal solution might be to do a detailed compile-time analysis of part of the program to see how the identifier is used in the block, and to deduce which of the alternative declarations is more appropriate.

Type errors

The rules regarding where values of various types may appear in a program are, in most cases, not context free. If an identifier has been declared in such a way that integers can be assigned to it, it is illegal in many languages to try and assign a character to it. For strongly-typed languages (e.g. Pascal, Ada) such an error can be detected at compile time with the aid of the symbol table.

In Pascal programs an integer value can always appear where a real value might be expected. For example, if x is declared as

var x : *real*

then the assignment

$x := 7$

would be legal and the implementation would be expected to convert the integer value 7 to the corresponding real value before assigning it to the variable x. Similarly a function or a procedure with a real formal parameter may have a corresponding actual parameter which is of type integer. However apart from the conversion of integer to real values no other automatic type changes (or coercions) can take place in Pascal.

In Ada there are no coercions possible in any situation. PL/1, on the other hand, allows extensive coercions, the philosophy of the language being that any 'reasonable' coercion may be applied to the value of an expressions to produce a value of an appropriate type. ALGOL 68, compared with PL/1, allows limited coercions defined by rather complicated rules. The conversion of a value to an appropriate type may involve a sequence of steps each producing an intermediate type and the detection of such coercion sequences is a major aspect of implementing ALGOL 68. Further details of implementing coercions in ALGOL 68 are given in Patel [1981].

When it is not possible to convert a value to a suitable type the compiler would be expected to output a message such as

TYPES NOT COMPATIBLE IN ASSIGNMENT

Other errors which correspond to non-context-free aspects of typical languages are:

1. Incorrect number of array subscripts.
2. Incorrect number of parameters for a procedure or function call.
3. Operator cannot be identified from its operands.

The compiler is usually able to give clear messages when these types of error occur.

12.6 Run-time errors

Fault conditions can occur in programs at run time which cannot possibly be anticipated at compile time. Explicit divisions by zero, e.g.

$m/0$

could of course be detected at compile time. But the expression

   m/n

could also involve division by 0 (if n happened to be zero when the expression was evaluated) and this could not (in general) be detected at compile time. Other possible run-time faults include:

1. An array subscript out of range.
2. Integer overflow (caused, for example, by trying to add together the two largest integers which the implementation allows).
3. Trying to read beyond the end of a file.

In languages with dynamic types a much wider class of errors will not be detectable until run time. These include type errors connected with assignments and the identification of operators.

Language designers usually try as far as possible to eliminate errors that cannot be detected until run time (see Uzgalis, Eggert and Book [1977]). One solution is to try and define away the problem. For example, the result of dividing anything by zero could be defined to be zero, an out of range subscript could be defined to be equivalent to some value within the subscript range, some standard action could be taken when an attempt is made to read beyond the end of a file, and so on. In COBOL the programmer is able to specify the action to be taken on reaching the end of a file and, in a similar way, the programmer might be able to specify the action to be taken on the occurrence of other run-time errors.

The danger of defining away the problem is that programming or data errors may go undetected. Presumably programmers do not normally expect division by zero to occur when their programs are run, and would wish to be told if this were to happen. However, they might not wish their program to stop being executed just because this had occurred. A compromise is to print out run-time error messages as they occur, but allow the program to take some default action so that it can continue running, thus allowing further run-time errors to be detected. This approach is analogous to providing error recovery in the parsing phase of compilation.

In Ada run-time errors are dealt with by means of exceptions which are 'raised' when errors occur at run time. For example the predefined exception

   CONSTRAINT__ ERROR

will be raised in situations such as an array subscript going out of range while the predefined exception

   NUMERIC__ ERROR

will be raised in situations such as an attempt to divide by zero.

When an exception is raised the program will either terminate with a suitable message or control will be transferred to an exception handler written by the programmer. The handler will be associated with a block enclosing the piece of code which caused the error and provides a means of terminating the block concerned without necessarily terminating the program.

In the case of a run-time error it is not always easy to tell the programmer, in terms he can understand, exactly what has gone wrong. The program by this time is in machine code, whereas the programmer is only likely to understand references to the source code version. For this reason the run-time system may have access to the identifier and other tables, and may keep track of the line numbers in the source program. The tables required for diagnostic purposes may not be in memory when the program is running but may be loaded on the occurrence of a run-time error. In addition to printing an error message it may be possible to print out a profile of the program when the error occurred, including the values of all variables, etc. This is particularly helpful in identifying errors caused by uninitialized variables.

12.7 Limit errors

We have assumed up till now that a compiler should be able to compile *any* program written in the appropriate source language. However, this cannot be so, if only because of the finite size of the machine on which it is running. A good compiler should have as few arbitrary limits as possible and limits, where they exist, should be such as to accommodate the majority of reasonable sized programs. Possible limits which may be reached include:

1. size of programs which can be compiled,
2. number of entries in the symbol table or identifier table,
3. size of the parse stack or other compile-time stack.

If the various tables share space it may be the total space available which may be the limitation, rather than the space for a particular table.

For each limit which exists there is a possibility of a program causing the compiler to exceed it. What is important is that, when this happens, the compiler should behave in a well-defined way by giving a clear message to the user as to which particular limit has been reached.

Exercises

12.1 Would you expect the implementation of a good error recovery method to slow down the compilation time of a program with no errors?

12.2 Some languages use 'reserved' identifiers as language words. What advantage does this offer as far as error detection is concerned?

12.3 Discuss language features which might encourage or discourage programmers to make errors.

12.4 Discuss language features which might or might not lead to helpful error messages.

12.5 Explain how the existence of the dummy statement (consisting of no symbols) in ALGOL 60 and Pascal can allow the misuse of semi-colons in these languages to go undetected.

12.6 What advantage do the commentary delimiters in Pascal ('{', '}') offer over those in ALGOL 68 (**co, co**) as far as error recovery is concerned?

12.7 Would you expect an error recovery strategy to be independent of the source language?

12.8 Possible sources of run-time errors could be detected at compile time. Do you think this would be a useful facility?

12.9 In some compilers it is possible to switch off subscript checking at run time. Why do you think this facility is offered and how useful to you think it would be?

12.10 Suggest how it might be possible to write a compiler with only one limit as far as space was concerned, i.e. programs would only fail to compile due to lack of space if *all* the space available to the compiler was exhausted.

Chapter 13

Writing Reliable Compilers

An early draft of this chapter was entitled 'Writing Correct Compilers'. However, on reflection, the title was much too ambitious. The idea of being able to say with any certainty that a compiler was correct in the sense that any input to it would produce the appropriate output (either object code or error messages) would appear to be beyond the state of the art at present. Most compilers are imperfect to the extent that at least a few programs will not be compiled correctly, will not be accepted by the compiler, or will cause the compiler to fail or go into a loop. In Chapter 1 we discussed possible design aims for a compiler, one of which was reliability. In this chapter we return to this aspect of compiler design in discussing the relationship between the formal definition of a language and its implementation, modular design, and compiler checking.

13.1 Use of formal definition

The formal definition of a language describes (1) its syntax and (2) its semantics. As far as the syntax is concerned it is convenient from the implementor's point of view to consider separately:

(a) context-free aspects,
(b) non-context-free aspects,

As we have seen, the context-free grammar, corresponding to the context-free aspects of the language, can usually be transformed into a context-free parser by means of a suitable parser generator. Moreover, the fact that this can be done by means of a program (rather than manually) gives one more confidence in the reliability of the resultant parser. We have seen in Chapter 2 that attribute grammars are extended context-free grammars and that it is possible to define the complete syntax of Pascal by means of an attribute grammar. Ada too has been defined by an attribute grammar (Drossopoulou *et al.* [1982]). The question we now ask is whether an analyser can be built from an attribute grammar. First we look at some properties of attribute grammars which are important from the analysers point of view.

From the occurrences of synthesized and inherited attributes in the productions of the grammar and the evaluation rules associated with these productions the attribute values present in a particular parse tree will depend on one another in certain ways. In general, however, it may not be possible to evaluate all the attributes from these dependencies. This would be the case for example if the dependencies were defined in a circular manner. An algorithm exists to test for this particular situation and we say that, if for any parse tree there is a method of evaluating all the attributes, the attributes are *well defined*. As a special case it may be possible to evaluate all the attributes in a single left to right scan over the source program for any program in the language. Alternatively a (finite) number of passes may be required in order to evaluate all the attributes for any program in the language. A third possibility is that the number of passes required to evaluate all the attributes will depend on the particular program and may be arbitrarily large. Clearly this last possibility does not lead to a satisfactory compiler/analyser. Fortunately algorithms exist to distinguish between the three possibilities and almost all programming languages can be generated by attribute grammars which belong to the first or second category. Pascal, for example, has an attribute grammar belonging to the first category.

A number of compiler generating systems based on attribute grammars have been used. Most parsing methods such as precedence, bounded context, and LR(1) have been extended to include attribute grammars. The method of recursive descent can also be extended to include 'one pass' attribute grammars. As usual each nonterminal of the grammar is replaced by a procedure call and any inherited attributes associated with the nonterminal become input parameters to the procedure while any synthesized attributes become output parameters. Rules associated with productions become checks or evaluation rules in the parser. In this way a (rather inefficient) context-sensitive parser can be produced. Apart from the inefficiencies normally associated with recursive descent parsing the introduction of attributes tends to introduce inefficiencies too. Copying attributes corresponding to complete symbol tables say from one node of a parse tree to another is wasteful of time and space and the introduction of global attributes can be used to avoid this. For multi-pass compilers the storage of large attribute parse trees can also be a problem. Koskimies *et al.* [1982] have made a careful comparison of the space requirements of analysers built from attribute grammars using the Helsinki Language Processor and conclude that if attribute grammars are used in a disciplined way and are implemented carefully they are a useful and efficient basis for constructing compilers.

Affix grammars (Koster [1974]) have also been used to produce analysers, an example being the Manchester ALGOL 68 compiler (Barringer and Lindsey [1977]). Attempts have also been made (Patel [1981]) to implement ALGOL 68 more or less directly from the Revised Report (van Wijngaarden *et al.* [1975]), the main understanding required of the compiler writer being what tasks should be performed in each compiler pass. The predicates in the Report for example can be readily transformed into rather inefficient procedures which can then be optimized by fairly standard techniques.

Clearly, from the compiler writer's point of view it would be preferable if the formal definition of the language were such that it could be implemented more or less directly, though to some extent this might conflict with other requirements for a formal definition. For a discussion of the relationship between the formal definition of a language and its implementation see Griffiths [1975]. For an article on how the non-context-free aspects of ALGOL 60 and BASIC can be expressed using a formal notation see Williams [1978].

13.2 Modular design

We have discussed in previous chapters the various processes which a compiler has to perform. In a one-pass compiler all these processes will be performed in parallel and even in a multi-pass compiler several processes may take place in parallel in the same pass. For example, one pass may include lexical analysis and syntax analysis while another pass may include storage allocation and code generation.

In the interests of reliability, ease of updating, etc., it is usually desirable that the code for the different phases of compilation contained in a single pass should be kept as separate as possible. This can often be done by making one phase call another as a procedure or function. A common example of this is where the syntax analyser calls the lexical analyser as a function. Alternatively, when the two phases have equal status, coroutines may be used or the phases may be regarded as cooperating sequential processes (Dijkstra [1968]).

Where the code of a particular pass consists largely of actions called by a parser, the actions themselves being elements of a **case** clause, the following strategy might be used to separate the code corresponding to the two (say) phases making up the pass. The **case** clause containing the actions called by the parser would be of the form

```
case i of
1 : action1 ;
2 : action2 ;
3 : action3 ;

    .
    .
    .

end
```

where *action1* might be of the form

```
begin prologue ;
    phase1(1);
    phase2(1);
    epilogue
end
```

where *phase1* was a procedure of the form

procedure *phase1* (*no* : *integer*);

begin case *no* **of**

      end
end

so that a call of *phase1* (*1*) would involve executing the first element of the **case** clause within *phase1*, being the aspects of *action1* involving *phase1*. The procedure *phase2* would be similar in form to *phase1* and *prologue* would contain any actions such as unstacking compile-time values required for both the *phase1* action and the *phase2* action. Similarly, *epilogue* would perform actions such as stacking values produced by *phase1* and *phase2*. The presence of *prologue* and *epilogue* is to avoid inefficiencies caused by the same sub-actions being performed by both phases.

Not only is it desirable that the code for distinct phases is kept as separate as possible but it is also preferable that phases know as little as possible about each other. The syntax analyser, for example, does not require to know how the lexical analyser assembles characters into symbols; all it requires is that it can call a routine which will deliver the next symbol. The code generator does not need to know how addresses are allocated as long as it can obtain them when necessary from the symbol table, while it is the storage allocator's job to allocate addresses and, where appropriate, insert the addresses in the symbol table. Neither the code generator nor the storage allocator needs to be aware of the structure of the symbol table as long as suitable routines are provided to access and update the table.

In languages such as Ada, which include modules or packages, it is possible to hide identifiers from parts of a program that do not require to access them. For example, compilers use stacks for a number of purposes and the facilities of Ada allow us to make use of a stack in a disciplined way by the declaration of a suitable package.

package *stackpack* **is**
    procedure *push* (*n* : *integer*);
    function *pop* **return** *integer*;   package specification
end *stackpack*;

package body *stackpack* **is**
    length : **constant** : = *50*;
    stack : **array** (*1* .. *length*) **of** *integer*;
    pointer : *integer* **range** *0* .. *length* : = *0*;

```
procedure push (n : integer) is
begin
    pointer : = pointer + 1 ;
    stack (pointer) : = n ;
end push ;
                                        package body
function pop return integer is
begin pointer : = pointer − 1 ;
    return stack (pointer + 1);
end pop ;
end stackpack ;
```

For simplicity we have implemented an integer stack but the generic facility of Ada could have been used to provide stacks of values of various types. We have also ignored any problems of stack overflow or underflow which could have been dealt with using exceptions in Ada.

A **use** clause

use *stackpack*

would make the procedure *push* and the function *pop* available but the array *stack* and the integer variable *pointer* would not be accessible since they were not in the specification part of the package. The idea of not allowing access to certain variables, etc., is referred to as information hiding. If for some reason the data structure used to represent the stack were to be altered, this would not require any part of the program outside the package to be changed as long as *push* and *pop* were suitably redeclared within the package body.

The detailed structure of a compiler symbol table need not be known except within the routines which access and update it. Indeed one module of a compiler may require to be able to update the symbol table using certain routines while another may only require to use routines to access the table but not to alter it. Language facilities which allow individual modules of a compiler to have only as much access as necessary to the details of the data structures they have to use are clearly desirable from the compiler writer's point of view.

It seems reasonable to expect that by keeping the various aspects of the compilation process as distinct as possible the chances of each aspect being implemented correctly will be increased. The overall design of the compiler of course should also be correct. The policies advocated in this section are not claimed to be particularly novel or original, but merely the application of good structured programming design techniques to the particular problem of compiler writing. It should also be noted that the choice of implementation language can contribute towards the reliability of the compiler.

13.3 Checking the compiler

As for other programs, a compiler should not be considered reliable until it has been thoroughly tested with sample input. Rather, however, than writing the complete compiler and then checking it, it is better to check each aspect individually as the compiler is being written, to eliminate most of the faults. It will also be necessary to test the complete compiler for overall design faults. Programs to check the compiler should, preferably, not be written by the implementors but by others not familiar with the details of the implementation. Alternatively, random programs may be generated for testing purposes with the aid of the parser (see Housais [1977]).

Exercises

These exercises are based on Chapters 1–13 inclusive. Most are of the essay type and solutions are not given.

13.1 Discuss the importance of identifying the design aims of a compiler project at the outset.

13.2 Discuss the factors involved in establishing the optimal number of programmers which should be involved in a particular compiler writing project.

13.3 A compiler-writing team has to produce a number of compilers to be run on the same machine. To what extent might they make use of source-language-independent modules to build the compilers?

13.4 Describe how you might go about choosing an implementation language for a compiler.

13.5 Is it necessary for a compiler writer to be thoroughly familiar with the language he is implementing?

13.6 Do you feel the various aspects of compiler construction have been dealt with in the correct order in this book? If so, justify the ordering. If not, suggest an alternative.

13.7 Suggest research topics in the area of compiler construction.

13.8 What difficulties would be involved in writing a compiler for the English language?

13.9 A *decompiler* translates from object code to source code. Discuss the problems involved in writing one.

13.10 Discuss aspects involved in writing a compiler for PL/1, FORTRAN or whichever language you are most familiar with.

Outline Solutions to Exercises in Chapters 1–12

Chapter 1

1.1 Arithmetic expressions would generate add, subtract, multiply instructions, etc. Conditionals and loops would generate branch instructions. Assignments would generate load and store instructions.

1.2 A compiler written in 1900 code which translates from ALGOL 68 into 1900 code (Figure E.1).

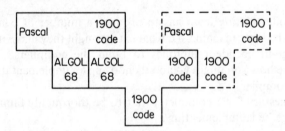

Figure E.1

1.3 (a) Almost essential, despite cost, in order to check that program logic does not lead to subscript errors.

  (b) Can be avoided if program logic is assumed correct, in order to make object code smaller and faster, but can still be dangerous.

1.4 1. and 2. and possibly 5. and 6.

1.5 (a) for stacks and tables,
  (b) rarely required,
  (c) for modularization.

1.6 1. To get clearer diagnostics.
  2. Small object code.

1.7 Possible incompatibility of the two compilers.

1.8 $a + b*c$

would normally be represented by the binary tree shown in Figure E.2,

236

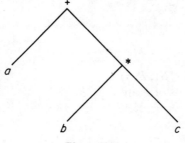

Figure E.2

but if + had been declared to have a higher priority than ∗ the tree would be as shown in Figure E.3.

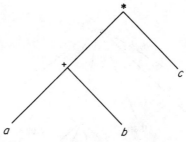

Figure E.3

Chapter 2

2.1 $G_1 = (\{a,b,c,\}, \{A,B,C,S\}, P,S)$
where the elements of P are

$$S \rightarrow ABC$$
$$A \rightarrow aA$$
$$A \rightarrow \varepsilon$$
$$B \rightarrow bB$$
$$B \rightarrow \varepsilon$$
$$C \rightarrow cC$$
$$C \rightarrow \varepsilon$$

$G_2 = (\{a,b,c,\}, \{T,C,S\}, P,S)$
where the elements of P are

$$S \rightarrow TC$$
$$T \rightarrow aTb$$

238

$$T \rightarrow \varepsilon$$
$$C \rightarrow cC$$
$$C \rightarrow \varepsilon$$

$G_3 = (\{a,b,x,y,\}, \{S\}, P, S)$
where the elements of P are

$$S \rightarrow xSy$$
$$S \rightarrow a$$
$$S \rightarrow b$$

2.2 L_1, since it corresponds to the regular expression

$a*b*c*$

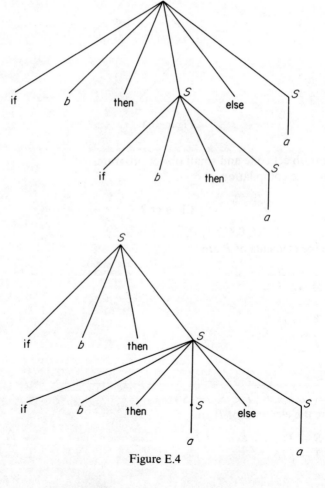

Figure E.4

2.3   Productions are

$$S \to xV$$
$$S \to yT$$
$$V \to xV$$
$$V \to bB$$
$$V \to b$$
$$T \to yT$$
$$T \to bB$$
$$T \to b$$
$$B \to bB$$
$$B \to b$$

2.4 $(xx^*|yy^*)\,bb^*$

2.5   The sentence

if b then if b then a else a

has two syntax trees (Figure E.4).

2.6   See Figure E.5.

2.7 $G = (\{0, 1\}, \{S\}, P, S)$

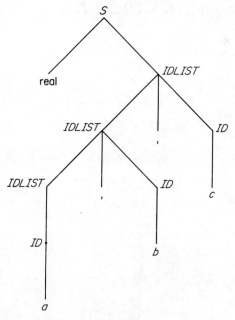

Figure E.5

where the elements of P are

$$S \to 0S$$
$$S \to 1S$$
$$S \to \varepsilon$$

2.8 $PROGRAM \underset{L}{\Rightarrow}$ **begin** $DECS$; $STATS$ **end**

$\underset{L}{\Rightarrow}$ **begin** d; $DECS$; $STATS$ **end**

$\underset{L}{\Rightarrow}$ **begin** d; d; $STATS$ **end**

$\underset{L}{\Rightarrow}$ **begin** d; d; s; $STATS$ **end**

$\underset{L}{\Rightarrow}$ **begin** d; d; s; s **end**

$PROGRAM \underset{R}{\Rightarrow}$ **begin** $DECS$; $STATS$ **end**

$\underset{R}{\Rightarrow}$ **begin** $DECS$; s; $STATS$ **end**

$\underset{R}{\Rightarrow}$ **begin** $DECS$; s; s **end**

$\underset{R}{\Rightarrow}$ **begin** d; $DECS$; s; s **end**

$\underset{R}{\Rightarrow}$ **begin** d; d; s; s **end**

2.9 (a) *letter* (*letter*|*digit*|) (*letter*|*digit*|) (*letter*|*digit*|)
        (*letter*|*digit*|) (*letter*|*digit*|)
    (b) $G = (\{letter, digit\}, \{R, S, T, U, V\}, P, S)$
        $S \to letter$
        $S \to letter\ R$
        $R \to letter\ S$
        $R \to digit\ S$
        $R \to letter$
        $R \to digit$
        $S \to letter\ T$
        $S \to digit\ T$
        $S \to letter$
        $S \to digit$
        $T \to letter\ U$
        $T \to digit\ U$
        $T \to letter$
        $T \to digit$
        $U \to letter\ V$
        $U \to digit\ V$
        $U \to letter$
        $U \to digit$
        $V \to letter$
        $V \to digit$

2.10 1. COBOL, Pascal solution—on reading from left to right each 'else' is associated with the nearest preceding 'then' not already associated with an 'else'.

    2. ALGOL 68, POP-2 solution—each conditional is terminated by **fi** or *CLOSE*.

    3. ALGOL 60 solution—sequence 'then if illegal: must have **begin** between them.

Chapter 3

3.1
$$S \rightarrow 1T$$
$$T \rightarrow 0V$$
$$V \rightarrow 1S$$
$$S \rightarrow 0U$$
$$U \rightarrow 1W$$
$$W \rightarrow 0X$$
$$X \rightarrow 0U$$
$$W \rightarrow 0$$
$$S \rightarrow \varepsilon$$

3.2 See Table E.0. S is starting state and S, X are finishing states.

3.3 See Figure E.6. S is starting state and S, F are finishing states.

3.4 See Figure E.7. S is starting state and S, F are finishing states.

3.5 A is sentence symbol and productions are

$$A \rightarrow 0A$$
$$A \rightarrow 1A$$
$$A \rightarrow 1B$$
$$B \rightarrow 1C$$
$$B \rightarrow 1$$
$$C \rightarrow 0C$$
$$C \rightarrow 1C$$
$$C \rightarrow 1$$
$$C \rightarrow 0$$

Table E.0

	States					
	S	T	U	V	W	X
0	U	V			X	U
1	T		W	S		

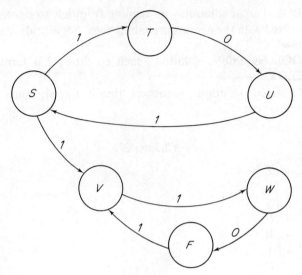

Figure E.6

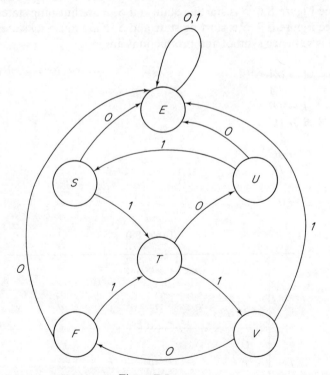

Figure E.7

The language consists of strings of zeros and ones containing at least two consecutive ones.

3.6
```
function doubleones : boolean ;
var n, p : integer ;
    ok : boolean ;
begin ok : = false ;
    read(n) ;
    p : = n ;
    read(n) ;
    while((n = 0) or (n = 1)) and not ok do
    if (n = 1) and (p = 1)
    then ok : = true
    else begin p : = n ;
             read(n)
         end ;
    while (n = 0) or (n = 1) do
    read(n) ;
    doubleones : = ok
end
```

The procedure assumes the string of zeros and ones is terminated by some other integer.

3.7
```
procedure fixed ;
var in : char ;
    dig : boolean ;
begin dig : = false ;
    read(in) ;
    if (in = ' + ') or (in = ' − ')
    then read (in) ;
    if digit (in)
    then begin dig : = true ;
             read(in)
         end ;
    while digit (in) do
    read(in) ;
    if in < > '.'
    then error
    else read (in) ;
    if digit (in)
    then begin dig : = true ;
             read(in)
         end ;
    if not dig
```

```
            then error;
            while digit (in) do
            read(in)
      end
```

The function *digit* and procedure *error* are assumed.

3.8
```
            procedure train;
            var in:rollingstock;
            begin readrs (in);
                  if in = engine
                  then readrs (in)
                  else error;
                  if in = engine
                  then readrs (in);
                  if in = truck
                  then readrs (in)
                  else error;
                  while in = truck do
                  readrs (in);
                  if in < > guardsvan
                  then error
      end
```

where *readrs* has been suitably defined.

3.9 An array of strings would be one possibility.

3.10 A boolean variable could be used to denote the two modes. Advantage—avoids overheads of recursion. Disadvantage—variable would have to be tested each time a compiler action was not identical for the two modes.

Chapter 4

4.1 (a) Deterministic since c denotes the middle of a string and the second half can be matched against the first half using a stack.

 (b) Not deterministic since the middle of the string cannot be determined on reading from left to right, therefore it is not known when to start matching.

 (c) Deterministic—similar to (a).

 (d) Deterministic—similar to (c).

 (e) Not deterministic—no way of knowing whether to take a '0' off stack for every '1' read or only for every second '1' read.

4.2 (a) Use the pumping lemma and assume language *is* context free. For sufficiently large k the string

$a^k b^k c^k$

can be written in the form

$uvwxy$

where $|vwx| \le k$ and $|vx| \ne 0$ and for $i \ge 0$ the string

$uv^i wx^i y$

is also in the language. Letting $i = 0$

uwy

is in the language. But uwy is obtained from $uvwxy$ by removing v and x and, since $|vwx| \le k$, v and x together cannot contain a's, b's, and c's (i.e. vwx cannot stretch across the k b's). Therefore uwy must still contain k a's or k c's but it cannot contain k a's, b's, and c's since $|vx| \ne 0$. Therefore, it cannot contain an equal number of a's, b's and c's and is not in the language. Thus we have a contradiction and the language is *not* context free.

(b) Use the pumping lemma and assume the language is context free. For a sufficiently large prime k,

$p = a^k$

can be expressed as

$uvwxy$

where $|vwx| \le k$ and $|vx| \ne 0$ and for $i \ge 0$

$uv^i wx^i y$

is in the language. Such strings are of length $p + i \times l$ where p is the length of uwy and l is the length of vx which is not zero. Not all these lengths are prime. For example,

$p + pl$

is not prime. Hence contradiction and language is not context free.

4.3   **procedure** E;
     begin T;
           G
     end;

```
procedure G
begin if in = ' + '
      then begin read(in);
                  T;
                  G
            end
end;

procedure T;
begin F;
      U
end;

procedure U;
begin if in = ' × '
      then begin read(in);
                  F;
                  U
            end
end;

procedure F;
begin if in = '('
      then begin read(in);
                  E;
                  if in = ')'
                  then read(in)
                  else error
            end
      else if identifier (in)
            then read(in)
            else error
end;
```

where 'forward' declarations have been omitted.

4.4   (a) This follows from (2).
      (b) Any s-grammar satisfies (1) and (2).
      (c) The transformation can be performed by repeatedly replacing left-
          most nonterminals using productions of the grammar until a q-
          grammar is obtained.

4.5   S is the sentence symbol in each case:

      1. $S \rightarrow 0S11$
          $S \rightarrow a$

2. $S \to 0S$
   $S \to 1T$
   $S \to \varepsilon$
   $T \to 0S$
   $T \to \varepsilon$
3. $S \to 1T$
   $S \to 0U$
   $T \to 0X$
   $U \to 1X$
   $T \to 1UU$
   $U \to 0TT$
   $X \to S$
   $X \to \varepsilon$

4.6 The productions for E and T prevent the grammar from being LL(1). Replace these productions by

$E \to TX$
$X \to + TX$
$X \to \varepsilon$
$T \to FY$
$Y \to \times FY$
$Y \to \varepsilon$

Table E. 1

	terminals	jump	accept	stack	return	error
1	$\{begin\}$	2	false	false	false	true
2	$\{begin\}$	3	true	false	false	true
3	$\{d\}$	4	true	false	false	true
4	$\{semi\}$	5	true	false	false	true
5	$\{d,s\}$	7	false	true	false	true
6	$\{end\}$	0	true	false	true	true
7	$\{d\}$	9	false	false	false	false
8	$\{s\}$	12	false	false	false	false
9	$\{d\}$	10	true	false	false	true
10	$\{semi\}$	11	true	false	false	true
11	$\{d,s\}$	7	false	false	false	true
12	$\{s\}$	13	true	false	false	true
13	$\{end, semi\}$	14	false	false	false	true
14	$\{end\}$	16	false	false	false	false
15	$\{semi\}$	17	false	false	false	true
16	$\{end\}$	0	false	false	true	true
17	$\{semi\}$	18	true	false	false	true
18	$\{s\}$	19	true	false	false	true
19	$\{end, semi\}$	14	false	false	false	true

Table   E. 2

	terminals	jump	accept	stack	return	error
1	$\{(,x,y\}$	2	false	false	false	true
2	$\{(,x,y\}$	4	false	true	false	true
3	$\{+,\perp,)\}$	7	false	false	false	true
4	$\{(,x,y\}$	5	false	false	false	true
5	$\{(,x,y\}$	19	false	true	false	true
6	$\{\times,+,\perp,)\}$	13	false	false	false	true
7	$\{+\}$	9	false	false	false	false
8	$\{\perp,)\}$	12	false	false	false	true
9	$\{+\}$	10	true	false	false	true
10	$\{(,x,y\}$	4	false	true	false	true
11	$\{+,\perp,)\}$	7	false	false	false	true
12	$\{\perp,)\}$	0	false	false	true	true
13	$\{\times\}$	15	false	false	false	false
14	$\{+,\perp,)\}$	18	false	false	false	true
15	$\{\times\}$	16	true	false	false	true
16	$\{(,x,y\}$	19	false	true	false	true
17	$\{\times,+,\perp,)\}$	13	false	false	false	true
18	$\{+,\perp,)\}$	0	false	false	true	true
19	$\{(\}$	22	false	flase	false	false
20	$\{x\}$	25	false	false	false	false
21	$\{y\}$	26	false	false	false	true
22	$\{(\}$	23	true	false	false	true
23	$\{(,x,y\}$	1	false	true	false	true
24	$\{)\}$	0	true	false	true	true
25	$\{x\}$	0	true	false	true	true
26	$\{y\}$	0	true	false	true	true

4.7   No, since x is a Director Symbol for both productions for S.

4.8   A sentence generated by an LL(1) grammar cannot have two leftmost derivations since this would imply that two alternative productions for some nonterminal had a common Director Symbol.

4.9   See Table E.1.

4.10 See Table E.2.

Chapter 5

5.1   (a) $S \rightarrow aYc$
      $Y \rightarrow Ybb$
      $Y \rightarrow b$

      (S is the sentence symbol).

      (b) $E \rightarrow E + T$
      $E \rightarrow T$

$$T \rightarrow T \times F$$
$$T \rightarrow F$$
$$F \rightarrow x$$
$$F \rightarrow (E)$$

(E is the sentence symbol).

5.2 (a) Not LR(1) since it is ambiguous. Grammar can be replaced by

$$E \rightarrow E + i$$
$$E \rightarrow i$$

 (b) Grammar is not LR(1) since language cannot be parsed deterministically. No corresponding LR(1) grammar exists.

 (c) Grammar can be shown to be LR(0) therefore LR(1) by constructing
parsing table.

5.3 See Table E.3. Grammar is SLR(1).

Table E. 3

	S	E	T	F	'('	')'	'+'	'×'	x y	'⊥'
1	HALT	S2	S3	S4	S5				S6	
2						S7				R1
3					R3	R3	S9			R3
4					R5	R5	R5			R5
5		S11	S3	S4	S5				S6	
6					R7/8	R7/8	R7/8			R7/8
7			S8	S4	S5				S6	
8					R2	R2	S9			R2
9				S10	S5				S6	
10					R4	R4	R4			R4
11					S12	S7				
12					R6	R6	R6			R6

5.4 Grammar is not LR(1) since on reading d with *semi* as lookahead it is
not known whether to reduce to *DECLIST* or not. An equivalent SLR(1)
grammar is

$$PROGRAM \rightarrow begin\ d\ semi\ X\ end$$
$$X \rightarrow d\ semi\ X$$
$$X \rightarrow s\ Y$$
$$Y \rightarrow semi\ s\ Y$$
$$Y \rightarrow \varepsilon$$

See Table E.4.

Table E. 4

	PROGRAM	X	Y	begin	semi	d	s	end	'⊥'
1	HALT			S2					
2						S3			
3					S4				
4		S5				S7	S10		
5								S6	
6									R1
7					S8				
8		S9				S7	S10		
9								R2	
10			S11		S12			R5	
11								R3	
12							S13		
13			S14		S12			R5	
14								R4	

Table E. 5

	S	F	ITEM	','	a	t	'⊥'
1	HALT				S2		
2						S3	
3		S4		S5			R3
4							R1
5			S6		S8	S10	
6		S7		S5			R3
7							R2
8						S9	
9				R4			R4
10				R5			R5

5.5 See Table E.5.

5.6 Grammar is not LR(1) since language cannot be parsed deterministically—no way of telling, for example, whether *01* should be reduced to *S* from past history and one symbol of lookahead.

5.7 (a) No.

(b) No.

5.8 Grammar is not LR(1) since on reading '*I*' with lookahead ':' an LR(1) parser does not know whether to reduce by production (4) or not. The problem can be avoided by replacing the sequence ':=' by a single symbol during lexical analysis.

5.9 Errors might be discovered at an earlier stage of the parse (in terms of reductions performed, though not in terms of symbols read) by having fewer reduce actions and more error indications in the parsing table.

5.10 Stacks could be merged since there are no parsing actions which add or remove an item from one stack and not the other. Strictly speaking the symbol stack is not required.

5.11 Each regular language corresponds to a deterministic finite automaton from which an LR(1) parsing table can be derived.

Chapter 6

6.1 The action after an identifier would be simply to print it. Each operator, however, would be stacked, and would be unstacked and printed at the end of the *TERM* or *FACT*.

6.2 $E \rightarrow E + T$

$E \rightarrow \langle A1 \rangle E - T$

6.3 No.

6.4 After an operator was read its priority would be checked before it was handed over to the parser.

6.5 1. Algebraic expressions.

2. Lists of names and addresses.

6.6 1. Finite width of paper only allows indenting to a certain depth.

2. Different programmers have different indenting conventions.

6.7 By use of the following grammar:

$$I \;\; \rightarrow + U$$
$$\rightarrow - U \langle M \rangle$$
$$U \rightarrow d \langle A \rangle$$
$$d \langle A \rangle U$$

where the actions are

$$\langle M \rangle$$
$$sum := - sum$$
$$\langle A \rangle$$
$$sum := 10 * sum + d$$

where *sum* is initially zero and *d* is the value of the last digit read.

6.8 No need for block structured tables as described in the chapter: arrays could be used.

6.9 1. More natural programming style allowing an identifier to be declared when it is required.

2. Fewer program errors caused by missing declarations.

6.10 Each call of an action will correspond to an extra element of the parse table.

Chapter 7

7.1 1. To provide a natural method of allowing mutually recursive procedures, etc.

2. To allow the overloading of certain symbols.

7.2 1. To keep the compiler small,

2. To optimize the object code produced.

3. To give good compile-time diagnostics.

7.3 For—the original source code is still available. Against—may be possible to give syntax error messages at an earlier point in the source program with a multi-pass compiler.

7.4 1. Recognizing routine headings in ALGOL 68.

2. Dealing with declarations in Pascal.

7.5 For—helpful in debugging compiler. Against—reading and writing between passes possibly inefficient.

7.6 May help explain subsequent error messages.

7.7 Time may be wasted by parser as a result of making an invalid assumption in an earlier pass.

7.8 1. Compiler might take advantage of machine features such as a hardware stack.

2. Optimizations performed by the compiler might relate to capabilities of the machine.

3. Design of code generator might depend on the number of registers available.

7.9 1. No machine dependencies in 'front end'.

2. Use of abstract machine easily implementable on most computers.

7.10 1. Structure of compiler might relate closely to definition of source language.

2. Compilation phases might be separated logically.

Chapter 8

8.1 (a) For—simple identifier table and simple hashing functions for symbol table.

(b) Against—cannot use mnemonic identifiers.

8.2 No, since default types can be overridden.

8.3 Identifiers might have been replaced by consecutive integers which could be used as indexes to table.

8.4 (a) Could be inserted in hash table before user-defined identifiers in fixed positions, which would not require to be recalculated for each program.

(b) Would be inserted in a special outermost block.

8.5 For—avoids clustering in the symbol table itself and symbol table can hold an arbitrary number of identifiers. Against—space taken up by the pointers.

8.6 Find the middle of the array and make this element the root of the tree. The left and right subtrees would be formed from the two halves of the array, and so on.

8.7 To declare mutually recursive procedures, etc.

8.8 For—saves space in the mode table. Against—for each new mode encountered a check must be made to see if it is already in the mode table.

8.9 Yes, since the same identifier can be used as a variable and as a field of a record in any block.

8.10 No.

Chapter 9

9.1 By declaring variables locally, where possible.

9.2 The process of accessing a value on the stack using *DISPLAY* involves adding an offset to the start address of *DISPLAY*, following a pointer, and adding another offset. This could be partly avoided by having a separate stack for static values if procedures did not have to be implemented.

9.3 Advantage—no need for extra compiler pass to make working stack offsets relative to start of frame. Disadvantage—complication of having multiple stacks at run time.

9.4 Global space could be allocated for the duration of the program and local space would be shared by the procedures. Total space required would be given by — global space + maximum space required by any procedure.

9.5 Array sizes are fixed at compile time.

9.6 Suppose *y* is the formal parameter of a procedure called by reference or value and result, and *x* is the corresponding actual parameter. Assign a new value to *x* within the procedure and print *y*. If *y* is called by reference the new value of *x* will be printed whereas if *y* is called by value and result the previous value of *y* will be printed.

9.7 They can usually be replaced by globals.

9.8 Garbage collection is not satisfactory in a real-time environment since it can cause the program to be stopped for an indeterminate time. The use of reference counters is more satisfactory even though the program may be slowed down a little as a result.

9.9 As described in the chapter, the more backward pointers there are the longer the algorithm is likely to take. A preliminary scan could be used to determine which end of the heap the algorithm should start at.

9.10 No need to use recursion or a stack.

Chapter 10

10.1 (a) $a + b$

$1 + c$

$d + e$

$3 + f$

2×4

(b) $a + b = 1$

$1 + c = 2$

$d + e = 3$

$3 + f = 4$

$2 \times 4 = 5$

10.2 So that the triples can be rearranged (e.g. during optimization) without altering the triples themselves.

10.3 To avoid ambiguity a monadic operator must be represented differently from the corresponding dyadic operator in the reverse Polish produced.

10.4 Advantage—removes operator precedence thus allowing simple algorithms to perform translation. Disadvantage—not optimal approach with regard to compile time.

10.5 No need for a type stack at compile time as long as brackets cannot be used to specify priorities.

10.6 *All* values have to be stacked at compile time until the right-hand side of the expression is reached, unless brackets are involved.

10.7 May save a certain amount of table lookup but will lengthen source text considerably.

10.8 An outline of how the Pascal case statement might be implemented:

1. Case selector is mapped on to type integer (if necessary).
2. Unconditional jump inserted from case selector to beyond all case elements.
3. Check inserted that selector is within the range of the case labels and equal to one of them.
4. Index jump inserted to provide jump back to appropriate case element.
5. Execution of case element.
6. Jump to end of case statement.

10.9 Main steps are:
1. Check label is in symbol table—cannot jump into block.
2. Generate code to adjust *DISPLAY* if jumping out of block.
3. Generate *jump* instruction.

10.10 Relatively inefficient if P-code is interpreted. Even if P-code is not interpreted extra instructions may be generated if the architecture is not stack based.

Chapter 11

11.1 Advantages—may be possible to use standard linker and assembler. Disadvantages—possibly less efficient, extra pass required.

11.2   Assuming $P = 2$ and $Q = 4$ the code generated would be

        LDX   2   DISPLAY + 2
        ADN   2   4
        ADN   1   1
        STO   2   0(1)

11.3   The code might be

        LDX   2   0(1)
        NEG   2
        STO   2   0(1)

11.4   Compact code is produced.
11.5   (a) Programming stage.
       (b) In the production of P-code.
       (c) In the production of assembly code from P-code.
11.6   When a single compile-time action generated more than (say) eight assembly code instructions.
11.7   Because of dynamic arrays and recursive modes.
11.8   To store the value of *DISPLAY* and to point to the foot of the current frame
11.9   It would be necessary to remember the last two assembly code instructions generated at all times.
11.10 Each unconditional jump would be checked to see if it led to an unconditional jump.

Chapter 12

12.1   No.
12.2   Errors may be detected at an earlier stage since the compiler will not confuse language words with user-defined identifiers as is possible in FORTRAN and PL/1.
12.3   Arbitrary rules tend to encourage errors. Research has shown that using the semi-colon as a separator rather than a terminator leads to more programming errors, as does the overuse of certain characters.
12.4   Strict typing tends to lead to clearer error messages; see also Exercise 12.2.

12.5   *x* ; **end**

       is interpreted as

            x

            semi-colon
            dummy statement
            end

12.6 The opening and closing commentary symbols are not identical.

12.7 No.

12.8 No—there would probably be too many.

12.9 To make the program run faster—useful, but dangerous.

12.10 It would be necessary to move tables, etc., as they filled the space originally allocated to them.

Bibliography

Aho, A. V. and Johnson, S. C. [1974]. 'LR parsing', *Computing Surveys*, **6**, 99–124.

Aho, A. V. and Ullman, J. D. [1972]. *The Theory of Parsing, Translation, and Compiling. Vol. 1: Parsing*, Prentice-Hall, Englewood Cliffs, N. J.

Aho, A. V. and Ullman, J. D. [1977]. *Principles of Compiler Design*, Addison-Wesley, Reading, Mass.

Ammann, U. [1974]. 'The Method of Structured Programming Applied to the Development of a Compiler. In A. Guenther *et al*, (Eds), *International Computing Symposium, 1973*, North Holland, pp. 93–99.

Ammann, U. [1981]. 'Code Generation for a Pascal Compiler.' In D. W. Barron (Ed.), *Pascal–the Language and its Implementation*, Wiley, Chichester.

Backhouse, R. C. [1979]. *Syntax of Programming Languages, Theory and Practice*, Prentice Hall, Englewood Cliffs, N. J.

Baker, T. P. [1982]. 'A Single-Pass Syntax-Directed Front End for Ada.' *Proc. SIGPLAN '82 Symposium on Compiler Construction*, SIGPLAN Notices, 17, No. 6.

Barringer, H. and Lindsey, C. H. [1977]. 'The Manchester ALGOL 68 Compiler, Part 1.' *Proc. 5th annual iii Conference, Guidel, France.*

Bauer, F. L. and Eickel, J. (Eds) [1974]. *Compiler Construction, an Advanced Course*, Springer-Verlag, New York.

Bauer, F. L. [1974]. 'Historical Remarks on Compiler Construction.' In F. L. Bauer and J. Eickel (Eds), *Compiler Construction, an Advanced Course*, Springer-Verlag, New York. pp. 603–621.

Bauer, H., Becker, S., Graham, S. and Satterthwaite, E. [1968]. *ALGOL W Language Description*, Computer Science Department, Stanford University.

Bochmann, G. V. [1973]. 'Semantic Evaluation from Left to Right.' *CACM*, **19**, 55–62.

Branquart, P., Cardinael, J. -P., Lewi, J., Delescaille, J. -P. and Vanbegin, M. [1976]. *An Optimised Translation Process and its Application to ALGOL 68*, Lecture Notes in Computer Science, **38**, Springer-Verlag, New York.

Bratman, H. [1961]. 'An Alternate Form of the UNCOL Diagram.' *CACM*, **4**, 142.

Brown, P. J. [1976]. 'Throw-Away Compiling.' *Software Practice and Experience*, **6**, No. 3, 423–434.

Brown, P. J. [1979]. *Writing Interactive Compilers and Interpreters*, Wiley, Chichester.

Cohen, J. and Roth, M. S. [1978]. 'Analyses of Deterministic Parsing Algorithms.' *CACM*, **21**, No 6, 448–458.

Dakin, R. J. and Poole, P. C. [1973]. 'A Mixed Code Approach.' *Computer Journal*, **16**, No. 3, 219–222.

DeRemer, F. L. [1971]. 'Simple LR(*k*) Grammars.' *CACM*, **14**, 453–460.

DeRemer, F. L. [1974]. 'Review of Formalisms and Notation.' In F. L. Bauer and J. Eickel (Eds), *Compiler Construction, an Advanced Course*, Springer-Verlag, New York pp. 42–56.

Dijkstra, E. W. [1968]. 'Cooperating Sequential Processes.' In F. Genuys (Ed.), *Programming Languages*, Academic Press, New York. pp. 43–112.

257

Drossopoulou, S., Uhl, J., Persch, G., Goos, G., Dausmann, M., and Winterstein, G. [1982]. 'An Attribute Grammar for Ada.' *Proc. SIGPLAN '82 Symposium on Compiler Construction*, SIGPLAN Notices, 17, No. 6.

Foster, J. M. [1968]. 'A Syntax Improving Device. *Computer Journal*, 11, 31–34.

Goos, G., Wulf, W. A., Evans, A., and Butler, K. [1983]. *DIANA Reference Manual*, Ada Joint Program Office, Contract number MDA 903–82–C–0148.

Gries, D. [1971]. *Compiler Construction for Digital Computers*, Wiley, New York.

Griffiths, M. [1969]. 'Analyse Déterministe et Compilateurs'. *Thesis*, University of Grenoble, October 1969.

Griffiths, M. [1974]. 'LL(1) Grammars and Analysers.', In F. L. Bauer and J. Eickel (Eds), *Compiler Construction, an Advanced Course*, Springer-Verlag, New York. pp. 57–84.

Griffiths, M. [1975]. 'Relationship between the Definition and Implementation of a Language.' In G. Goos and J. Hartmanis (Eds), *Software Engineering—An Advanced Course (Munich 1972)*, Lecture Notes in Computer Science, Springer-Verlag, New York.

Hall, P. A. V. [1975]. *Computational Structures*, MacDonald and Jane's/American Elsevier.

Hansen, W. J. and Boom, H. [1977]. 'The Report on the Standard Hardware Representation for ALGOL 68.' *SIGPLAN Notices*, 12, No. 5, 80–87.

Hopcroft, J. E., and Ullman, J. D. [1979]. *Introduction to Automata Theory, Languages and Computation*, Addison-Wesley, Reading, Mass.

Horning, J. J. [1974a]. 'LR Grammars and Analysers.' In F. L. Bauer and J. Eickel (Eds), *Compiler Construction, an Advanced Course*, Springer-Verlag, New York. pp. 85–108.

Horning, J. J. [1974b]. 'Structuring Compiler Development.' In F. L. Bauer and J. Eickel (Eds), *Compiler Construction, an Advanced Course*, Springer-Verlag, New York. pp. 498–524.

Housais, B. [1977]. 'Verification of an ALGOL 68 Implementation.' *Proc. Strathclyde ALGOL 68 Conference*, SIGPLAN Notices, 12, No. 6, 117–128.

Hunter, R. B., McGettrick, A. D., and Patel, R. R. [1977]. "LL versus LR parsing with illustrations from ALGOL 68.' *Proc. Strathclyde ALGOL 68 Conference, SIGPLAN Notices*, 12, No. 6, 49–53.

Jensen, K., and Wirth, N. [1978]. *Pascal User Manual and Report*, 2nd Edition, Springer-Verlag, New York.

Knuth, D. E. [1965]. 'On the Translation of Languages from Left to Right.' *Information and Control*, 8, 607–639.

Knuth, D. E. [1967]. 'The Remaining Trouble Spots in ALGOL 60.' *CACM*, 10, No. 10, 611.

Knuth, D. E. [1968a]. 'Semantics of Context-free Languages.' *Maths Systems. Theory*, 2, No. 2, 127–145.

Knuth, D. E. [1968b]. *The Art of Computer Programming, 1, Fundamental Algorithms*, 1st ed. Addison-Wesley, Reading, Mass.

Knuth, D. E. [1971]. 'Topdown Syntax Analysis.' *Acta Informatica*, 1, 79–110.

Knuth, D. E. [1973]. *The Art of Computer Programming, 1, Fundamental Algorithms*, 2nd ed. Addison-Wesley, Reading, Mass.

Koskimies, K., Raiha, K-J., and Sarjakoshi, M. [1982]. 'Compiler Construction using Attribute Grammars.' *Proc. SIGPLAN '82 Symposium on Compiler Construction*, SIGPLAN Notices, 17, No. 6.

Koster, C. H. A. [1974]. 'Using the CDL Compiler-Compiler.' In F. L. Bauer and J. Eickel (Eds), *Compiler Construction, an Advanced Course*, Springer-Verlag, New York. pp. 366–426.

Ledgard, H. F. [1974]. 'Production Systems: or Can we do better than BNF?' *CACM*, 10, No. 2, 94–102.

Lucas, P., and Walk, K. [1969]. 'On the Formal Description of PL/1.' *Annual Review Automatic Programming*, 6, No. 3, 105–182.

McGettrick, A. D., [1980]. *The Definition of Programming Languages,* Cambridge University Press, Cambridge.

Marcotty, M., Ledgard, H. F., and Bochmann, G. V. [1976]. 'A Sampler of Formal Definitions.' *ACM Computing Surveys,* **8**, No. 2.

Minsky, M. L. [1967]. *Computation: Finite and Infinite Machines,* Prentice-Hall, Englewood Cliffs, N. J.

Morris, J. B. [1976]. *A Manual for the MODEL Programming Language.* Los Alamos Scientific Laboratory, Los Alamos, New Mexico.

Naur, P. (Ed.) [1963]. 'Revised Report on the Algorithmic Language ALGOL 60.' *CACM,* **6**, No. 1, 1–17.

Naur, P. [1964]. 'The Design of the GIER Algol Compiler.' *Annual Review Automatic Programming,* **4**, 49–85.

Nelson, A. [1979]. 'A Comparison of Pascal Intermediate Languages'. *Proc. SIGPLAN Symposium on Compiler Construction,* SIGPLAN Notices, 14, No. 8.

Patel, R. R. [1981]. 'An Implementation of ALGOL 68 based on the Revised Report.' *Ph.D. Thesis,* University of Strathclyde, 1981.

Poole, P. C. [1974]. 'Portable and Adaptable Compilers.' In F. L. Bauer and J. Eickel (Eds), *Compiler Construction, an Advanced Course,* Springer-Verlag, New York. pp. 427–497.

Richards, M. [1971]. 'The Portability of the BCPL Compiler.' *Software Practice and Experience,* **1**, 135–146.

Rohl, J. S. [1975]. *An Introduction to Compiler Writing,* MacDonald and Jane's/American Elsevier.

Simonet, M. [1977]. 'An Attribute Description of a Subset of ALGOL 68.' *Proc. Strathclyde ALGOL 68 Conference, SIGPLAN Notices,* **12**, No. 6, 129–137.

Simpson, D. S. [1976]. Efficient Code Generation for an ALGOL 68 Compiler. *Ph.D. Thesis,* Department of Computer Science, University of Manchester.

Strasen, V., [1969]. 'Gaussian Elimination is not Optimal.' *Numerische Mathematik,* **13**, 354–356.

Tanenbaum, A. S., Stevenson, J. W., and van Staveren, H. [1980]. 'Description of an Experimental Machine for use with Block Structured Languages.' *Informatica Rapport IR-54,* Vrije Universiteit, Amsterdam.

Uzgalis, R., Eggert, P., and Book, E. [1977]. Report for System Development Corporation, Sunnyvale, California.

van Wijngaarden, A., Mailloux, B. J., Peck, J. E. L., Koster, C. H. A., Sintzoff, M., Lindsey, C. H., Meertens, L. G. L. T. and Fisker, R. G. [1975]. 'Revised Report on Algorithmic Language ALGOL 68.' *Acta Informatica,* **5**, Nos. 1–3.

Warshall, S. [1962]. 'A theorem on Boolean matrices.' *JACM,* **9**, 11–12.

Watt, D. A. [1974]. 'Analysis-oriented Two-level Grammars.' *Ph.D. Thesis,* University of Glasgow.

Watt, D. A. [1977]. 'An Extended Attribute Grammar for Pascal'. *Report No. 11,* Computing Department, University of Glasgow.

Williams, M. H. [1978]. 'Static Semantic features of ALGOL 60 and BASIC.' *Computer Journal,* **61**, No. 3, 234–242.

Index

Absolute address, 170
Abstract machine, 149
Action, 122, 125–136, 144–147, 152, 196, 197, 200–207, 222, 224, 227, 232, 233
Action name, 197
Actual parameter, 178, 179, 226
Ada, 1, 2, 4, 13, 55, 135, 141, 143, 148–152, 161–165, 175–181, 197, 226, 227, 230–234
Ada module, 140, 225
Ada package, 162
Address, 7, 13, 54, 150, 155, 168, 172–179, 186, 196, 200–206, 211, 213, 233
Address field, 7
Address type, 178
Adjacency matrix, 77
Admissible symbol, 222, 224
Affix grammar, 41, 231
Aggregate, 141
Aho, A. V., 4, 26, 103
ALGOL 60, 4, 6, 15, 140–143, 153, 175–181, 217, 218, 232
ALGOL 60 Report, 30, 131, 138
ALGOL 68, 1–5, 13, 16, 30, 54–58, 66, 86, 87, 95, 120, 121, 139, 143–153, 160–165, 175–181, 197, 207, 213, 218, 220–222, 226
ALGOL 68 analyser, 165
ALGOL 68 compiler, 143, 146
ALGOL 68R, 138
ALGOL W, 179
ALGOL W report, 30
Algorithm, 27, 38, 73, 76, 78, 80, 85, 114, 119, 126, 134, 145, 147, 156, 157, 184–190, 195, 223, 231
Alphabet, 20, 26, 27
Alphabetical order, 153, 156
Alteration of symbols, 223
Ambiguity, 23, 29, 30, 56, 119, 143–145, 225

Ambiguous grammar, 38, 119, 120, 222
Ammann, U., 150, 164, 170
Analyser, 11, 30, 34, 69, 136, 153, 225, 230, 231
Analysis, 1, 11, 54, 125, 146–148, 192
Anonymous variable, 181
APL, 5
Applied occurrence, 13, 33, 130–134, 140, 144–148, 160, 200, 206, 224
Arbitrary length constant, 54
Arbitrary length identifier, 53
Arctan, 205
Arithmetic expression, 125
Arithmetic if statement, 56
Arithmetic operation, 6, 7
Arithmetic unit, 7
Array, 5, 54, 73, 74, 144, 153, 154, 173, 176, 177, 179, 201, 206
Array access, 175
Array base address, 150
Array bound, 175, 224
Array descriptor, 176, 177
Array element, 172–177, 206
Array subscript, 226, 227
Array type, 163, 164
Assembler, 7
Assembly code, 7, 11, 192, 209–211, 213
Assembly code instruction, 209
Assembly code subroutine, 209
Assignment, 3, 5, 12, 28, 29, 56, 165, 178, 183–185, 193, 202, 206, 220, 224–227
Assignment compatible, 34
Assignment statement, 200
Attribute, 30, 33, 151, 231
Attribute grammar, 30, 32, 34, 41, 230, 231
Attribute parse tree, 231
Attribute value, 231
Augmented configuration, 118
Automata theory, 60
Automaton, 29, 44–49, 63

261